Fognet's Field Guide to

OpenView
Network Node Manager

2nd Edition

Mike Peckar

Fogbooks®
West Boylston, Massachusetts

**Fognet's Field Guide to OpenView Network Node Manager
Second Edition**

Mike Peckar

Printed in the United States of America, Spain, and the United Kingdom
ISBN 0-9785627-2-0

Publisher contact, feedback, and orders: www.fogbooks.com

Contents at a Glance

Table of Contents

5. Discovery via *netmon* 39

6. Status Polling - *netmon* 54

8. Traps, Events and Alarms.................97

9. Interpreting Events 111

10. Event Correlation 122

11. SNMP Functions 139

12. Systems Management 148

13. Data Collection and Thresholds 153

14. Notifications.....................................164

15. Fault Analysis Tools 175

16. Third Party Tools 182

17. Cisco Devices 185

18. *ovw* Map Operations.......................198

21. Dynamic Views 240

24. High Availability and Backup.........281

25. Firewalls and Security.....................291

1. Introduction

This *vade mecum* is written for field consultants, users and administrators of the HP Network Node Manager (NNM) software product. The second edition covers information that is relevant for NNM product versions 6.0 through 7.53 with Intermediate Patch 20. It does not cover NNM 8i, which is an entirely new and different product (see page 295). It was written for those who seek a shortcut to commonly used product info that is either missing or obfuscated in the product docs, and it covers practical implementation information that can't be found in any product documentation or the fine product manual or reference pages. This guide was gleaned from OpenView users and from the author's fifteen years of compiled notes on the product.

So, what is NNM? NNM is a scalable enterprise network fault management tool that provides SNMP manager features, network discovery, OSI layer 2 and layer 3 topology mapping, network device status polling, third party integration APIs and some limited reporting, performance and trend analysis capabilities. It is the most popular enterprise-class network management tool for managing IP networks.

The terms "OpenView" and "NNM" have been used synonymously for many years, but it has never been accurate to mix these terms. NNM is a discreet product within the OpenView software product suite. A list of some of the more popular and relevant HP Software products are listed on page 308.

Shortly after its acquisition of Mercury Interactive in 2007, HP dropped the use of "OpenView" in all its software products and branded all software under the HP umbrella "HP Software." "HP OpenView Network Node Manager" thus became "HP Network Node Manager." The author's expectation is that NNM will still be referred to as "OpenView" for at least another decade.

The second edition contains expansions, corrections and coverage of new features released in NNM 7.51 and 7.52 and 7.53 and intermediate patches. Almost all acronyms used within this guide are expanded in an attempt at a comprehensive glossary starting on page 314. Feedback on this guide is welcomed and encouraged and can be submitted to the author through the publisher.

Acknowledgements

Rachel proved indispensable as chief editor for this book. The author's sister Sue Wiedorn did the wonderful cover art. The author's children, Molly, Jake and Charlie suffered greatly from a severe lack of attention during the writing and updating of this book. Special thanks for input into the 2nd edition go to Kevin May. Tusen takk to Nils Johannessen for providing cover to cover editing for the 2nd edition and contributed some great additional material. Kevin Smith of HP has provided valuable insights for both editions. Finally, Tracy Avent of HP provided both technical and moral support and is just too nice of a fellow to skip a credit herewith.

Much of this work would have been impossible without the mentorship of some of the elder statesmen and stateswomen of the OpenView Forum listserv and greater OpenView community. In 2007, OVForum was renamed/rebranded to VivIt (vivit-worldwide.org)

About Fognet and the author

Mike joined Digital Equipment Corp in 1987 and in 1993 began work on the DEC/IBM OEM'd ports of NNM 3.31 to Alpha OSF/1 and NT/Alpha called PolyCenter and Tivoli NetView. Following that, Mike worked for HP as a senior post-sales OpenView consultant. He founded Fognet in 1998 as a consultancy focused on enterprise management. Fognet is an IT consulting service company, delivering enterprise management product implementations, training, architecture and integration with a primary focus on the OpenView NNM and Operations products. Visit Fognet's web site at www.fognet.com.

Conventions used in this guide

Background and foreground processes are listed *italics*. Commands are listed in `Courier` font. File names are listed in regular font.

2. General Information

This section covers some basic information and procedures which are most frequently used to administer NNM.

Paths

The paths to files used in this guide are shown using NNM standard environment variables. The convention in this guide is to mix UNIX and Windows-like paths with the understanding that the reader will make the appropriate translation for that reader's platform. Thus the UNIX path for $OV_CONF/C/trapd.conf, when used in this guide is the equivalent of %OV_CONF%\C\trapd.conf on the Windows platform. For Windows platform users, the use of environmental variables helps interpret paths without care as to the directory in which NNM was originally installed. Under Windows, all NNM directories are relative to the installation directory. This is not the case with the UNIX paths, where per OSF conventions; files are laid out as follows:

/etc/opt/OV/share	Configuration files
/var/opt/OV/share	Files that "grow"
/opt/OV	Optional or program files

Default passwords

The following passwords are used to access various NNM subsystems:

SNMP read community string:	public
Web GUI user:	ovuser
Web GUI password:	ovuser
Data Warehouse DB user:	ovdb
Data Warehouse DB password:	ovdb

The Extended Topology configuration GUI password is in:

$OV_AS\webapps\topology\WEB-INF\dynamicViewsUsers.xml

3

OpenView environment variables

To activate the environment variables on Windows so they can be used to find directories from the command line, enter:

```
ov.envvars.bat
```

The absolute path shouldn't be necessary since the OpenView bin directory is placed in the path upon product install. On UNIX, use the appropriate shell-specific script in the NNM bin directory. The following scripts can be called from the appropriate command line shell or from other scripts that themselves invoke these shells:

```
ov.envvars.sh
ov.envvars.csh
ov.envvars.pl
```

The complete list of environmental variables can be found within the files above. Selected environment variables for UNIX include:

OV_BACKGROUNDS	/etc/opt/OV/share/backgrounds
OV_BIN	/opt/OV/bin
OV_BITMAPS	/etc/opt/OV/share/bitmaps
OV_CONF	/etc/opt/OV/share/conf
OV_CONTRIB	/opt/OV/contrib
OV_DB	/var/opt/OV/share/databases
OV_DOC	/opt/OV/doc
OV_FIELDS	/etc/opt/OV/share/fields
OV_HELP	/var/opt/OV/share/help
OV_JRE	/opt/OV/jre/jre1.4
OV_LIB	/opt/OV/lib
OV_LOG	/var/opt/OV/share/log
OV_LRF	/etc/opt/OV/share/lrf
OV_MAN	/opt/OV/man
OV_NEW_CONF	/opt/OV/newconfig
OV_REGISTRATION	/etc/opt/OV/share/registration
OV_SHARE_LOG	/var/opt/OV/share/log
OV_SNMP_MIBS	/var/opt/OV/share/snmp_mibs
OV_SYMBOLS	/etc/opt/OV/share/symbols
OV_WWW	/opt/OV/www
OV_ANALYSIS_CONF	/etc/opt/OV/share/conf/analysis
OV_SHARE_HTDOCS	/var/opt/OV/www/htdocs
OV_WWW_REG	/etc/opt/OV/share/www/registration
OV_AS	/opt/OV/tomcat/jakarta-tomcat-4.0.4

Extending OV environment variables

There are no restrictions to adding custom variables to the shell-specific script in `$OV_BIN/ov.envvars.*` on either the UNIX or Windows server nodes.

Note that Windows environmental variables are not case sensitive whereas UNIX environmental variables are.

NNM environment variables usage restrictions

Environment variables *cannot* be used in action callbacks. Environment variables *can* be used in trustedCmds.conf files.

Customize daemons via local registration files (LRF)

Local registration files are used to set options and behaviors for OpenView's background daemons. LRFs are read by the commands `ovaddobj` and `ovdelobj` to register or deregister an NNM managed process with *ovspmd*.

LRF changes that correspond to daemon command line options are found between the second and third set of colons in the file. So in the following ovwdb.lrf file line, the command line argument is "`-O`".

```
OVs_YES_START::-O:OVs_WELL_BEHAVED:15:PAUSE
```

When updating an LRF, the general procedure to make the change effective is:

- Backup the original LRF
- Edit the LRF and enter changes
- Run:
  ```
  ovaddobj $OV_LRF/<daemon>.lrf
  ovstop <daemon>
  ovstart <daemon>
  ```

A common error is that either the `ovaddobj` command is not run from the $OV_LRF directory, or the full path to the LRF file is not specified. Some OpenView daemons have dependencies on each other, so when an `ovstop` is issued for a particular daemon, several other daemons may also be shut down.

Dependent daemons are listed in the second colon-separated field in the LRF file. In general, it is a good practice to stop all user GUI sessions when issuing `ovstop` commands. To make sure that all appropriate daemons are running after starting or starting any daemons, run `ovstatus -c`.

Debug any process configured in a LRF by using the `-debug x` option in the forth LRF field. "x" as a value between 1 and 5 with increasing levels of verbosity.

A history of `ovaddobj` and `ovdelobj` operations is held in the $OV_CONF/ovsuf file. In some cases, this file can grow large, as in when `ovaddobj` and `ovdelobj` operations are used in user-customized scheduled operations to control NNM behaviors like discovery, etc. In this case, the ovsuf should be cleared out on occasion to improve performance. When doing this, preserve the one line lowest in the file for each daemon listed.

Application registration files (ARF)

Any file placed in $OV_REGISTRATION/C is read by the *ovw* process to register *ovw* GUI menu-bar items. The syntax is described in detail in the OVwRegIntro man/ref pages. Use these simple rules to guarantee sure smooth sailing:

1. Make backup copies of registration files to be modified, but do not store the backups in the registration directory tree as they will be read and cause errors
2. Any filename supported by the OS is read by *ovw*
3. Test syntax when making changes using:
   ```
   regverify -arf <arf filename>
   ```
4. See page 214 for procedure to create alternate ARF trees

The Menu Bar item attributes in ARF files include: Selection capabilities based on object DB fields, Hotkeys, Precedence number, and Selection rule specifications. The MIB Application Builder is front-end ARF file generator designed to work with SNMP MIB values. The following directory is reserved for MIB application builder apps:

$OV_REGISTRATION/C/ovmib

For some excellent examples, see the NNM manual:

Creating_and_Using_Reg_Files.pdf

Symbols, OID types and fields (FRF)

oid_to_sym provides the mapping of device types to the symbol used to represent those devices. oid_to_type and HPoid2type provide the mapping of device types to how to treat the devices in the IPMAP topology. In version 7.0 and greater, the oid_to_sym_reg database was introduced to facilitate better integration with NNM ET. For backward compatibility, the oid_to_sym configuration file is still read first when IPMAP starts.

Field registration files (FRFs) define all the fields in the object (*ovwdb*) database. FRF updates are necessary when a new symbol mapping is desired or to add uniquely identifying attributes to the object database.

The oid_to_type and HPoid2type mappings use two object database field values: "vendor", and "SNMP agent", to assign topology rules for devices which map to those fields. For almost all NNM deployments, there would probably be agents and vendors that are not listed in oid_to_type, so it may be desirable to add these missing values via the FRF process.

If there is a need simply to make sure devices for an undefined SNMP agent are mapped properly in IPMAP, it is not required that FRFs be updated. A shortcut is to assign pre-existing Vendor and SNMP agent values to the newly added SNMP agent OID in the oid_to_type files that is already associated with a symbol that satisfactorily represents the object. The only problem with this shortcut is that object and topology database searches and reports might produce incorrect results.

When adding a new entry, determine if the vendor and/or agent is already in the object database (a pre-requisite) by performing find operations in the *ovw* GUI. Alternatively on UNIX, issue following two commands:

```
ovobjprint -e `ovobjprint -f |grep vendor |cut -f1`
ovobjprint -e `ovobjprint -f |grep SNMPAg |cut -f1`
```

Summary of oid_to_type and HPoid2type topology attributes:

B	Bridge
D	Cisco HSRP (ip addr's not in ip.ipAddrTable)
S	2ndary addrs. Do not delete 2ndary If's

7

N	Ignore unnumbered interfaces on these devices
d	Dormant oper status - Cisco ISDN
G	Gateway
H	Hub
I	Ignore SNMP
L	Allow Loopback connections
M	Not a Gateway
T	Terminal Server
U	Discover as unmanaged

The following global defaults for oid_to_type and HPoid2type are used to specify global topology treatment for classes of devices that don't otherwise map to specific OID entries in the file:

DEFAULT_SNMP -- Supports SNMP but does not have a more specificOID entry
DEFAULT_IP -- Supports IP and otherwise would not have a matching entry
DEFAULT_IPX -- Supports IPX and otherwise would not have a matching entry
DEFAULT -- Any node which otherwise would not have a matching entry

For example, to instruct NNM to discover SNMP-supported nodes that are not listed in the files as unmanaged, use:

DEFAULT_SNMP:::U

To unmanage Windows servers and/or workstations with SNMP turned on, change these entries:

```
1.3.6.1.4.1.311.1.1.3.1:Windows NT:U   # Pre NT SP2
1.3.6.1.4.1.311.1.1.3.1.1:Workstation:Windows NT:U
1.3.6.1.4.1.311.1.1.3.1.2:Server:Windows NT:U
1.3.6.1.4.1.311.1.1.3.1.3:PDC:Windows NT:U
```

To add a "vendor" FRF:

Edit the file $OV_FIELDS/C/ovw_fields and add the new vendor, an example of the section follows :

```
Field "vendor" {
        Type    Enumeration;
        Flags   capability, general, locate;
        Enumeration "Unset",
                "Hewlett-Packard",
                "3Com",
                "ACC",
                "Allied Telesyn"
```

To add an "SNMP agent" FRF:

Edit the file $OV_FIELDS/C/snmp_fields and add the new agent, an example of the section follows:

```
Field "SNMPAgent" {
        Type Enumeration;
        Flags    capability, general, locate;
        Enumeration   "Unset",
                  "HP 3000/XL",
                  "HP 386",
                  "HP 700/[R]X X-Terminal",
                  "HP 9000/HP-UX",
                  "HP Bridge",
```

To make sure no syntax errors have been introduced, run the following command and look for errors:

Windows:	`regverify`
UNIX:	`ovw -verify >/dev/null`

Once syntax has been verified, update the object database using:

```
ovw -fields
```

Once valid Agent and Vendor fields are registered, the new field entries can be used in the oid_to_type file and newly-discovered devices should be mapped according to the rules.

To update already discovered objects without having to rediscover them, exit *ovw* and run:

```
ovstop netmon
ovtopofix -u -o <sysObjectID>
ovstart netmon
```

To add customized symbols, see the procedure "Create a Symbol Registration File" in the Appendix of the NNM Guide: Managing Your Network.

Application defaults update procedure (app-defaults)

UNIX: Edit the appropriate file in the $APP_DEFS directory.

Windows: Edit the appropriate registry key under:

HKEY_LOCAL_MACHINE if the value is global for all users, or:
HKEY_CURRENT_USER, if different users need to be able to use different application default values.

The assorted classes are found under:

> HKLM\SOFTWARE\ or HKCU\SOFTWARE\
> \Hewlett-Packard\OpenView\Network Node Manager

The app-defaults files (UNIX) or classes (Windows) are:

OVw	*ovw* GUI settings, e.g. Map colors, fonts
XNm	GUI settings for MIB browser, collector, etc
XNmappmon	GUI settings for tables and forms
XNmevents	GUI settings for alarm browser
XNmgraph	GUI settings for grapher
XNmtrap	GUI settings for event configuration

Troubleshooting Windows paths

In NNM event configuration action callbacks, backslashes must be escaped and spaces must be quoted, for example:

```
C:\\"Program Files"\\"HP OpenView"\\program.bat
```

In NNM filter files, the colon must be escaped and the backslashes replaced with regular slashes.

```
servers "servers" {d\:/ov/conf/coreservers.txt}
```

In NNM ARF files, quotes are needed for spaces and must be escaped, but all the following examples will work:

```
Application "Wordpad" { Command "C:/\"Program
    Files\"/Windows\" \"NT/Accesories/wordpad";}
Application "wordpad" { Command "\"C:/Program Files/Windows
    NT/Accesories/wordpad\""; }
Application "webpage" { Command "C:\\PROGRA~1\\
    INTERN~1\\iexplore.exe http://webpage.html" }
```

Finally, if none of the above seems to work, add the directory location of the executable to the system path, or use the 'AppPath' registry key, then simply call the executable name without specifying the path.

Force or restart an ET discovery

Before attempting this operation, check to see if a discovery is currently running: from Home Base, select the Discovery Status tab. Check discovery status from the command line by running:

```
ovstatus -v ovet_disco
```

Restart or force ET discovery only when underlying configuration changes have been made that may require such an action. Make sure that any devices that may be the target of a force ET discovery are properly discovered by *netmon* first.

ET discovery can be initiated from Homebase: select Discovery Status, then ET Configuration, then Initiate Full Discovery Now. This can also be accessed from *ovw* via: Options->Extended Topology Configuration. Or, the web URL is:

```
http://<nnm server>:7510/topology/etconfig
```

To force ET Discovery from the command line, run:

```
          etrestart.ovpl
  or:
          etrestart.ovpl -verbose -disco
```

Be prepared to wait a while for discovery to complete.

The progress of discovery can be followed on the Discovery Status page. If changes have been made that require an ET rediscovery, and a discovery is already in progress, use:

```
          etrestart.ovpl -force
```

To refresh Homebase and APA status views, run:

```
          ovstop ovas
          ovstop ovet_poll
          ovstart ovas
          ovstart ovet_poll
```

By default, ET waits until *netmon* has found 2500 changes in a network before ET runs a new discovery. To change this so it runs at a scheduled time, go the ET configuration (see above) and turn off "Enable discovery for a specified number of NNM changes."

Then turn on "Enable recurring discovery." Schedule a discovery daily, and click Apply. Note that lowering the threshold may have a performance cost.

11

If ET rediscovery isn't properly discovering particular devices, see the section on improving ET discovery on page 229.

Re-do discovery (start from scratch)

Re-do discovery after making major changes such as switching from files-based lookups to DNS, or to recover from suspected corruption of the object, map, topology, or ET databases.

Before performing this operation, consider exporting maps to save customizations (see page 284).

Review any additional changes that may profoundly affect topology, such as reclassifying the treatment of a major class of connector devices by OID, DNS changes, etc.

To just delete the databases, run the following command:

```
$OV_CONTRIB/deleteOVDB/deleteOVDB.ovpl
```

To manually start from scratch:

1. Important: close all OpenView GUIs
2. `ovstop -c`
3. Remove the databases & log files:
4. UNIX: `cd $OV_DB; rm -rf openview; rm -rf nnmet`
   Windows: delete all the directories below:
   \databases\openview
   \databases\nnmet
5. If exporting topology, run: `ovtoposql -R i|o -C`
6. Clear the SNMP cache: `xnmsnmpconf -clearCache`
7. Restart all the OV daemons: `ovstart -c`
8. Start the user interface: `ovw &`
9. Re-initiate ET: `setupExtTopo.ovpl`

Logging NNM errors to Windows event log

The *ovtracelog* utility is provided for logging NNM exceptions through the Windows tracing and logging facility. See the *ovtracelog* reference or man page for details.

Running `ovstart` and `ovpause` as non-root (UNIX)

Use the following steps to allow non-root users to issue the `ovstart` and `ovstop` as well as `ovpause` or `ovresume` commands.

1. Make sure root is the owner of `ovstart` and `ovstop`
2. `chmod 4555 ovstart ; chmod 4555 ovstop`
3. Create a file called $OV_CONF/ovstart.allow
4. `chmod 400 ovstart.allow ; chown root ovstart.allow`
5. In the file put a user name or UNIX user ID
6. `chown root:sys ovstart ovstop ovstatus`
7. `chown root:sys ovpause ovresume`
8. `chmod 666 $OV_LOG/ovstart.log`
9. Consult the $OV_LOG/ovstart.log for possible errors.

Common log files

The following are common log files is $OV_LOG:

Setup.log	Troubleshoot installation (Windows)
ovactiond.log	Troubleshoot automatic actions
ovalarmsrv.trace	Troubleshoot xnmevents
ovcapsd.log	Troubleshoot DMI/RDMI (Windows)
ovrepld.log	Troubleshoot MS-CS updates
ovbackup.log	Troubleshoot ovbackup.ovpl actions
Pmd.log0	Troubleshoot postmaster daemon
snmpCol.trace	Troubleshoot raw data collection
ovdw*.log	Troubleshoot data warehouse and reporting

The following are common log files is $OV_PRIV_LOG:

httpd*.log	Troubleshoot web server
ovas_err.log	Troubleshoot Dynamic Views
ovrequestd.log	Troubleshoot Data Warehouse feeds

NNM product documentation

User manuals are found in:

$OV_WWW/htdocs/C/Manuals

Online help:

13

Unix:

    http://<nnmserver>:3443/OvCgi/OvWebHelp.exe

Windows:

    http://<nnmserver>/OvCgi/OvWebHelp.exe

Under Windows, the online help facility can be invoked directly even if NNM is not running:

    %OV_HELP\C\NNM.hlp

Download user manuals:

    http://ovweb.external.hp.com/lpe/doc_serv

Additional ECS Manuals: $OV_DOC/ECS/C
Selected RFC's: $OV_DOC/RFC
White Papers: $OV_DOC/WhitePapers
Release Notes: $OV_WWW/htdocs/C/ReleaseNotes/
Release Note Updates (V7.5):

  http://ovweb.external.hp.com/nnm/NNM7.5/relNoteUpd/relNoteUpdate.htm

Man Pages (Linux)

Man pages for daemons and certain commands are placed under /opt/OV/man/man1m for NNM and /opt/OV/man/man1m.Z for ECS tools. The 1m and 1m.z manual sections may not be defined by default under Linux varients. Specify the section in the command line to get around this issue, for example:

```
man 1m netmon
man 1m.Z ecsmgr
```

Alternatively, 1m and 1m.Z may be added to the MANSECT variable in the /etc/man.config file, for example:

    MANSECT 1:8:2:3:4:5:6:7:9:tcl:n:l:p:o:1m:1m.Z

NNM patch information

Email notifications for patch updates:

    http://support.openview.hp.com/emailReg.jsp

Determining what patches are installed:

Windows: Control Panel-Add/Remove Programs
UNIX: swlist -l fileset | grep "^# PH"

3. Common Issues

This section covers some of the more common issues encountered during initial installation and setup-up of NNM.

Troubleshooting resources

The following tool can be used on any NNM platform to check patch levels. Always try to keep NNM up-to-date on patch levels:

```
$OV_SUPPORT/checkPatch.ovpl
```

The most comprehensive database of solutions to common NNM problems is located at the HP IT Resource Center at:

www.itrc.hp.com

Using the ITRC-embedded search engine, however, is often slow and yields poor results. Fortunately, the entire ITRC database is mined by Google, so when an error occurs that is very generic, adding "ITRC" to the search term in Google can often help narrow down the issue.

Another excellent resource is the VivIt (formerly OVForum) listserv at:

www.vivit-worldwide.org (formerly www.ovforum.org)

The forum provides a few special interest groups, but by far, the most active is the general forum which covers all OpenView products. In practice, most of the traffic pertains to NNM. The ovforum listserv is maintained by the OpenView Forum International users group, which is an independent organization that has no direct ties to HP. For this reason, it is a good place to submit questions that are less biased by HP. For example, questions pertaining to comparaisons of OpenView with competing products or discussions about the quality HP products and services. Also, user experiences and customizations are more likely to be found on the listserv. Conversely, very few HP employees participate in the ovforum listserv. Questions posed to the ITRC, however, are very likely to be answered directly by HP subject matter experts.

Licensing issues due to upgrades, migrations, homing

License updates are required from HP under the following circumstances:

- When upgrading from 6.x to 7.x
- When changing IP address
- When changing server OS

If an NNM server has more than one IP address, the preferred IP address can be specified using the NNM_INTERFACE keyword in the following file: $OV_CONF/ov.conf

Changing NNM server hostname or IP address

Generally, changing the NNM server name or IP is something to avoid, mostly because NNM registers itself (if it can) as a trap recipient on SNMP agents it discovers, but also for all the reasons listed in the section on NNM and Name Services (see page 25). Changing IP address means that traps may be lost, particularly if trap destinations have been set manually for many devices. Be aware that on many devices, if adding a trap recipient by FQDN, this is converted to the IP address in the devices configuration. An IP address change also requires that the product license be updated. To change the hostname and/or IP address:

1.   Stop NNM processes using `ovstop`
2.   Change the name in: $OV_DB/openview/ovwdb/ovserver
3.   Change the name in all the $OV_CONF/*auth* files
4.   Change the server name in the OS
5.   Run: `xnmsnmpconf -clearC`
6.   Update license if IP Address changed
7.   Update agent trap destinations if IP address changed
8.   Start processes using `ovstart`

Installation issue: virtual directories not created

Symptoms are that "the page cannot be found" or "Under construction" appears when the web GUIs first launched. This happens on Windows installations when NNM 7+ is installed into an environment where anti-virus software prevents VBscripts from running.

To resolve this issue, disable any programs that block vbscripts then locate the `setupIIS.vbs` script from the newconfig subdirectories on the installation media, then run:

```
cscript setupIIS.vbs "C:\Program Files\HP OpenView\NNM" -
```

If issues persist, installation registry file entries may need to be updated. There are articles which describe the update procedure on ITRC.

Installation issue: *ovas* not running

Typically, the root cause is with the web server's configuration. There are many possible things that can go wrong. In troubleshooting, always look to the web server's health first. Is it running? Does the event log (or syslog) contain pertinent information? Do the web server logs look O.K.?

Check the ovas.log file. *ovas* is the daemon that serves dynamic views. If ovas.log shows an error like this:

```
ld.so.1: ovas: fatal: relocation error: file
/opt/OV/jre/jre1.4/lib/sparc/libjava.so: symbol
VerifyFixClassname: referenced symbol not found
```

The problem is that LD_LIBRARY_PATH is not set correctly, possibly set by another application (e.g. Checkpoint). Reset it to:

/opt/OV/lib

Another common problem causing *ovas* to fail to start is that another application (probably one that uses Tomcat) has grabbed the Tomcat server port. In NNM V7.01+ this is port 8005. To resolve, change the Server Port number from 8005 to some other unused port number, then restart the *ovas* daemon. The Server Port is specified in the following file:

$OV_AS/conf/server.xml

Installation issue (UNIX): Using NFS mounted CDs

When exporting a remote CD drive to be used for installing NNM, 'root' access to the drive must be granted. Use a line similar to the following on the machine that has the CD drive installed on it:

- *HP-UX in* /etc/exports:
  <mount_point_of_CD> -ro,root=<machine_name_1[:machine2]>
- *Solaris* in /etc/dfs/dfstab
  share -F nfs -o root=<machine_name> <mount_point_of_CD>
- *Red Hat Linux Advanced Server 2.1* in /etc/exports
  <mount_point_of_CDROM> <machine_name> (ro,all_squash)

Installation issue (Windows): Non-standard directory

NNM inserts information about its install location into the registry. If NNM is be installed in a non-standard location (other than %SystemDrive%/Program Files/HP OpenView), that subdirectory should be created prior to installation. This will allow the non-standard location to be used to store data (rather than in %SystemDrive%/Program Files/HP OpenView/data). Create the <install location>/data directory before installation.

Installation issue (Windows): Terminal Services

When installing Network Node Manager 7.5x under Terminal Services, problems might exist where %SystemRoot% does not correctly resolve in Command Prompt windows. If this occurs, a reboot is necessary.

Unable to download JRE through firewall

Recent versions of NNM (7.01+) do not come bundled with JRE and automatically detect if a compatible version is installed on the server. If not, the install process may attempt to access sun.com to download the bits. Some firewall rules require a resolvable DNS name for the download, but the Sun download site for JRE returns a virtual host. Resolvable locations for JRE are available and can be found in a web search. One such site is:

http://download.au.kde.org/pub/java-sun

If firewall rules won't even permit that, try to download and run the "Windows Offline Installation" of the runtime environment from:

http://java.sun.com/j2se/1.4.2/download.html

Devices discovered in unmanaged state

Objects that are beige in the maps are unmanaged objects. Whenever a node or interface is discovered whose IP address is in a subnet that was previously undiscovered by *netmon*, a new network symbol is placed on the internet map in the unmanaged state. This is to prevent runaway discovery. New networks need to be selected and then managed from within the *ovw* map.

When random devices are discovered as unmanaged, it could be that the server's license limit has been reached. Run the following command to determine the number of discovered objects and licensed object count: `ovtopodump -l`. Finally, devices may be placed on the map in the unmanaged state due to the "-U" configuration flag in the oid_to_type or HPoid2type files. See page 7 for more info on these files. Use a *netmon* seed file as a way to allow for the discovery of selected networks as managed. Also, scripts that search for unmanaged devices and then manage them externally can be written to simulate the NNM version 3.31 behavior of discovering the entire network by default.

See page 43 for information about managing objects externally and page 44 for more about seeding *netmon*.

Cleaning orphaned objects from object database

NNM database irregularities may manifest themselves in several ways. For example, an error message indicating that a particular object cannot be added to the topology using `loadhosts` is one indication the object exists in one or more NNM databases but has something wrong with it or is out of sync with another NNM databases.

These sorts of issues are also common in environments where DNS is very dynamic or sometimes misconfigured. It is a good general practice to repeat this procedure occasionally:

```
Open all existing maps and allow them to synchronize, close.
ovstop netmon
xnmsnmpconf -clearC
ovw -mapcount -ruDv
ovtopofix -a
ovstart netmon
Open all existing maps and allow them to synchronize.
```

Daemons ovet_da* not running (ovstatus)

After enabling Extended Topology, new daemons are registered through the ARF object manager. The `ovstatus` command may return "Not Running" for daemons with names like ovet_daDetails, ovet_daCDP, ovet_disco, etc. These daemons are supposed to be not running most of the time, and might only display as running when they are called to run during an ET discovery cycle.

They may also show as running soon after an `ovstart` command is issued, but they may subsequently show as not running when and `ovstatus` command is issued.

Netscape and NNM co-existence (UNIX)

Netscape might allocate the entire color map when started, which may whack out *ovw* colored icons and cause the error seen immediately below. To force Netscape to use a private color map, start it up using:

```
netscape -install
```

Alternatively, the maximum number of colors, and/or the use of a private color map can be specified in the X App Defaults resource files for Netscape.

Cannot allocate 128 colors - using monochrome images

On UNIX platforms, a message similar to above may occur when there are not enough colors allocated to the colormap that NNM is requesting to properly display icons, etc. A similar message may be:

Allocation errors: 32 colors (128 requested).

To resolve, from within CDE, bring up the Style Manager. Under Color, there is an option for "Number of Colors." There should be an option under that to set "More colors for applications." Also, see the section immediately above and use the "-install" Netscape option, if using netscape. If running X over a virtual windowing server such as Exceed or Reflections, be sure the server application is configured to use a color depth of 24.

Unable to load any useable font set (UNIX)

Symptom: When launching an xnmgraph window:

```
Warning: Cannot convert string "-dt-interface system-medium-r-
normal-m*-*-*-*-*-" to type FontSet
Warning: Unable to load any useable fontset
```

To resolve, run:

```
xrdb -merge /usr/lib/X11/app-defaults/Xnmgraph
```

xterm: unable to locate a suitable font (UNIX)

Create a file in the home directory of the user called .Xdefaults and include the following line in the file:

```
xterm*Font:-*-lucidatypewriter-bold-r-*-*-12-*-*-*-*-*-*-*
```

Missing charsets in string to fontset (Solaris)

Symptom: On launch of *ovw*, the following errors return:

```
Warning: Cannot convert string "-dt-interface system-medium-r-
normal-s*-*-*-*-*-" to type FontSet
Warning: Missing charsets in String to FontSet conversion
Warning: Unable to load any usable fontset...
```

Resolution:
1. Startup the font server on the Solaris workstation:
   /usr/openwin/bin/fslsfonts -server <NNM Server>:7000

2. Enable the font server on the Solaris workstation:
   /usr/openwin/bin/xset+fp tcp/<NNM Server>:7000/all

Missing charsets in string to fontset (HP-UX)

Symptom: On launch of *ovw*, the following errors return:

```
Warning: Cannot convert string "-dt-interface system-medium-r-
normal-s*-*-*-*-*-" to type FontSet
Warning: Missing charsets in String to FontSet conversion
Warning: Unable to load any usable fontset...
```

Resolution: To turn on the HP-UX font server:

1.   On the HP-UX server, edit: /etc/X11/fs/config
2.   Append the following to the end of the "catalog=...." line:
        /usr/dt/config/xfonts/C
3.   Save the file and edit: /etc/rc.config.d/xfs
4.   Set the following variable in the above file:
        RUN_X_FONT_SERVER=1
5.   Save the file and run the following commands:
        /sbin/init.d/xfs stop

```
/sbin/init.d/xfs start
```
6. On the target system enter:
```
xset +fp tcp/<Server IP Addr>:7000 1>/dev/null
xset fp rehash
```
7. If xset is not in the path, append $XDIR environment variable.

NTLM - password needed - firewall: unknown

Often seen as an installation issue, this is a known issue with JAVA 1.4.2_01. To resolve, explicitly set the proxy server by selecting "Bypass proxy server for local addresses" dialog under LAN settings under the connections tabs in IE Internet Options when using a script for proxy detection. Similarly, if the local user account specified for anonymous IIS access is disabled due to site security policies, this needs to be changed.

Troubleshooting daemons using ovstart and ovstatus

To get more status for a daemon: `ovstatus -v <daemon>`
To get highest verbosity (UNIX only): `ovstart -v -V -d <daemon>`

Automatically detect and restart OV daemons that die

The following log-only OpenView enterprise event can be used to detect and log failing daemons that are registered via ARF and "Well-Behaved":

```
OV_AppUngracefulExit .1.3.6.1.4.1.11.2.17.1.0.59179058
```

The fourth varbind contains the name of the daemon that exited ungracefully, so in addition to logging this event, set up an automatic action that executes: `ovstart $4`

Filtering on custom *ovwdb* fields

The NNM Guide to Scalability and Distribution Appendix A Table A-2 lists objects and attributes that can be used in a filter. The IPMAP_FILTER_FROM_OVW environment variable allows filtering on customized field values and those added by third party products. See page 3 for information on setting environment variables.

Working with multiple JAVA versions

Multiple versions of JAVA may be installed on the NNM server or on any clients that are used to access the NNM server. See the support matrix on page 304 to determine which version of JAVA is required for a particular version of NNM. On the client side, the environment that invokes NNM needs to be configured to point to the appropriate version of JAVA.

On UNIX systems set the environment variable $JAVA_HOME to point to the binary directory for the supported JAVA installation, for example: /opt/java1.4/bin. On Windows systems, set the compatible version via: Control Panel->Java Plug-in. Often, other JAVA applications require different versions than those that are compatible with NNM. Some users resort to configuring multiple vendors' browsers with separately-configured versions of JAVA. While certainly inconvenient, it solves some cross-application issues. It is advisable when installing multiple JAVA versions to install them incrementally from lowest to highest version.

Note that Microsoft Internet Explorer browsers support only a single installation onto any one system. Many other browsers, however, can be installed multiple times onto the same system, so each installed instance can be configured to point to separate versions of JAVA.

Client-side support for multiple JAVA versions is improved with Version 1.5 and greater. The process is to copy the directories for the pre 1.5 versions from where they were installed to a new location. Deinstall all pre 1.5 versions (Control Panel, Add/remove programs) then install a 1.5+ version, which can be found at:

www.java.com/en/download/windows_ie.jsp.

Copy/move the previous version directories to a subfolder of the newly installed 1.5+ version. Start Control Panel/Java. Select Java/View under Java Application Runtime Setings. Choose Find, and search and find the `javaw.exe` for the previous version(s), Verify that the application detects correct info under Platform and Product. Select OK to exit Java Control Panel.

4. NNM and Name Services

NNM relies heavily on lookups for mapping names to addresses and vice versa. The section on *netmon* discovery on page 38 explains the importance of stable and accessible name services to NNM.

Using /etc/hosts or LMhosts files based lookups works well, but provides very limited ability to use naming services as a tool for associating multiple interfaces with devices when NNM cannot do so otherwise via SNMP. WINS-based naming is supported, but generally is not a best practice, since Microsoft itself is moving away from it in favor of DNS. If the WINS server is not close to the NNM server, a network outage could render NNM practically unusable if it can't reach the WINS server.

The same is true of DNS servers, but DNS is automatically cached locally under Windows and caching DNS is often recommended for UNIX NNM servers. DNS is the preferred name service for NNM. Other naming services have trouble with the situation where a router cannot be addressed by SNMP and NNM would otherwise create separate nodes for each interface since it has no other way to know the interfaces belong to the same device.

DNS can provide the mapping of multiple interfaces to a single node name. Hosts files can't do this, nor can WINS.

How node objects are named

Objects are assigned IP Hostnames based on whether *netmon* can find a name by descending through the following checks:

- A non-migratable uniquely-named software loopback interface (not 127.0.0.*). Determined by querying ifType for softwareLoopback
- `gethostbyaddr` results on Preferred IP (see below)

- SNMP sysName returned on Preferred IP (see below)
- Preferred IP:
  - Lowest numbered IP Address
  - Lowest Software loopback IP address (not 127.0.0.*)
  - NAT address (introduced in V6.4x)
  - Lowest non-migratable IP Address
- Use the IPX server address (Windows only)
- Use "lowest" IPX address (Windows only)
- LLa address (MAC Address)
- A migratable name
- The current name (if present in DB)
- The NNM UUID

The best practice is to assign software loopback addresses wherever possible. The address that responds to SNMP and is the preferred address/interface for management, should be given the A record in DNS, and a corresponding PTR in its reverse zone. If other conventions are used, there may be a mismatch in a node's name and the name used by NNM for traps from that node. In all cases, reverse lookups are heavily used by NNM so PTR records should always be in place for all interfaces that NNM can't associate with a node through SNMP. The PTR's for all other interfaces but the one used for management, should be a standalone PTR pointing to the FQDN configured in the A-record

Assigning software loopbacks has benefits other than for NNM alone. Using a loopback interface in OSPF can make OSPF networks more stable. Cisco in fact recommends using them. Other uses for loopbacks include load balancing between BGP peers over two or more interfaces on Cisco routers. Cisco Works uses much the same rules as NNM for selecting a preferred SNMP address

SNMP sysname for any device can be written from the NNM server if an SNMP write community is enabled for the device. This can be done from the SNMP MIB browser or from the command line using:

```
snmpset -c <writeString> <target> sysName.0 octetstring
<nameString>
```

Note: Loopback addresses on routers in the same subnet can cause routing to not work properly. This is avoided by using 32 bits masks.

If the routers support it and they are running a classless routing protocol, a full 32-bit mask for the loopback IP can be used to save on IP address space. This works fine with any version of NNM after 6.2, and Cisco routers with post 12.3 IOS. On prior versions of NNM, the following errors may be seen: From loadhosts: "WARNING: Invalid broadcast IP Address 255.255.255.255, ignoring entry for <target>." From the GUI, the error is: "The IP address is the broadcast address for this network." For more on this, see the section on 31 and 32-bit netmasks on page 49.

It is important to draw the distinction between names and labels in NNM. Names are things that must be unique in the object database (*ovwdb*) and topology (ovtopmd) database. In NNM, nodes have two kinds of names: IP Hostnames and Selection Names. Labels are the strings that show up on the node in a map.

How preferred IP address for SNMP is chosen

The preferred SNMP address for a node is chosen according to the above procedure. This is the address used to access the SNMP agent on the node.

The preferred IP address used can be manipulated using the options listed on page 29.

How node objects are labeled

Node selection names are by default the same as the IP Hostname, which is determined according to the rules above. Users (and third party applications) can change the selection name. If the selection name for two objects conflict, a numeric ID string is appended to one of the selection names in order to achieve uniqueness. Node labeling rules, in descending order of precedence, are:

- If the node has an IP hostname, truncate it to the basename (strip off domain and subdomain names)
- If the node has a NetWare server name, use it, otherwise, use the network number of the internal server address
- If the node reports an SNMP sysName value, use it, truncating after any blanks in the returned value
- If the node supports IP, the IP address is formatted as string

- If the node supports IPX, the host-address portion is used
- If the node has a LLA/MAC, the physAddr is formatted as a string

In environments where the use of SNMP sysName is preferred over any names assigned to the device in name services, use the ipNoLookup.conf, described on page 29.

How interface objects are named by *netmon*

In NNM 6.2 and later, if the agent supports the ifAlias MIB variable and it is non-blank and unique on the node, it should be used, otherwise a non-blank response for ifName is used. If this isn't available, ifDescr will be used, but only the first part up to any blanks (up to V7.51 Intermediate Patch 18, see section below). To force the use of ifName/ifDescr only, use the *netmon* LRF setting "-k useIfAlias=false". ifAlias is found in :

```
ifMIB.ifMIBObjects.ifXTable.ifXEntry.ifAlias
```

If a duplicate ifAlias is detected for a node, NNM generates an alarm. Either resolve the duplicate naming issue (preferred solution) or force ifName globally with the *netmon* LRF switch mentioned above. See page 5 for instructions on using the LRF procedure.

When changing the ifAlias, or when changing the LRF switch, a demand poll to the node may or may not properly update the object's label. There was a known problem with NNM 6.2 and ifAlias changes that was addressed via patches. If it doesn't update properly, the node should be deleted from all maps and rediscovered.

ifDescr naming restrictions

NNM V7.51 Intermediate Patch 18 added support for white spaces in the ifDescr SNMP variable. Prior to this, the text after the first white space was truncated. To allow the complete text of ifDescr to be used, set the following environmental variable to a value of "true:"

```
OV_NNM_IFLABEL_IFDESCR
```

How network objects are named

When a new network object is discovered by *netmon*, the networks file or DNS is searched for matching names. If none are found, the IP network address for the network is used. The files are:

Windows:	\windows\system32\drivers\etc\networks
UNIX:	/etc/networks

To change the name of an existing network name in NNM after updating the networks file, run:

```
ovtopofix -u <previous name for network object>
```

Node and interface naming restrictions

The only allowable characters in a label for a host name in NNM are ASCII letters, digits, and the dash character. The underscore character is illegal. In essence, NNM, like many other applications, enforces pre-RFC 2181 rules with respect to allowable characters in hostnames. More recent versions of NNM may have relaxed some of these restrictions.

Labels may not be all numbers, but may have a leading digit (e.g. 3com.com). Labels must end and begin only with a letter or digit, to a maximum of 63 characters. Letters are case-insensitive, though pre-NNM 5.0 versions preserved case. NNM uses this convention based on RFC1034 section 3.5.

Less stringent naming conventions apply to interfaces, however. Problems may arise from the use of certain characters in ifName and ifAlias entries, and interface name lengths are limited to 63 characters as well.

ipNoLookup.conf, snmpnolookupconf, excludeip.conf

ipNoLookup.conf is a configuration file which specifies IP addresses against which lookups will not be performed.

snmpnolookupconf is a command line utility which maintains the SNMP No Lookup cache, which is part of the SNMP configuration database (ovsnmp.conf). IP hostname entries in the No Lookup cache will not have name service queries issued to them.

If the above tools do provide the desired results, for example, to address naming issues stemming from the lowest IP address being used, use the excludeip.conf configuration file to manipulate the selection of the preferred IP address.

General DNS considerations

netmon discovers IP addresses first. To determine hostnames, *netmon* performs reverse lookups on the IP addresses using the *gethostbyaddr* system call. Reverse lookups in DNS-configured environments will fail unless PTR records are explicitly defined within DNS. Failure to populate PTR records in DNS is one of the most common causes of name service related issues in NNM.

To use DNS to force a particular address to be chosen over what NNM defaults to (often the name associated with the lowest numbered IP address), use the following procedure. Create an ordinary A-record for the primary interface with a corresponding PTR-record in the reverse zone. For all other IP addresses, one can make another name record (A-record) for the node, without a PTR pointing back. But for all those addresses, make a PTR pointing at the A-record for the primary name.

Preferrably, in the PTR records, take each of the node's IP Addresses and point them back to the common A-record. Then alias the other IP addresses in the forward lookups with CNAME records. If the reverse lookup does not map back to the A-record, then NNM misses the connection back to the node when an SNMP trap does not come from the A-record's IP address.

Cache-only DNS

As mentioned above, there are several reasons why a cache-only DNS server should be considered on the NNM server. The main reason is to provide local control of device naming for network management purposes. A local cache-only DNS used to be more frequently recommended for NNM server performance improvements, but HP made some reductions to NNM's use of lookups as well as added some levels of user control over lookup behavior (see above). Still, a local DNS server would increase lookup speed and reduce network load, as NNM is still a heavy user of DNS.

Another compelling reason for a local DNS server is to eliminate the scenario where the network link between the NNM server and the DNS server are severed. NNM functions are severely hampered by the loss of name services during normal operations. NNM provides some caching of lookup data through the SNMP configuration *cachedb*, which is part of the ovsnmp.conf database. This doesn't cache all lookup data, however, particularly discovery-related lookups.

Note also that Windows 2000 and above servers (and workstations) provide a DNS client that acts as a cache-only DNS server, but this does not provide any configurability. It does bring into question the reason to install a cache-only DNS server on NNM servers solely for performance improvements or to prevent service disruptions, however.

Split horizon DNS

Split Horizon DNS configurations may offer greater flexibility and ease of control for network management purposes over cache-only DNS. In general, there are three architectures for split horizon DNS: Two separate content DNS servers, each with different databases; a single content DNS server serving up multiple databases; and a single content DNS server serving up a single database whose records are tagged for visibility to specific clients.

With NNM, any of above options can be used to achieve finer control over network management naming while not compromising network applications or security. In fact, network management is often the primary reason for using Split Horizon DNS.

Another common practice in this regard is to configure a local DNS for a subdomain of devices, where that DNS server is then authoratative for devices only of interest to the network managers and caching for all other devices.

BIND-based DNS implementation troubleshooting

The first versions of BIND 9 broke the ability to coerce sortlist order for resource record sets that was possible in BIND 8 using the RRSET option shown below. Dropping RRSET meant that random-cyclic behavior determined which DNS record would be returned first in the list, which is what NNM uses to determine IP Hostname. The option was re-instated in BIND 9.2.3. The BIND 8 and BIND 9.2.3 (or later) method for fixing return order within the options block in named.conf is:

```
rrset-order {class IN type A "hostA.local" order fixed;};
```

The following named.conf logging options are useful for tracing what DNS queries are being generated by NNM:

```
logging {
        channel "queryfile" {
```

31

```
                    file "/var/log/dns-query.log" versions 4 size
    5m; # 20MB rolling logs
                    print-time yes;
                    print-category yes;
                    print-severity yes;
                    severity info;
        };
        category "queries" {
                    "queryfile";
        };
    };
```

BIND-based DNS on Windows

Microsoft's built-in caching "DNS Client" service may not provide enough flexibility and control, as it is not at all user-configurable. Microsoft's DNS Server is also difficult to work with (according to some). ISC BIND is easy to install on the NNM server as a cache-only DNS server that provides full control, and is free. Be aware, however, that BIND, like SNMP, has been the subject of security vulnerabilities in the past. More info can be found on this through SANS.

The following steps outline configuring ISC BIND on Windows:

1. Download BIND binary and docs from www.isc.org
2. Extract and install package
3. Run: `rndc-confgen -a`
4. Create configuration files; see examples in docs or on web
5. Check configuration files with `namedcheckconf`
6. Start ISC BIND service and monitor App Log events
7. Test forward and reverse lookups with `nslookup`
8. Disable Windows DNS Client Service
9. Reboot and check event log again

Note: When making major changes to name services that the NNM server subscribes to, always expect some issues with NNM's topology and general stability. Often, it is advisable to start discovery from scratch is such cases. See page 12 for this procedure.

"Name services are performing poorly" alarms

This OpenView enterprise event is generated when NNM's internally-generated lookups are taking too long or constantly timing out. If nodes are being polled via *netmon*, the following command may provide some information about lookup performance:

```
    ovstatus -v netmon
```

See the appropriate section below to address performance issues with name services, and also refer to the NNM "Managing" guide in Appendix E and other sections.

Tuning lookup performance (Windows)

NNM uses *gethostbyname* and *gethostbyaddr* system calls, but default NT settings for these requests can be very long. By default, NT should perform a NetBIOS lookup first, then a hosts file (\windows\system32\drivers\etc\lmhosts) lookup. A NetBIOS lookup timeout is 4.5 seconds, based on the following registry values:

HKLM\System\ControlSet001\Services\NetBt\Parameters:

NameSrvQueryTimeout=1500 msec
NameSrvQueryCount=3

If DNS or WINS is configured, typically these might be called on first, and then NetBIOS and hosts lookups would be performed. Make sure "Enable DNS for Windows Resolution" is checked, and "Enable LMHosts Lookup" is unchecked.

The recommended registry parameter settings are as follows:

HKLM\System\ControlSet001\Services\NetBt\Parameters:

Set NameSrvQueryCount to 0
Set NameSrvQueryTimeout to 100 to 500
Set NodeType to 2 (i.e. P-node)

NameSrvQueryTimeout should be set based on the overall latency in the network. Note that with these settings, access to other NT servers does not appear to be affected, however access to LAN Manager servers does.

Control the search order using the following keys under:

HKLM\System\CurrentControlSet\Services\TcpIP\ServiceProvider:

DnsPriority
LocalPriority
HostsPriority
NetbtPriority

These should have values assigned to them the range of -32768 to 32767. The *lower* the number the *higher* the priority. The priority order determines the order that they are used. localPriority affects the name lookup using the lmhosts file.

There is also another key:

HKLM\System\CurrentControlSet\Services\TcpIP\Parameters\DnsNbtLookupOrder

This affects whether DNS has priority over NetBIOS. A value of 0 indicates DNS has priority, a value of 1 indicates NetBIOS does. See MS document Q120642 for more information. A best practice is to simply disable NetBIOS over TCP/IP (NetBT). If this is done, it should only compromise file sharing to/from NT 4.0 servers.

If not disabling the NetBT, set the NNM server as an H-Node or P-Node for NetBT resolution. This way, if a name isn't resolved by one of the other methods, the server should do a query directly to a WINS server, which is more likely to succeed on a large network than a broadcast. A P-Node does not do a broadcast before giving up, but is not allowed on some networks. This is set in:

HKLM\SYSTEM\CurrentControlSet\Services\Tcpip\ServiceProvider

with the key name being Class. A value of 8 makes the computer an H node. The Class value for B node is 1, for P node is 2, and for M node is 4. Keep in mind that most Windows DNS servers are configured to do a WINS query themselves if a name or address isn't in their zones. WINS name resolution failures can be made to fail faster by adjusting:

HKLM\SYSTEM\CurrentControlSet\Services\NetBT\Parameters:

    BcastNameQueryCount
    BcastQueryTimeout
    NameSrvQueryRetries
    NameSrvQueryTimeout.

If Active Directory is involved Windows uses the DNS servers known to Active Directory first, even if they are different then the configured DNS servers. To switch to a locally-controlled DNS server, get the NMS Server out of the Active Directory tree and point it at a DNS Server that is not known to Active Directory, preferably on the same subnet. Active Directory is not required to run NNM..

Tuning lookup performance (UNIX)

The most important configuration entry point for UNIX name services tuning is the /etc/nsswitch.conf file. This file sets the order and failover behavior for several services including name services.

The nslookup command operates differently on HP-UX and Solaris. On HP-UX, nslookup queries DNS, NIS, or hosts; on Solaris, nslookup queries DNS only. On Solaris, use getent hosts <target> queries to test how lookups are affected by nsswitch.conf.

On HP-UX and Solaris, DNS timeouts can be tuned directly in the /etc/resolv.conf file. By default, the timeout is calculated using the RES_RETRANS parameter whose default is 5000 milliseconds (HP-UX) and 5 seconds (Solaris) and RES_RETRY whose default is 4.

The following entries limit the timeout 1s per failed lookup:

```
domain <domain>
nameserver <primaryNameServer>
nameserver <secondaryNameServer>
retrans 1000  # value in milliseconds
retry 1
```

NNM doesn't detect DNS changes (Windows)

With Windows 2000, Microsoft introduced a local caching-only DNS server that gets queried first for any DNS lookups, regardless of lookup order. This is the DNS Client service, and it is installed and runs automatically by default.

Odd values could still be returned from the local client after another DNS server is updated. Disabling the DNS Client service if running a caching-only DNS on the NNM server, is recommended on the NNM server as NNM already caches queries via the SNMP Configuration database. That cache can be cleared using:

```
xnmsnmpconf -clearC
```

To dump and then clear the contents of the local DNS cache , run:

```
ipconfig /displaydns
ipconfig /flushdns
```

To A record or not to A record

Newer versions of NNM have more intelligence and flexibility for picking the preferred management IP address (aka primary IP address). For primary IP Addresses, always add an A record and a PTR record for the resverse zone.

Adding A records for secondary IP addresses is generally not necessary for NNM's purposes, but may be desirable for other reasons. When adding A records for secondary IP addresses, instead of adding a PTR record pointing back to that A record's name, use the name associated with the A record for the primary IP address.

A record compare issue on Solaris platform

Solaris implements special logic in *gethostbyaddr* such that after the OS requests the PTR from the DNS and gets the A record back, it issues a subsequent request for the A record and compares the results to the IP address originally requested. If this additional request isn't returned, the whole call returns NULL. This logic was instituted as IP spoofing protection.

This can be problematic on multi-homed hosts that do not have A records for every IP address defined for the node in the case where A records cannot otherwise be entered for all interfaces in DNS due to issues with round robin, application requirements, etc. Work-arounds include only entering the loopback address for the device in DNS or using a combination of noIpLookup.conf and `snmpnolookupconf`. See page 29 for more on these settings.

nscd issues on Solaris

The Name Server Cache Daemon, *nscd*, is intended to speed up name service lookups, whether from NIS, NIS+, DNS, or local files. In some cases, however, *nscd* can slow DNS lookups, and some administrators choose to disable it. Moreover, *nscd* interferes with round robin (*nscd* caches records in one order and doesn't rotate them). Some important /etc/ncsd.conf file tunables are:

Toggle host lookup caching:	`enable-cache hosts <yes	no>`
TTL positive results:	`positive-time-to-live hosts <sec>`
TTL negative results:	`negative-time-to-live hosts <sec>`

Name resolution support commands:

Use the following commands to determine if NNM is performing poorly with respect to name services:

```
$OV_SUPPORT/gethost <hostname>
$OV_SUPPORT/gethost -v <host>    (fwd and reverse lookup)
$OV_SUPPORT/gethost -a <IP Address>
xnmsnmpconf -resolve <target>
xnmsnmpconf -dumpcache all
xnmsnmpconf -clearC
snmplookupconf -dumpC
snmplookupconf -t[est] <target>
$OV_SUPPORT/checkDNS.ovpl
ovstatus -v snmpCollect
ovstatus -v netmon
```

NNM DNS tracing

Set the following environment variable to enable DNS tracing to the specified file, then restart the OpenView daemons:

```
OV_NS_LOG_TRACE=<directory>;0.0;2;
```

See page 3 for information on setting environment variables. Logfile entries have the following form:

N:2:N:...	Hostname to IP Address lookup
N:2:A:...	IP Address to Hostname lookup

Name services-related documentation

NNM 6.2 patches introduced DNS performance improvements which are discussed in the following white papers:

HP's White Paper: $OV_DOC/WhitePapers/DNSandOpenView.pdf
D. Stevenson's DNS White Paper: www.fognet.com/ds-dns.doc

NNM in demo, DHCP or mobile environments

From an SNMP management perspective, the NNM server needs to be a fixed IP address that doesn't change often. Changing the IP address of the NNM server causes SNMP devices to generate traps to all the addresses that NNM discovers them from, because the NNM server sets itself as a trap destination when it can.

If NNM is to be installed on a laptop that is moved around, or it is a demo system where the IP address is expected to change, set the USE_LOOPBACK=ON parameter in the following file to keep

NNM daemons from crashing when the network becomes unavailable: $OV_CONF/ov.conf. Typically, in this scenario, the NNM license is instant-on, otherwise it would report an error if the licenced IP changed.

5. Discovery via *netmon*

NNM has two discovery engines and two polling engines, each of which address OSI level 2 and level 3 respectively, and each of which has overlap onto the other layer. *netmon* is the level 3 discovery and polling engine and is a legacy product element. *ovet_disco* and *ovet_poll* are the newer level 2-focused discovery and polling daemons.

The ET pollers depend on *netmon* for discovery, and the `ovet_bridge` process is responsible for keeping the separate topology databases synchronized. Distributed NNM architure is build mostly on legacy level 3 topology and discovery, and ET discovery is not necessarily easily compatible with distributed installations.

When NNM is first installed, *netmon* discovery occurs automatically unless disabled during dialog at installation. To get layer2 topology disovered, the *ovet_disco*-based discovery must be enabled using the following command:

```
setupExtTopo.ovpl
```

Similarly, the *ovet_poll*-based poller and the advanced problem analyzer, if desired, must be enabled using the following command:

```
ovet_apaConfig.ovpl -enable APAPolling
```

Prior to running *ovet_disco*-based discovery, at least some of the environment should be properly discovered by *netmon* first. Similarly, prior to enabling the *ovet_poll*-based poller, the *ovet_disco*-based discovery must be run first. All *netmon* polling options that can be set in the Options-Network Polling Configuration menus can be controlled from the command line as well using the xnmpolling command. For example, to toggle *netmon* discovery on or off, use:

```
xnmpolling -ipDiscoveryOff or xnmpolling -ipDiscoveryOn
```

Preparing for NNM discovery

The HP documentation covers this well, but here is a review of some important steps to take before setting NNM loose on the network:

1. Make sure SNMP community strings are properly configured
2. Make sure name services are OK. Read the section on naming
3. Populate netmon.noDiscover file with undesirable devices
4. Populate netmon.noDiscover file with HSRP devices (skip if running NNM 7.? or above, or use netmon.migratable)
5. Have any edge routers? Consider –R *netmon* LRF switch
6. Make sure firewalls are open to desired areas (see page 291)
7. Check for cut SNMP tables on key devices
8. Set loopback addresses on routers, map to DNS (see page 25)
9. Run: `nmcheckconf` (UNIX) to probe network configuration
10. If there are nodes with many interfaces that are not desirable to discover/manage, consider using netmon.interfaceNoDiscover

After NNM discovery

After initial automatic discovery by NNM, perform these steps to expand the discovered environment:

1. Select desired unmanaged networks (beige) and select Map- Manage Objects to discover into adjacent networks
2. Run the following and compare to entries in oid_to_type, oid_to_sym, and HPOid2Type (command is case sensitive):
    ```
    ovobjprint -a "SNMP sysObjectID"
    ```
3. See the script on page 47 for a way to automate the above step
4. Check totals on objects discovered by running: `ovtopodump -l`
5. Once `ET Discovery is complete, compare ovtopodump -l` output with `ovet_topodump -info` output

Discovery process in a nutshell

netmon queries the SNMP MIB of the NNM Server to determine its IP address, subnet mask, its default router's IP address and its local ARP cache. *netmon* reads the ARP cache of the default router via SNMP, then sends an ICMP `ping` to each IP address learned from the ARP cache. See page 51 for a list of the specific MIB variables queried for this information.

Those nodes that respond to SNMP get an SNMP request for sysObjectId for each discovered node, and a series of other queries (listed below) to determine other attributes and capabilities. To determine the node type, NNM maps the agent OID to the oid_to_type or HPoid2type file for vendor, SNMP agent and other topology flags that determine where in the map the node object should be placed. The oid_to_sym is then queried to map a symbol to the node. Additional name service queries are made and the node is assigned a selection name according to the rules on page 25.

Discovery polls vs. other types of *netmon* polls

Discovery polls focus on finding new nodes that haven't been found before. The discovery poll looks at the routing table, etc., and if it finds something new, *netmon* issues subsequent capability and topology checks, otherwise it doesn't.

A configuration check or configuration poll combines a capability poll and a topology check, this combo being the equivalent of issuing the nmdemandpoll command. The capability poll looks at object DB capabilities.

The topology poll looks at topology MIB tables such as the bridge MIB, etc. The topology poll is only issued to those to connector nodes, and can be configured to occur more frequently in the polling options.

Understanding *netmon*-based level 2 discovery

As mentioned above, there are some vagaries in this legacy poller. The switches and options that affect *netmon's* discovery, polling, and subsequent topology placement in IPMAP are numerous. For the most part, it is best to leave NNM's L2 settings alone.

For the brave, the level2conf white paper explains much of the aforementioned vagaries. Because it typically raises more questions than it answers, this white paper was removed from later distributions of NNM. In fact, it has been purged from all of HP's public pages, but it can still be found at several sites via web search.

Limiting discovery

$OV_CONF/oid_to_type has global options to limit discovery, for example, of all non-SNMP supported devices. All systems matching OID's placed in that file can also be configured to be ignored by NNM discovery. Details on using oid_to_type can be found on page 7.

To disable automatic discovery, toggle the "Discover New IP Nodes" radio button in the IP Discovery configuration area of the Options-Network Polling Configuration menu bar item. The same can be accomplished from the command line with:

```
xnmpolling -ipDiscoveryOff
```

To limit discovery by IP address range, IP address wildcard, or by MAC addresses, see the man/ref pages for netmon.noDiscover and netmon.noMACdiscover. Any changes to these files require that *netmon* be restarted using `ovstop` and `ovstart` and only apply to new nodes being discovered.

To limit discovery of interfaces based on ifType, name, description etc, use netmon.interfaceNoDiscover (available in NNM 7.5+). This will prevent the interfaces from being discovered both by netmon and ET disco. See Page 55 for more information on this.

Limiting export of nodes from *netmon* to ET is configured in the bridge.noDiscover file in $OV_CONF. See the bridge.noDiscover man/ref pages for more information on this.

With the release of NNM 6.31, HP introduced the ability of filters to be used to prevent discovery of whole classes of nodes based on standard NNM filters.

A discovery filter uses NNM filter definition language (see page 277) to discard or include only those nodes which pass the filter. For example, to discover only nodes with Cisco and Extreme SNMP agents, build a filter like this:

```
DiscoInclude "Cisco, Extreme" {
    ("SNMP sysObjectID" ~ "1.3.6.1.4.1.9.*") ||
    ("SNMP sysObjectID" ~ "1.3.6.1.4.1.1916.*")
}
```

Or to exclude Microsoft nodes from discovery:

```
DiscoExclude "Microsoft: {
    { isNode && ( vendor != "Microsoft" )
}
```

Run `ovfiltertest` to see the results of the filter if any of the devices to include or exclude have already been discovered.

To activate the discovery filters, use the menu bar pull down: Options:Network Polling Configuration:IP. Select Configuration Area: General. Select Use Discovery Filter, then enter the filter name, for example, DiscoExclude.

The following external commands can be used to deploy and control a discovery filter named <filter-name>:

```
xnmpolling -discFiltName <filter-name> -discFiltOn
xnmpolling -discFiltName <filter-name> -discFiltOff
```

Once the filter is configured, tested, and added to the polling configuration, all nodes to be excluded must be deleted from the topology and all existing maps must be opened. Once they are deleted, they will not be rediscovered.

Externally managing or unmanaging objects

Objects are typically managed or unmanaged using map operations in the GUI, but here are four commands used to manage or unmanage objects externally (in increasing order of complexity):

```
xnmtopoconf
ovtopofix
topology URLs
ovautoifmgr
```

See page 241 for information on adding, deleting, managing or unmanaging objects via topology URLs. Note that none of the above tools can be used to control discovery by ET or polling by APA. In NNM 7.5 and above, use ovet_toposet.ovpl to unmanage nodes, boards and interfaces from being status polled by the APA. More information on ovet_toposet.ovpl can be found on page 77.

xnmtopoconf can be used to manage or unmanage individual nodes from the command line. xnmtopoconf is only available on NNM editions supporting DIM (i.e. not NNM Standard Edition). Use ovtopofix -G/g to manage/unmanage objects by OOID. For example, get OOIDs for all interfaces whose name is Se0/1.1, then pass to ovtopofix -G:

```
ovobjprint -a "SNMP ifName" "SNMP ifName"="Se0/1.1"
```

The following two commands, respectively unmanage (-g) and manage (-G) objects:

```
ovtopofix -g <OOID>
ovtopofix -G <OOID>
```

Use *ovautoifmgr* to automatically manage or unmanage interfaces based on filters. For example, an administrator may want to manage only interfaces with IP addresses assigned on switches. First, set up two filters for the ovautoifmgr.conf file, one that passed the nodes whose interfaces are to be scanned by the second filter. In the filters file, define two filters:

```
Switches "Switches Node Filter" { isBridge }
NonIpInt "Non-IP Interfaces filter" { !isIP }
```

Then, in the ovautoifmgr.conf file, add: `Switches NonIpInt`

Stop discovery of non-IP interfaces for a device class

Use the –N flag in the oid_to_type file. Changes affect only newly-discovered devices, or run: `ovtopofix -o <OID>`. Details on using oid_to_type can be found on page 7.

Stop all SNMP discovery/polling to a device class

On some devices, it is not desirable to have SNMP visibility, but simple ICMP status to the node is OK. Use the –I flag in the oid_to_type file to force ICMP-only status. Changes affect only newly-discovered devices, or run: `ovtopofix -o <OID>`. Details on using oid_to_type can be found on page 7.

Discovery hints

A command line option to provide *netmon* discovery hints was added in intermediate patch 18 to V7.51. This allows hints to be entered directly from the command line and can reduce or illiminate the need to use seeding (see below) and is a more direct method that using the `loadhosts` command (page 47). To add a hint to *netmon*, issue the following command:

```
netmon -h <ip addr>
```

Seeding discovery

Use a *netmon* seed file in environments where rediscovery of the network is frequent and devices cannot be discovered by *netmon* due to network or SNMP access. Entries in the seed file should be populated into previously-undiscovered networks as managed networks. This can save time where otherwise, new networks must be manually managed from the GUI.

A seed file might also speed the discovery process. A seed file has the form of a standard hosts file and is configured using the -s <seedfile> LRF switch to netmon.lrf. See page 5 for LRF instructions. Note when specifying a file in the switch for Windows-based servers, the colon must be escaped, for example:

```
-P -s "c\:\seedfile.txt" -k segRedux=true
```

Configuring multiple SNMP community strings

The netmon.cmstr file supports an ordered list of communities to use when contacting SNMP agents for read-only access. Here is an example for a list of five communities to attempt to use in ascending order to contact all SNMP agents:

```
"cs1", "cs2", "cs3", "cs4", "cs5" : : : :
```

Preferred SNMP management address

If a configuration poll fails to reach a node's preferred SNMP address as set in the SNMP configuration DB, *netmon* issues a special "pickSnmpAddrPoll" that attempts to find a valid alternative SNMP preferred address. This can cause issues with data collections and could cause the target's node name to change in NNM.

If loopbacks are not widely implemented, pickSnmpAddrPoll is a useful tool to help manage changing SNMP management addresses. Also, see page 27 and subsequent sections for tips on using DNS to understand the best network naming conventions to most efficiently SNMP manage networks.

Defining loopback addresses on network devices also may obviate the need to worry about the preferred SNMP management address changing, since most network devices will re-assign the configured loopback to an active interface if the current interface fails. If this is the case, follow the steps below to disable preferred management address picking which is enabled by default.

To disable the pickSnmpAddrPoll feature, set the following LRF (see page 5) switch in *netmon*:

```
-k pickSnmpAddrPolls=false
```

45

Another –k netmon lrf option was added in NNM 7.53 that should also be disabled to stop netmon from switching preferred management addresses. The difference between this newer one and pickSnmpAddrPolls is that the above option affects general SNMP polls while the new option affects *netmon*-based SNMP status polls:

```
-k adjustNodeSnmpAddr=false
```

Forcing the SNMP address for a node

Use this method if all other mechanisms for picking the correct preferred SNMP address fail. If using the APA, see page 94 for how ET and the APA can affect preffered management SNMP address. To force NNM to change the SNMP Address to a different one, follow these steps:

1. If using APA, disable polling using:
   ```
   ovet_apaConfig.ovpl –disable APAPolling
   ```
2. In the IPMAP topology map, temporarily unmanage all the interfaces for the target node except the interface that is to be set as the SNMP Address
3. Demand Poll the device
4. Unless the *netmon* –k pickSnmpAddrPolls was set to false, the preferred SNMP address will now be set to the managed interface.
5. Run: ovtopodump –l |grep "SNMP ADDRESS"
6. Re-manage the rest of the node's interfaces
7. Re-enable APA using:
   ```
   ovet_apaConfig.ovpl –enable APAPolling
   ```

If there is the need to perform this task for more than a handful of nodes, a command line tool called topodbpoke can be used to change the preferred SNMP Address in the *ovw* topology. topodbpoke was shipped with NNM 7.53 in the $OV_SUPPORT directory. Instuctions for using it can be found in the following document under "Change Incorrect IPv4 Management Address" in this white paper:

$OV_DOC/whitepapers/ETandAPADeploymentGuide.pdf

If running V7.53, this documentation can also be found in the Guide to Using Extended Topology user manual. Before NNM 7.53, the tool was available through HP support. The author had a need for this tool in October 2007 and opened a case with HP, but HP support was unable to locate the utility. For this reason, and for folks running earlier versions of NNM, the author has posted the `topodbpoke` code for all platforms except Linux here:

www.fognet.com/topodbpoke.zip

netmon's auto-adjusting discovery polling algorithm

Discovery polls are basically SNMP requests to routing tables to find nodes that haven't been discovered before. All nodes start at 15 minute intervals for new node polling. If *netmon* discovers no new nodes during a poll, then five minutes are added to the polling interval. If more than 5 nodes are discovered during a poll, the polling interval is halved. When a new node is discovered, a configuration poll is issued. Subsequent configuration polls are issued every 24 hours by default.

PERL script: find OIDs not listed in oid_to_type

This script produces a list of SNMP OIDs that have been discovered by *netmon*, but do not have corresponding entries in the oid_to_type or HPoid2type files. Consider adding the resulting OIDs to the files and setting desired topology flags for their treatment. Note that on Windows, the results produced are not made unique.

```
#!/usr/local/bin/perl
open IN1,"c:\openview\conf\oid_to_type";
open IN2,"c:\openview\conf\HPoid2type";
@oids1 = <IN1>; @oids2 = <IN2>;
close IN1; close IN2;
@oids = (@oids1,@oids2);
open CMD,qq(ovobjprint -a "SNMP sysObjectID" |);
@objdb = <CMD>;
close CMD;
foreach (@objdb) {
    s/.*\"\.1.3.6.(.+)\"/1.3.6.$1/ or next;
    chomp;
    next if $oidhash{"$_"};
    $oidhash{"$_"} = 1;
    my @found;
    foreach $x (@oids) {
        push @found, $x if $x =~ /^$_/;
    }
    print "$_ not in oid_to_type\n" unless @found;
}
```

loadhosts

The `loadhosts` command is useful for adding nodes to the NNM topology outside of the discovery process, but it can produce unintended results. If adding a node into a network that does not yet exist in the map, be particularly careful, since NNM may make certain assumptions about the "classfullness" of the network.

47

In the past, `loadhosts` was the preferred method for forcing discovery for a node or set of nodes that *netmon* couldn't otherwise discover. Since the release of Intermediate Patch 18 to V7.51, the best practice to accomplish this is to give *netmon* discovery hints using the "-h" option to *netmon*. See page 44 for details.

To make sure `loadhosts` honors the "classfulness" of the network of the device being added. Use the "–m" option to specify the netmask for the network the device lies in if it is in a network not already present in NNM topology. Still, `loadhosts` may complain, so it may be necessary to manually create a network symbol in ovw with the correct mask and then manually add the device using map operations. To do this, see page 204.

If adding less than 100 addresses, remember to use the –n 1 switch. Page 241 provides information on adding, deleting, managing or unmanaging objects via topology URLs. This facility was designed to provide a secure remote front end for `loadhosts`. `loadhosts` is designed to take input from a file, but when invoked from the command line, should take standard input. This means that after input is entered for the `loadhosts` command, the prompt might hang until it is interrupted with a "Ctrl C" command.

`loadhosts` has many command line options, but the best practice is to load a host with minimal switches and let *netmon* discover the rest. For connectors, it is best to use the address associated with the software loopback to seed *netmon*, but in some environments, it is better to use the address associated with the DNS name assigned to the device.

Name services may be used by *netmon* to determine what interfaces are associated with a particular host if it can't otherwise determine this through SNMP.

`loadhosts` bypasses *netmon*'s normal discovery sequence, so upon loading, a new node may not receive a full configuration check. This means that the icon may not be properly represented on the map. Force the configuration poll using the GUI, `nmdemandpoll`, or use the "-o" option to `loadhosts` to force an oid_to_type lookup if the device's SNMP agent OID is listed there. `loadhosts` will not succeed in entering a particular node into the topology if the network it is loaded into is in the unmanaged state.

Batch load hosts having a subnet mask of 255.255.255.248, where the file contains an /etc/hosts-like list of IP addresses and hostnames:

```
loadhosts -bvpm 255.255.255.248 <filename>
```

To add a single node via piping (works on Windows, too):

```
echo "192.168.1.9 patchy" | loadhosts -V -v -m 255.255.255.0
```

`loadhosts` operations may fail for a variety of reasons. A typical error message might say that the subnet mask is invalid. The most common cause is that there is an incorrectly classed network defined (see page 211). There are other reasons `loadhosts` may fail, such as firewalls, etc. In this case, add the objects manually using the procedure on page 204. In general, if the object can be reached via ICMP or SNMP, it can be loaded into the topology. Objects that can't be reached by either protocol may be added, but can never be automatically connected in the topology or given a status by *netmon* or the APA.

Discovery of 31 and 32 bit subnetworks

Both 31 and 32 bit networks use the network address as an IP Address. These are IP networks with a subnet masks of, respectively, 255.255.255.254 and 255.255.255.255. The NNM topology manager has trouble with these, since it uses the network address to name network level objects. To properly handle this situation, the -1 and -2 switches were added as LRF switches to the ovtopmd daemon. These switches get around the naming problem by appending /31 or /32 (as appropriate) to the network object name in the object database. See the ovtopmd man/ref page for more details and see page 5 for information on modifying LRF files.

Discovery of HSRP, clusters, and multilinked routers

Legacy NNM handles migrating or duplicate IP addresses very poorly. NNM requires forcing interfaces that share the same IP address to go undiscovered by NNM's IPMAP topology by placing them in the netmon.noDiscover file.

Alternatively, the devices that run HSRP can be configured with "D" flag in the oid_to_type file, which assumes that if the floating address is not in the ipAddrTable, then the address should go undiscovered. Unfortunately, Cisco started reporting floating addresses in the active router's ipAddrTable with IOS 12.1(14) and greater and 12.2(13) and greater, so the netmon.noDiscover file is the best bet.

In NNM 7.5 the following two LRF flags were added to the *netmon* daemon:

    -k migrateHsrpVirtualIP=true
    -k doNotDiscoverDuplicates=true

The first allows the automatic population of virtual group IP addresses into the netmon.migratable file during discovery. The second allows duplicate IP addresses to be populated into the netmon.noDiscover file during discovery. Both are set to false by default.

These settings, once applied, will only affect newly-discovered devices. Note that there was a bug with migrateHsrpVirtualIP that was addressed with an early patch to V7.5.In some cases, the use of the netmon.migratable file can be used for clustered nodes. HSRP virtual group IP addresses can also be placed in that file.

Cisco's implementation of multilink PPP and Juniper's Multi-Router Automatic Protection Switching feature both create active interfaces that share a single address. In essence, *netmon* cannot accommodate the duplicate interface addressing between the router pairs involved because both interfaces are active at the same time. Contrast this to an HSRP-like situation where a single virtual address is only active in one place at one time. These are best managed using the netmon.migratable file.

See the *netmon* man/ref page for more information and see page 5 for how to update LRF flags. See the procedure on page 7 for configuring oid_to_type. See page 251 for details on how ET handles VRRP. See page 253 for more info on how ET handles HSRP. See page 289 for details on managing migratable IP addresses.

Summary of *netmon* configuration files

The following external files influence *netmon's* behavior, but the main settings for *netmon* are controlled through the *xnmpolling* and *xnmsnmpconf* interfaces available from the Options menu of *ovw*:

    $OV_CONF/polling
    $OV_LOG/netmon.trace
    $OV_CONF/oid_to_type
    $OV_CONF/HPoid2type
    $OV_CONF/excludeip.conf
    $OV_CONF/netmon.noDiscover

$OV_CONF/netmon.MACnoDiscover
$OV_CONF/netmon.interfaceNoDiscover
$OV_CONF/netmon.migratable
$OV_CONF/netmon.cmstr
$OV_CONF/netmon.equivPorts
$OV_CONF/netmon.snmpStatus
$OV_CONF/netmon.statusIntervals
$OV_CONF/netmon.statusMapping
$OV_CONF/nmdemandpoll.ports

Undocumented *netmon* LRF switch settings

See page 5 for details on the LRF procedure.

-A	Automatically manage networks when created.
-H0	Don't do http discovery (UNIX only)
-H1	Do http discovery (UNIX only)
-2	Don't use SNMPv2C
-k configPollDelay <#> (see below)	

Implementing the –H0 and –H1 switches improves the performance and scalability of discovery polls and of configuration polls. The equivalent for Windows-based NNM servers is to add the -nohttp and -nohttpmg switches to the ovcapsd.lrf file. The HTTP discovery simply sets a capability flag if the target responds to a poll to port 80. The only purpose of this flag is to allow searching and reporting based on that capability. It is a good general practice to disable this polling if there is no use for this extra data in the object database.

V7.51 Intermediate Patch 18 introduced the -k configPollDelay <#> option to allow a delay of <#> seconds for the configuration poll if the state of the SNMP address is down when the poll initiates. This was introduced to address the case where a system with multiple SNMP subagent took some time for all subagents to start after a reboot in order to populate the interface tables properly.

SNMP queries issued by *netmon*

Queries issued during a *netmon* discovery/capability poll. This list may vary with NNM version:

.1.3	Test for SNMP Support
.1.3.6.1.2.1.1.2.0	sysObjectID
.1.3.6.1.2.1.1.1.0	sysDescr
.1.3.6.1.2.1.1.5.0	sysName
.1.3.6.1.4.1.11.2.3.1.6.1.1.2.1.2	hpClusterTable
.1.3.6.1.2.1.17.1.1.0	dot1dBaseBridgeAddress
.1.3.6.1.2.1.17.1.2.0	dot1dBaseNumPorts

.1.3.6.1.2.1.17.1.3.0	dot1dBaseType
.1.3.6.1.2.1.4.20.1.1	getnext ipAdEntAddr
.1.3.6.1.2.1.4.20.1.3	ipAdEntNetMask
.1.3.6.1.2.1.4.20.1.2	ipAdEntIfIndex
.1.3.6.1.2.1.2.1	ifNumber
.1.3.6.1.2.1.2.2.1.1	ifPhysAddress
.1.3.6.1.2.1.2.2.1.3	ifType
.1.3.6.1.2.1.2.2.1.2	ifDescr
.1.3.6.1.2.1.2.2.1.8	ifOperStatus
.1.3.6.1.2.1.2.2.1.7	ifAdminStatus
.1.3.6.1.2.1.31.1.1.1.1	ifName
.1.3.6.1.2.1.31.1.1.1.18	ifAlias
.1.3.6.1.2.1.17.1.4.1.1.0	dot1dBasePort
.1.3.6.1.2.1.17.1.4.1.2.0	dot1dBasePortIfIndex.
.1.3.6.1.2.1.4.1.0	ipForwarding
.1.3.6.1.2.1.1.6.0	sysLocation
.1.3.6.1.2.1.1.4	sysContact
.1.3.6.1.2.1.4.21.1.7.0.0.0.0	ipRouteNextHop
.1.3.6.1.4.1.11.2.17.4.1.1.1.0	hpOVDStnType
.1.3.6.1.4.1.11.2.36.1.1.1.1.0	managementURL
.1.3.6.1.2.1.4.21.1.7	ipRouteNextHop
.1.3.6.1.2.1.4.21.1.8	ipRouteType
.1.3.6.1.2.1.4.21.1.2	ipRouteIfIndex
.1.3.6.1.2.1.4.21.1.1	ipRouteDest
.1.3.6.1.2.1.4.21.1.11	ipRouteMask
.1.3.6.1.2.1.4.22.1.3	ipNetToMediaNetAddress
.1.3.6.1.2.1.4.22.1.2	ipNetToMediaPhysAddress
.1.3.6.1.2.1.4.22.1.1	ipNetToMediaIfIndex
.1.3.6.1.2.1.4.22.1.4	ipNetToMediaType
.1.3.6.1.2.1.3.1.1.3	atnetAddress
.1.3.6.1.2.1.3.1.1.2	atPhysAddress
.1.3.6.1.2.1.3.1.1.1	atIfIndex
.1.3.6.1.2.1.16	rmon mib
.1.3.6.1.2.1.16.20	rmonConformance
.1.3.6.1.2.1.10.18	DS1 mib
.1.3.6.1.2.1.10.30	DS3 mib
.1.3.6.1.2.1.10.32	frameRelay mib
.1.3.6.1.2.1.10.39	SONET mib
.1.3.6.1.2.1.37	ATM mib
.1.3.6.1.4.1.9.9.23.1.3.1	cdpGlobalRun
.1.3.6.1.2.1.10.166.2.1.9	mpls
.1.3.6.1.3.96	Cisco mpls
.1.3.6.1.4.1.9.9.106.1.2.1.1.11	HSRP
.1.3.6.1.2.1.55	IPV6
.1.3.6.1.2.1.14.1.1	OSPF
.1.3.6.1.2.1.15.3.1.1	BGP4
.1.3.6.1.2.1.68	vrrpMIB
.1.3.6.1.2.1.17.2.1	STP
.1.2.840.10036	wireless

Queries issued during a *netmon* topology poll:
  ifMib (RFC 1573):

.1.3.6.1.2.1.31.1.1.1.1   ifXTableifName

Mau MIB (RFC 1515):
.1.3.6.1.2.1.26.1.1.1.1   rpMauTablerpMauGroupIndex
.1.3.6.1.2.1.26.1.1.1.2   rpMauPortIndex
.1.3.6.1.2.1.26.1.1.1.4   rpMauType
.1.3.6.1.2.1.26.4.x   dot3MauType

Repeater MIB (RFC 1516):
.1.3.6.1.2.1.22.3.3.1.1.1   rptrAddrTrackGroupIndex
.1.3.6.1.2.1.22.3.3.1.1.2   rptrAddrTrackPortIndex
.1.3.6.1.2.1.22.3.3.1.1.5   rptrAddrTrackNewLastSrcAddr
.1.3.6.1.2.1.22.3.3.1.1.4   rptrAddrTrackSourceAddrChanges
.1.3.6.1.2.1.22.3.3.1.1.6   rptrAddrTrackCapacity

Repeater MIB (RFC 2108):
.1.3.6.1.2.1.22.1.4.1.1.1   rptrInfoTablerptrInfoId
.1.3.6.1.2.1.22.1.4.1.1.2   rptrInfoRptrType
.1.3.6.1.2.1.22.1.4.1.1.3   rptrInfoOperStatus
.1.3.6.1.2.1.22.3.1.1.1.1   rptrAddrSearchTablerptrAddrSearchLock
.1.3.6.1.2.1.22.3.1.1.1.2   rptrAddrSearchStatus
.1.3.6.1.2.1.22.3.1.1.1.3   rptrAddrSearchAddress
.1.3.6.1.2.1.22.3.1.1.1.4   rptrAddrSearchState
.1.3.6.1.2.1.22.3.1.1.1.5   rptrAddrSearchGroup
.1.3.6.1.2.1.22.3.1.1.1.6   rtprAddrSearchPort
.1.3.6.1.2.1.22.3.1.1.1.7   rptrAddrSearchOwner
.1.3.6.1.2.1.22.3.3.1.1.1   rptrAddrTrackGroupIndex
.1.3.6.1.2.1.22.3.3.1.1.2   rptrAddrTrackPortIndex
.1.3.6.1.2.1.22.3.3.1.1.5   rptrAddrTrackNewLastSrcAddr
.1.3.6.1.2.1.22.3.3.1.1.4   rptrAddrTrackSourceAddrChanges
.1.3.6.1.2.1.22.3.3.1.1.6   rptrAddrTrackCapacity

Bridge MIB (RFC 1493):
.1.3.6.1.2.1.17.1.1   dot1dBasedot1dBaseBridgeAddress
.1.3.6.1.2.1.17.1.2   dot1dBaseBridgeNumPorts
.1.3.6.1.2.1.17.1.3   dot1dBaseBridgeType.1
.1.3.6.1.2.1.17.1.4.1.1   dot1dBasePort
.1.3.6.1.2.1.17.1.4.1.2   dot1dBasePortIfIndex
.1.3.6.1.2.1.17.2.15.1.1   dot1dStpPort
.1.3.6.1.2.1.17.2.15.1.3   dot1dStpPortState
.1.3.6.1.2.1.17.2.15.1.8   dot1dStpPortDesignatedBridge
.1.3.6.1.2.1.17.2.15.1.9   dot1dStpPortDesignatedPort.
.1.3.6.1.2.1.17.4.3.1.1   dot1dTpFdbTabledot1dTpFdbAddress
.1.3.6.1.2.1.17.4.3.1.2   dot1dTpFdbPort
.1.3.6.1.2.1.17.4.3.1.3   dot1dTpFdbStatus

6. Status Polling - *netmon*

This section covers the functions within *netmon* that deliver status. *netmon* is also responsible for discvoery and configuration polling, and those functions are discussed in Section 5, Discovery.

ICMP and SNMP idiosyncrasies and "brown-outs"

When a node is not responding to pings or SNMP requests, NNM generates events and sets topology status. But there are other reasons that may cause ICMP or SNMP requests to fail that might produce the same events and status in NNM when in fact the node may be perfectly healthy. Some NNM users might change the text of status events from "node down" to "node not responding to polls" to more accurately reflect this reality. The list below provides just some examples.

- Routers drops packets due to high CPU utilization coupled with low priority for ICMP and/or SNMP. Assign higher priorities to ICMP and/or SNMP on routers. Check out Cisco's Priority Queueing.

- Network congestion over WAN links is slowing response times. For example, if polls are traversing frame relay links, then check FECN, BECN, and packets marked DE.

- If an NNM status poll goes through a T1 link running AMI, the packet is dropped. This is due to the fact that NNM's ICMP payloads are set to 64 bits of all zeros, and the older AMI coding, which is intended for use in voice circuits, is designed to make sure there is at least one 1-bit for every 8 bits to reduce potential line harmonics. The solution is to set up the links affected to use B8ZS instead of AMI coding.

- The route that SNMP or ICMP packets take to the source and from it back to the NNM server can be different, and at least one router may be configured to drop the protocol somewhere along the way. Use `traceroute` or `tracert`, Problem Diagnosis, `rping`, and `rnetstat` to determine the source of the problem.

Adjusting ICMP and SNMP status polling intervals

Both SNMP and ICMP polling intervals are set in the SNMP Configuration GUI for *netmon*-based polling settings. ET-based polling intervals and other settings are configured through XML files, the primary of which is paConfig.xml. Like *netmon*, ET polling configs are combined for both status and topology/discovery.

SNMP configuration settings are employed exactly as configured. ICMP configuration settings, however, are rounded out the nearest second, so the default timeout of 0.8 is actually rounded out to 1 second for ICMP polls. The timeout interval is re-doubled for every retry. A configuration of 0.8 timeout and 2 retries means that when an ICMP poll is issued, it should take 7 seconds to fail (first poll times out in 1 second, first retry times out in 2 seconds, and second retry times out in 4 seconds). An SNMP poll to the same node should time out in 5.6 seconds.

netmon.noDiscover and netmon.MACnoDiscover files

Use these files to enter IP address and MAC addresses individually, by ranges, or by wildcards to prevent subsequent discovery after restarting *netmon*. Any addresses that have been previously discovered will have to be manually deleted from the topology.

To make sure an address is not in the topology, use the Find application from the *ovw* menu bar and Find by Attribute: IP Address. Entries found can be highlighted from the Find application and then deleted from the Edit menu bar after choosing View: Select Highlighted.

If populating the netmon.MACnoDiscover file, it may be of interest to also set the –k FilterLLAOnlyNodes=true LRF flag to the *netmon* daemon. Setting this flag will force *netmon* to stop using MAC addresses in the netmon.MACnoDiscover file as hints for discovery. See page 5 for how to set LRF flags.

netmon.interfaceNoDiscover file

The file $OV_CONF/netmon.interfaceNoDiscover is used to define how to restrict the set of interfaces to be discovered for a node. This configuration file was introduced in intermediate patch 12 to V7.5. In V7.51, the InterfaceFiltering.pdf white paper was added in $OV_DOC.WhitePapers. In V7.53, this information was rolled into the Using_Extended_Topology.pdf user manual.

Unlike netmon.noDiscover, netmon.interfaceNodiscover will truncate the SNMP tables used to populate interface data on connector nodes, greatly improving discovery and polling performance. Not only can specific interfaces be explicitly excluded (example #2 below), but in truncate mode (example #1 below), no additional interfaces will be subsequently discovered once a specified interface is discovered. Be careful with example #1 below (truncate) if you are not quite certain that all uninteresting interfaces will have a highlighted ifIndex than the first one matching the example. Filters can be defined that are exclusive or inclusive.

Important: netmon.interfaceNoDiscover is used both by *netmon* and ET/APA, so interfaces defined in netmon.interfaceNoDiscover will be deleted both from the the node object in NNM and in ET. If removing a large number of interfaces (thousands), consider not taking too many at the same time because the process of deleting interfaces is very CPU-intensive. Consider stopping netmon temporarily, let ET finish deleting the interfaces and then start up netmon again.

In the file, an asterick represents any number of characters up to the next period. For example, *.corp.com matches pc.corp.com. A question mark matches a single character. Brackets match a single character, characters in a range, or characters not within a range if '!' is the first character within the brackets. For example: [bf]an.fognet.com matches ban.fognet.com and fan.fognet.com; [b-d]an.fognet.com matches ban.fognet.com, can.fognet.com and dan.fognet.com; and [!c-z]an.fognet.com matches only aan.fognet.com andban.fognet.com. Use the `netmon -a 117` command to trace *netmon's* parsing of the netmon.nodiscover and netmon.noInterfaceDiscover files. See page 69 for details on *netmon* tracing. Below are some examples. There are more examples in the white paper mentioned above:

```
# Truncate the interface table when an interface with
# ifType of 135 is found on node 10.162.191.146
10.162.191.146 1 ifType=135


# Ignore the interfaces with ifType of 135 or 53 for
# nodes within the address range:
10.162.191.* 2 ifType=135,53


# For nodes with a name ending in "core",
# Ignoreinterfaces with ifDescr containing the string
# "VLAN" or "virtual" for node names matching "core:
*core 2 ifDescr="*VLAN*","*virtual*"
```

Commonly used *netmon* LRF switch settings

There are dozens of LRF switches for *netmon*, each a layered bit of added functionality that has been added with each subsequent version of NNM. Some switches are preserved for backward compatibility and are obsolete. Some of those pertain to Layer 2 topology representation. See page 5 for details on using the LRF update procedure.

`-b <num>`	Send burst of <num> pings, 1 per sec after retries
`-q <num>`	Increase ICMP receive queue length, see man/ref
`-Q <num>`	Increase SNMP receive queue length, see man/ref
	Note: –q or –Q set too high may overload buffers
`-H 0`	Disable HTTP polls to speed configuration checks
`-k bridgeMIB=false`	Reduce segments created from RFC 1493
`-k snmpTimeoutImplies=unknown`	Default is critical
`-k nonIPStatusPolls=false`	Reduces SNMP switch queries

Be sure to carefully read the man or reference page entries for these and other *netmon* LRF switches since changing them can profoundly change the IPMAP topology and the granularity of status polls.

netmon global status polling default

The global default for discovery polling defined in SNMP configuration is 15 minutes, but the object-based polling introduced in NNM version 6.2 overrides this for most devices of interest (routers, switches, etc).

netmon object-based polling (V6.2+)

Object-based polling allows different intervals for different devices classes. It also allows different intervals for primary vs. secondary interfaces as determined by *netmon*'s critical path analysis (more on this below). Objects are defined via NNM's standard filter definition language, and accessed via the Poll Objects configuration GUI, available as a button in the polling configuration. This GUI is a front-end to the netmon.statusIntervals file.

In general, object-based polling tightens the default polling intervals for Routers, Bridges, Hubs, and loosens the default polling intervals for Nodes to 1 hour (V6.4+).

Dynamically-adjusting status polling by *netmon*

Prior to NNM V6.0, *netmon* status polling was static. NNM V6.0 introduced the first dynamic polling enhancement to support ConnectorDown ECS and the critical path analysis, where polls to nodes flagged as secondary failures would be reduced by the status reduction multiplier, which equals 2 by default. This means the polling interval to these nodes will be multiplied by two as long as the primary node remains down.

V6.31 introduced two important *netmon* enhancements that dynamically adjust polling intervals to support new event correlations. These are built into *netmon*, so they should continue to take affect even if those new correlations are disabled.

This first new dynamic polling change in V6.31 is if one interface changes on a connector, then all of that connector's interfaces are immediately polled. This is non-configurable and affects any node in the object database with the capability flag isConnector set. This second new dynamic polling change in V6.31 is that any interface on a connector that has changed status is re-polled according to the two new *netmon* –k switches below (configured via LRF, see page 5):

```
-k shortPollTime=120
-k shortPollDownCount=2
```

The shortPollTime is the interval for the re-poll, and the shortPollDownCount is the number of re-polls to issue. Per the defaults shown above, all connector interfaces changing status will be re-polled at 2 minutes and again at 4 minutes after the status change.

netmon layer 2 polling algorithms

Status based on layer 2 is very limited in *netmon* when compared to Extended Topology. *netmon* utilizes SNMP queries to Bridge, MAU, Repeater and some VLAN MIBs to determine layer 2 status.

Un-numbered interfaces are inferred from the port table, then polled via ARP. Contrast this with ET which has proprietary MIB extension data for hundreds of devices.

For *netmon*, in V5-V6.1, default status for "down" ports is Critical. In NNM V6.2 through V6.41, the default status for "down" ports is

Unknown. In NNM V7.0 and above, layer 2 polling is disabled in *netmon* and layer 2 topology is conveyed via ET.

Because ET is not enabled by default in NNM 7.0 and above, there is no layer 2 polling of any sort turned on by default in these later versions. Previous versions, however, have layer 2 polling turned on by default under *netmon*.

netmon layer 2 status is determined by polling standard MIB2 SNMP tables for ifAdminStatus and ifOperStatus. Default SNMP status mapping is based on the table below and is customizable via the netmon.statusMapping in NNM 6.2+. In versions prior to V6.2, status mapping is fixed per the table:

ifAdminStatus	ifOperStatus	OV Status
down	any	DISABLED
testing	any	TESTING
up	up	NORMAL
up	down	CRITICAL
up	testing	TESTING

APA-based layer two status is entirely different. All alarms are log-only by default and topology status is only reflected under Dynamic Views maps. The only statuses reflected are: Up (green), Contents Down (yellow), Unknown (secondary failure), and Disabled (adminStatus is down) (brown).

Non-IP unconnected port status (*netmon*)

The default status for non-IP (layer2) unconnected interfaces (unconnected switch ports for example) is Unknown instead of Critical since NNM 6.2, regardless of ifOperStatus and ifAdminStatus and netmon.statusMapping file settings. To restore the pre-V6.2 behavior set either or both of the following LRF switches in *netmon* (page 5):

```
-k ConnectorL2Ports=legacy
-k nonConnectorL2Ports=legacy
```

In NNM 7.53 Intermediate patch 19, a new option for netmon's -k connectorL2Ports parameter of "connected" was created which causes *netmon* to check for connectivity within the topology database. By default, netmon uses bridge forwarding table to determine connectivity.

netmon SNMP-based status for nodes

The ability to poll for primary status via SNMP vs. ICMP was introduced to allow polling across firewalls where ICMP is not allowed but SNMP may be. It is very limited in its abilities and is exclusive – that is if a device is polled for primary status via SNMP, it should no longer be polled by ICMP.

netmon.snmpStatus is the configuration file for defining Level 3 IP address ranges to poll via SNMP.

Use the following *netmon* –k LRF switch (see page 5) to control the behavior of SNMP polling timeouts:

```
-k snmpTimeoutImplies=[status]
```

where status is one of: unknown, unchanged, critical (default).

Determine *netmon*-based polling intervals for a device

The following command shows the base polling settings for a given node. It does not report on any dynamic polling changes that might be in effect:

```
xnmsnmpconf -resolve <node>
```

netmon critical path analysis

netmon maintains an in-memory route to every interface. This list is only updated when the *netmon* daemon is started, but a demand poll (*nmdemandpoll*) forces a critical path recalculation for a given path if issued to any node on that path. When an interface doesn't respond, *netmon* looks at all interfaces within the critical route and marks the closest as primary and all the distance ones as secondary failures.

ECS correlates subsequent alarms to the primary failure using the ConnectorDown correlation and *netmon* increases the status polling interval for secondary failures. Failure status for secondary nodes is configurable through the polling configuration. The Important Node filter defines nodes that are always to be considered primary by *netmon*. The path chosen by *netmon* to a particular device may not be the desirable path when there are multiple paths available. To hard-code a path, use the following *netmon* LRF switch (see page 5):

```
-c <critical-route-seedfile>
```

To dump the complete list of all critical route paths maintained by *netmon*:

```
snmpwalk <server> .1.3.6.1.4.1.11.2.17.4.4.2.1.1.5
```

To dump verbose information about the target node to $OV_LOG/netmon.trace, including the critical path:

```
netmon -n <target>
```

To dump verbose information about the target node to $OV_LOG/netmon.trace, including the critical path:

```
netmon -i <IP>
```

Node status events – interpretation

IPMAP topology, which is reflected in the *ovw* topology maps, is hierarchical in nature. All status for IPMAP topology originates at the interface level, that is, interface-level events are at the root of all other status events reflected in the topology. A "node down" event really means that all the interfaces within that node are either unreachable or unknown, etc. The status colors reflected on container objects in the topology is tied to the below list of status events using the default status propagation rules as set in the map properties. Some of these are logged by default, most of them are not, but the status is reflected in the topology regardless of the logging behavior of the events.

OV_Node_Up:	All Ifs are up or unknown
OV_Node_Warning:	One If is down
OV_Node_Marginal:	One If is down and >1 If is up
OV_Node_Major:	One If is up down
OV_Node_Down:	All Ifs are down or unknown
OV_Node_Unknown:	All Ifs are unknown

Handling multiple OV_Node_Up events

The OV_Node_ Up event is generated by *netmon* when it detects that all the node interfaces are up. As a side-effect, when one of the node's interfaces goes critical and after a while returns to normal, the OV_Node_Up event is generated without an intermediary OV_Node_Down. This may not be the desired behavior; an OV_Node_up is sometimes only wanted after an OV_Node_down. (All interfaces down).

To change this behavior to there is a one-to-one correspondence between the OV_Node_Up and OV_Node_Down events, ow these steps:

Modify the OV_Node_Down event: (Specific 58916865) to add an action callback to the Create_NodeDownFile.ovpl script (listed below). Send varbind $3 and $2 to the script as respective arguments, for example:

```
OVHIDESHELL Create_NodeDownFile.ovpl $3 $2
```

Modify the OV_Node_UP event: (Specific 58916864) to add an action callback to the Check_NodeDownFile.ovpl script (listed below). Send varbind $3 and $2 to the script as respective arguments, for example:

```
OVHIDESHELL Check_NodeDownFile.ovpl $3 $2
```

Create the scripts listed below and assure they are configured as Trusted Commands (See page 164 for details on Trusted Commands).

```perl
#!/opt/OV/bin/Perl/bin/perl
# Create_NodeDownFile.ovpl objectID [information]
# Create a file: $OV_TMP/NodeDown_objectID.txt with optional
additional information
# as contents and also appends info to the $OV_TMP/NodeDown.log
file.
# (This information can be used to store the IP-address,
downtime etc...)
use OVvars;
sub log {
 my ($logstring)= @_;
 open (LOGFILE, ">>$OV_TMP/NodeDown.log") ||
    die ("Cannot create/open $OV_TMP/NodeDown.log\n");
 print LOGFILE "$logstring\n";
 close LOGFILE;
}
if  ($#ARGV >= 0) {
 $objectID = $ARGV[0];
 $downfile = "$OV_TMP/NodeDown_$objectID.txt";
}
else {
```

```perl
 &log ("Create_NodeDownFile.ovpl called without parameters");
 exit 1;
}
open (DOWNFILE, ">$downfile") || die ("Cannot create/open
$downfile\n");
if ($#ARGV >= 1) {
 $information = $ARGV[1];
 print DOWNFILE ($information);
}
&log ("Created $downfile $information");
close DOWNFILE;
exit 0;


#!/opt/OV/bin/Perl/bin/perl
# Check_NodeDownFile.ovpl object_ID [information]
# Check if a file: $OV_TMP/NodeDown_objectID.txt has been
created previously.
# If present, a real OV_Node_Down has occured previously and
now a real OV_Node_Up
# message should be displayed in the Alarm browser and the file
has to be deleted to rearm
# the mechanism. The file contents and given information can be
used as desired.
# (e.g. display nodename, calculate the downtime etc.)
# Also append info to the $OV_TMP/NodeDown.log file.
use OVvars;
sub log {
 my ($logstring)= @_;
 open (LOGFILE, ">>$OV_TMP/NodeDown.log") ||
    die ("Cannot create/open $OV_TMP/NodeDown.log");
 print LOGFILE "$logstring\n";
 close LOGFILE;
}
if  ($#ARGV >= 0) {
 $objectID = $ARGV[0];
 $downfile = "$OV_TMP/NodeDown_$objectID.txt";
}
else {
 &log ("Check_NodeDownFile.ovpl called without parameters,
can't check filename");
```

```
 exit 1;
}
open (DOWNFILE, "$downfile") || die ("Cannot open and check
$downfile\n");
$contents = <DOWNFILE>;
if ($#ARGV >= 1) {
 $information = $ARGV[1];
 $message = $information;
}
else {
 $message = $contents;
}
$category = "Status Alarms";
$localhost = "Localhost";
$message = "Node UP event for Object ID $objectID $message";
&log ("$message for category: $category ");
$cmd = "ovevent -c \"$category\" \"\"";
$cmd .= " .1.3.6.1.4.1.11.2.17.1.0.58916872";
$cmd .= " .1.3.6.1.4.1.11.2.17.2.1.0 Integer 14";
$cmd .= " .1.3.6.1.4.1.11.2.17.2.2.0 OctetString
\"$localhost\"";
$cmd .= " .1.3.6.1.4.1.11.2.17.2.4.0 OctetString \"$message\"";
`$cmd`;
close DOWNFILE;
unlink "$downfile";
exit 0;
```

Status event variable bindings of interest

The table below lists some *netmon* interface and node event varbinds:

IF Status Varbind #	Node Status Varbind #	Description
$2	$2	Hostname of node that caused event
$5	$5	Timestamp event occured
$7		Interface Name or Label
$8		IP Address of Interface or "0"
$11		Number of bits in the subnet mask
* $12		Interface ifAlias

*	$13	*	$8	Local list of capabilities
*	$14	*	$9	Name of primary failure host
*	$15	*	$10	Name of primary failure entity
*	$16	*	$11	OV OID of primary failure entity
*	$17	*	$12	Description of primary failure entity
*	$18	*	$13	Primary failure list of capabilities

* = New as of NNM V6.31

For example, here are two status event texts from NNM V6.31+:

```
IF $7 Down $12, Capabilities: $13 Root Cause $14 $15
Node Down  Capabilities: $8  Root Cause: $9 $10
```

Contrast these with the same status event texts in versions prior to V6.31:

```
IF $7 Down
Node Down
```

ICMP burst polls

The -b <seconds> LRF option to *netmon* (see page 5 for LRF instructions) sends a burst of pings, one per second to any object after the regularly-issued set of timeouts and retries have been exhausted.

ICMP redirects

If netmon -a 3 shows messages similar to this:

```
unexpected ICMP message 5 code 1 from 192.168.1.1
```

...where the IP is the NNM Server's default gateway, then the default gateway is probably improperly configured. This sort of error causes NNM's polling waitlist to get severely backed up. More information on ICMP redirects can be found in RFC 792.

ICMP type 5 message codes are:

```
0 Redirect datagrams for the Network
1 Redirect datagrams for the Host
2 Redirect datagrams for Type of Service and Network
3 Redirect datagrams for Type of Service and Host
```

ICMP re-directs may also happen when nodes that are redirected are on the other side of an internal router have a route to a subnet that the hosts and are on via a non-persistent WAN link. When this WAN link goes down, that route disappears from the router's route table. So, when *netmon* polls the node, the router sends an ICMP redirect to NNM pointing it towards another server because the router doesn't have the route to that node anymore. The other server to which is redirecting is likely to be the redirecting router's own default route, which is different than the NNM server's default route.

Within NNM, the node may be reported down because *netmon* is trying to reach it through the redirecting gateway's default route, which may be a firewall. If this is the case, one solution is to have a separate segment for the firewall from the router with no other nodes on it. That way, traffic should be forced to go through the internal router regardless of whether the WAN link to the nodes is down or not.

netmon vs. APA poller

netmon provides discovery, configuration, and topology as well as status polling. In V7.0 and later, a new APA poller was made available to take over *netmon's* status polling functions, to take advantage of ET's more comprehensive picture of status via SNMP and to get around *netmon's* limitations due to legacy architecture.

In general, *netmon*-based polling is ICMP-based except for non-IP and devices specifically set to be polled via SNMP in the netmon.snmpStatus file. APA polling generally combines ICMP with SNMP-based status polls, is massively multi-threaded, and the device type dictates how the device should be polled. Also, the APA is "neighbor aware" in how it handles failures. The APA however, requires the extended topology is enabled and is dependent on ET discovery to work properly. In some environments, ET remains problematic to deploy and maintain.

netmon Cons
- Single-threaded, single protocol, legacy issues (IP, DNS)
- Polls via ICMP *or* SNMP, never both, SNMP polls limited
- Secondary status determination mechanisms rudimentary
- Rudimentarily dynamic in adjusting to neighbor status
- Cannot poll into OAD's; not good in handling HSRP, NAT, etc.
- Cannot separate IP address from a physical interface
- Is not "connection aware," rudimentary path analysis
- Unique path to each interface to determine primary
- Disparate configuration switches, files, and dependencies
- Provides status at only two entity levels: interface, node

netmon Pros
- Behavior is 100% characterizable and configurable, less FUD
- Still scales well when properly tuned/controlled
- GUIs available for polling customization/configuration
- Preservation of investment in *netmon*-based status
- Doesn't depend on ET discovery

APA Cons
- Analysis engine complex, difficult to characterize/control
- APA requires ET enabing and timely ET discovery
- Customization via XML files; no configuration GUI included
- *netmon*-based customizations not inherited by APA, e.g.:
  - Poller settings in SNMP Configuration GUI ignored
  - Interfaces unmanaged in NNM topology or by ovautoifmgr still may be polled
  - Object based polling settings based on NNM filters (APA uses ET filters)
- Separate definition files/filters for Important Nodes
- nmdemandpoll, ovet_toposet, checkPollCfg N/A in 7.01
- Cannot be used in DIM environment MS (CS only)
- Incompatible with LAN/WAN Edge & MPLS SPI in 7.01 (ok in 7.5+)
- IPX polling not available after switching to APA
- Initial setup can cause floods of events (mostly log-only)
- IPMAP topology status from APA can be problematic
- Interface count increases if formerly not managing Level 2

APA Pros
- Multi-threaded, multi-protocol (ICMP & SNMP, others)
- Switched-topology-aware, dup IP-aware, neighbor-aware
- Provides status at multiple entity levels:
  - Address, Interface, Node, Connection, Board, AgPort
- Provides more dynamic polling based on queued status:
- Provides connection-oriented and device-oriented status
- Provides more accurate & timely status than *netmon*
- Less reliant on ECS, more correlation at the source
- Generates fewer log-only and embedded status events
- Polls OAD, HSRP, and other IP address sharing interfaces
- Fewer, more intelligent and more timely status events
- More granularity in entity-based polling via XML files
- Reduces need to use distributed NNM
- Vendor-spesific agents gives better information for various types of equipment

netmon polling statistics

netmon polling statistics can be viewed from the command line by running:

```
ovstatus -v netmon
```

Statistics can also be graphed from *ovw* by selecting the NNM server icon in the map and running Performance > Network Polling Statistics.

Trends of negative numbers indicate that *netmon* isn't keeping up with its list of objects to be polled. Very frequently, this condition on new installations is indicative of issues with DNS lookup performance.

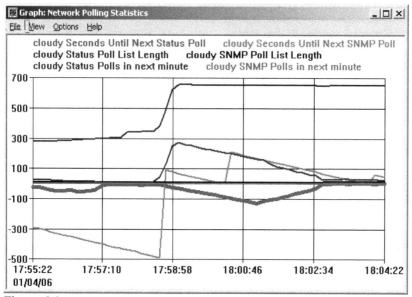

Figure 6-1

The graph in figure 6.1 shows an example trend for a from-scratch discovery of a network consisting of 650 interfaces. The top line represents status poll list length and under normal circumstances this line should remain flat. This graph was started shortly after a fresh installation and *netmon* had already discovered about 300 interfaces. The second line from the top, status polls in the next minute, abruptly rises then trends back to zero.

SNMP was misconfigured and the lowest line, seconds until next SNMP poll was woefully behind. After that, the SNMP issue was addressed, and *netmon* was able to discover another 350 interfaces. The seconds until next SNMP poll recovered nicely but then the seconds until next status poll started to trend negative, a normal reaction to a burst of new-node discovery.

The thick line that hovers below zero is seconds until next status poll,. Anytime that the values for this metric are below zero, it indicates that some nodes are not getting polled within their defined status polling intervals – *netmon* is falling behind. Under normal operating conditions, this line stays near zero.

netmon troubleshooting, tracing and dumping

Run: `netmon -M <mask>` to send an event to the running *netmon* to turn on tracing. Once tracing is enabled, run: `nmdemandpoll <node name>` or perform some other action to get *netmon* to perform the task to trace. Trace output is written $OV_LOG/netmon.trace. Run: `netmon -M 0` to turn off tracing as *netmon*.trace grows without bounds and can easily fill up a disk with more verbose tracemasks. Tracemasks are additive, so to trace both SNMP requests and SNMP replies and timeouts, use a tracemask of 12 (4+8). Several tracemasks are listed in the *netmon* man/ref page; the following are some additional tracemasks:

0x00000100	Trace effects of netmon.cmstr file
0xffffffff	Turn on all masks – uses lots of disk/CPU

`netmon -a <action-number>` dumps *netmon* internal data structures such as ping lists and SNMP lists to $OV_LOG/netmon.trace. Use the following command to dump a list of all action-numbers and their meanings: `netmon -a ?`

`netmon -n <target>` dumps verbose information about the target node to $OV_LOG/netmon.trace, including the critical path.

`netmon -i <IP>` dumps verbose information about the target Interface to $OV_LOG/netmon.trace including the critical path.

7. Status Polling - APA

Introduced in NNM 7.01, the APA polls HSRP and OAD by default, and can be configured to take over for *netmon* status polling. Before enabling APA polling, read the pros and cons of *netmon* vs. APA polling on page 66.

There were several changes to the APA between V7.01 and V7.5 and in subsequent patches to V7.5 and V7.51. These changes concern performance, scalability, granularity, and the ability to characterize polling behaviors. If using the APA, always make sure the latest updates are applied.

APA Architecture

Polling policies are labeled as Class Specifications in the paConfig.xml file. The three primary "parameters" that are user configurable are snmpEnable, pingEnable, and interval. For each object (like an address, interface or node), APA begins parsing the paConfig.xml from the top down looking for a polling policy match for the object and the parameter setting. It also looks for match for its parent objects and applies logic to make a decision about how to poll the object.

For snmpEnable and pingEnable parameters, this is a logical AND. For interval, its more of an if/else statement as detail below. If it can't find an explicit policy match for the object, it reverts to the default setting.
Note that default settings are "typeless", meaning there isn't a separate default for nodes, interfaces and addresses. They all share the same default settings.

The APA then does the same algorithm for the parent object and performs a logical AND of all the results. In APA, Node is the parent of Interface which is the parent of Address.

Node <- Interface <- Address

To find a polling policy for an address in paConfig.xml, it will look for explicit polling policies for the address, the parent interface and the parent node. It would look something like this:

(Address Setting) AND (Interface Setting) AND (Node Setting)

So, for a given address, APA begins looking through the paConfig.xml file for a policy match for the address. If it doesn't find one, it reverts to the default setting which is PingEnable=true. Now it goes to the parent object which is an interface. Suppose it matches on "unconnected interfaces on routers" and that configuration is set to PingEnable=false. Now it goes to the parent object which is a node and it finds one for routers and the configuration is set to PingEnable=true. AND all these values together and you'll get:

True AND False AND True = False

Therefore the address in not pinged. Now, for the interval parameter, the logic is similar but rather than ANDing the values together, it just takes the first value it matches and doesn't try the default until all parents are exhausted. So the logic is:

(Addr Interval) else (Intf Interval) else (Node Interval) else (default)

For example, a set of routers has a polling interval of 120 seconds and there are no polling intervals set for any Interfaces and no polling intervals set for addresses. Suppose the default polling cycle is set to 300 seconds:

(undefined) else (undefined) else (120s) else (500s) = 120s

APA vs *netmon* status architecture

The following diagram shows the major subsystems of both legacy NNM and ET and their relationships to status. This relates only to NNM 7.x versions:

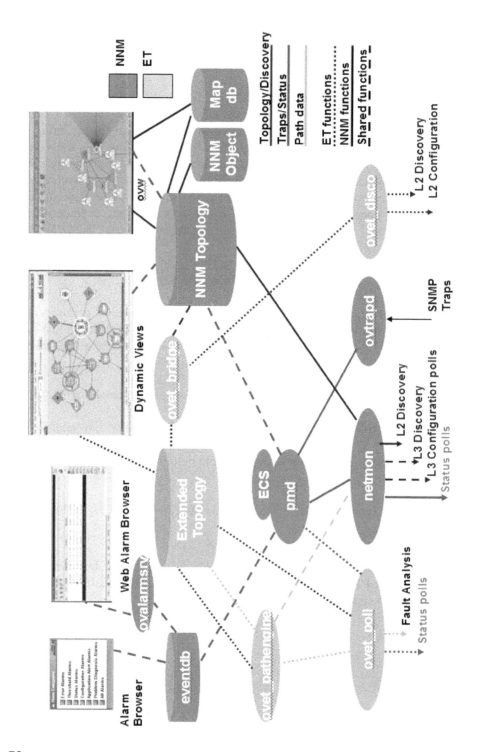

APA and Smart Plug-Ins

Both the Smart Plug-in for Frame Relay (version 2.0) and the Smart Plug-in for MPLS IP VPN (version 1.0) are incompatible with the APA and require netmon to be the daemon that polls objects in order to work properly. Do not enable the APA if these plug-ins were purchased.

Turn APA polling on or off ("the big switch")

To enable APA, follow these steps:

1. Read $OV_DOC/whitepapers/Active_Problem_Analyzer.pdf or the Using_Extended_Topology user manual after V7.53
2. Exit GUI sessions
3. Run: `setupExtTopo.ovpl`, then `etrestart.ovpl`. Wait
4. Run `ovet_apaConfig.ovpl -enable APAPolling`
5. Watch ovstatus carefully:
   `ovstatus -v netmon`   Should say "Polling 0 interfaces"
   `ovstatus -v ovet_poll` Should say "Polling devices"
6. If *netmon* is still polling, run: `ovstop` and `ovstart`

To disable the APA, run:

`ovet_apaConfig.ovpl -disable APAPolling`

Determine poller control

To unambiguously determine whether *netmon* is polling for status or the APA, run:

`ovet_apaConfig.ovpl -query APAPolling`

APA configuration in a nutshell

The following xml files are used to configure the APA:
$OV_CONF/nnmet/paConfig.xml
$OV_CONF/nnmet/topology/filter/TopoFilters.xml
$OV_CONF/nnmet/topology/filter/APANoPollNodes.xml
$OV_CONF/nnmet/topology/filter/MyHostID.xml

The following tools are used to tune APA settings:
```
/opt/OV/bin/ovet_topodump.ovpl
/opt/OV/support/NM/checkpollcfg
/opt/OV/bin/ovet_demandpoll.ovpl
```

Demand polling using ovet_demandpoll.ovpl

The GUI-based "poll node" and the underlying command nmdemandpoll should force a *netmon* discovery poll, but not a status poll for APA nodes. In NNM 7.01 and up, ovet_demandpoll.ovpl is available for forcing APA status polls. If issued with the -d option, detailed information about the internal states of the device being polled will be dumped, but the actual device will not be actively polled. Below are all options, some of which are not supported in earlier releases of NNM:

-o	Specify a specific object (supply OID)
-d	Dump the status of the object
-t	Timeout to wait for 1st response
-r	Specify the Overlapping Domain ID
-V	Verbose
-v	Use to show HSRP virtual IP
-B	Force sync between legacy and ET databases
-s	Generate summary reports
-P	Enable logging of polling activity (requires –o)
-p	Disable logging of polling activity (reguires –o)
-g	Create sample islandGroup config file

The –g option above was added in NNM 7.53 and is discussed in the section below on Island Group Monitoring.

The –d option above changes after installing NNM 7.51 Intermediate Patch 15, providing more detailed info on use of ET filters.

Example ovet_demandpoll.ovpl -d <node> output:

```
OBJ_TYPE        SHORT_OBJECT_NAME  snmpEnable  ET_FILTER
--------------------------------------------------------------
all-types       *                  true        DEFAULT
NODE            nodename           true        isRouter
Composite       nodename           true        Node Value

OBJ_TYPE        SHORT_OBJECT_NAME  pingEnable  ET_FILTER
--------------------------------------------------------------
all-types       *                  true        DEFAULT
NODE            nodename           true        isRouter
Composite       nodename           true        Node Value

OBJ_TYPE        SHORT_OBJECT_NAME  interval    ET_FILTER
--------------------------------------------------------------
all-types       *                  300         DEFAULT
NODE            nodename           300         isRouter
```

```
Composite        nodename           300         Node Value
```

Note in the above output, the results show the SNMP, Ping, and interval settings for each interface on the node.

Example `ovet_demandpoll.ovpl -d <interface>` output:

```
OBJ_TYPE         SHORT_OBJECT_NAME  snmpEnable  ET_FILTER
-----------------------------------------------------------
all-types        *                  true        DEFAULT
NODE             nodename           true        isRouter
INTERFACE        nodename[0[1]]     true        UnconnectedIF
Composite        nodename[0[1]]     true        InterfaceVal
```

If `ovet_demandpoll.ovpl` is issued with the `-V` option, detailed information will be dumped about the actively issued poll. If issued with the –B option, the status bridge will be force-updated. Use this to help update stale status that is showing in the IPMAP topology or if the Dynamic Views maps show inconsistent status with the *ovw* map's status for a particular object.

On windows, the ovet_demandpoll.ovpl script calls an executable called $OV_SUPPORT/NM/ovet_demandpoll.exe. Due to the way this is structured, output from the script can't be redirected to standard output. To work around this, copy ovet_demandpoll.exe into the $OV_BIN directory and then run ovet_demandpoll.exe instead of ovet_demandpoll.ovpl. The arguments are identical and the output can be redict4ed, for example to a file:

ovet_demandpoll.exe –d patchy.fognet.com > c:\temp\patchy.dmp

APA Island Group Monitoring

Introduced in NNM 7.53, this feature provides a method for handling "islands of connectivity" that result from ET's inability to discover connectivity through WAN clouds. The feature is enabled by default, but configuration of the island group names is necessary in order to properly identify the island group names that NNM will report on. This reporting is conveyed through the following two new APA events:

OV_APA_ISLAND_GROUP_DOWN
OV_APA_ISLAND_GROUP_UP

The Group Down alarm might look like the following:

Remote Site Node Group Down 3   Capabilites: isIPRouter,isSwicth,

The 2 varbinds passed after the "Group Down" text are the group number and the group name, which by default mean little unless those attributes are explicitly coded per the procedure below.

ET discovers nodes and their connectivity, but not the groups. The APA builds groups when loading data from ET. By default, a single node in the group, typically a router is selected to represent the group. A label which by default is blank is then available to name the group. To customize this behavior, follow these steps:

1. Run ovet_demandpoll.ovpl –g to create a sample configuration file called $OVCONF/nnmet/paIslandGroupNameSample.txt
2. Edit the file to add group names and, if desired, change the representative node for the group. The default name chosen by APA can be used if desired. The name may contain spaces.
3. Restart *ovet_poll* using `ovstop/ovstart`

WAN connections where ET can determine connectivity, like frame relay links where CDP is running over them, will not be considered islands. But remote sites that are connected through MPLS clouds will be considered islands, since ET can't resolve that particular sort of connectivity. Island Group Monitoring is enabled (default) or disabled via the paConfig.xml file parameter `disableIslandGroupDiscovery`.

APA status events

APA-generated status events are different from *netmon*-based status events, for example: `OV_APA_IF_DOWN` (OpenView enterprise specific event number `58983012`). With APA polling, ICMP and/or SNMP polls relate to address, interface, Aggregated Interface, Node, Connection, and Board. In the APA, polling granularity is defined by ET Topology filters. "Unreachable" is the term used in the APA to describe secondary entity failure status.

APA status from SNMP traps

APA listens for the below SNMP traps generated by devices to speed and add intellignce to the APA status. In many environments, these traps are disabled at the source to reduce SNMP chatter. Assuring that these traps are turned on at the device level for critical devices may increase the speed and accuracy of APA status.

```
CiscoColdStart          1.3.6.1.6.3.1.1.5.1
CiscoLinkDown           1.3.6.1.6.3.1.1.5.3
CiscoLinkUp             1.3.6.1.6.3.1.1.5.4
CiscoWarmStart          1.3.6.1.6.3.1.1.5.2
ColdStart               1.3.6.1.6.3.1.1.5.1
WarmStart               1.3.6.1.6.3.1.1.5.2
HSRPState               1.3.6.1.4.1.9.9.106.2.0.1
LinkDown                1.3.6.1.6.3.1.1.5.3
LinkUp                  1.3.6.1.6.3.1.1.5.4
chassisChangeNotifOID   1.3.6.1.4.1.9.5.11.2.0.2
StackMIBModuleDown      1.3.6.1.4.1.9.5.0.4
StackMIBModuleUp        1.3.6.1.4.1.9.5.
```

Suppress/allow APA status polling

To suppress or allow APA polling to interfaces/ports using Dynamic Views, use the Port Admin Tool (page 257) if running NNM V7.53.

To suppress or allow polling to any APA-polled entity (nodes, interfaces, connections, boards and addresses), use the `ovet_toposet.ovpl` command. This will work only for APA nodes in NNM 7.50 and up:

`-a`	Option allows APA polling for that entity
`-s`	Option suppresses APA polling for that entity
`-o`	Specify a particular object as the target

Use this command in conjunction with `ovtopofix -G` to unmanage devices on the *netmon* side. Nodes that have been suppressed will eventually be removed from both the ET and legacy databases. In typical environments, this takes about 7 days. For example, to stop polling to a particular interface on a node:

1. Confirm polling status of interfaces by running:
   `$OV_SUPPORT/NM/checkPollCfg -o <node>`
2. To map interface IP to interface names, run:
   `ovet_topodump.ovpl -nodeif <node>`
   When the interface name is too long, for example "HP NC7781 Gigabit Server Adapter," the OID string can be used instead of the ifName string when specifying the interface in the command `ovet_toposet` below. To get the OID string, run:
   `ovet_topodump.ovpl -nodeif -detail <node>`
3. Disable polling on interface hme1:
   `$OV_SUPPORT/NM/ovet_toposet -s -nodeif <node> -if hme1`
4. Repeat step 1 to confirm polling configuration change

APA status events

Selected APA varbinds of interest:

Varbind #	Description
$2	Timestamp event occured
$3	Hostname of node that caused the event
$5	Label of the responsible interface
$6	ifAlias of the responsible interface
$8	ifIndex of the responsible interface
$9	ifDescr of the responsible interface
$10	Responsible Level 3 address or port #
$11	Responsible Level 2 address
$12	Subnet Mask
$13	Route Distinguisher
$15	Capabilities
$16-$28	Double-object failure varbinds if connector
$29-$42	Primary failure varbinds if secondary

Example APA Event texts:

```
IF Down:            $5 $10 $6 Capabilities: $15
Address Down:       $5 $10 $6 Capabilities: $15
Connection Down:    $5 $10 connected to $16 $18
Node Down:          $10 Capabilities: $15
```

APA status as reflected in ovw maps

APA status is much more accurate and representative of the polling entities in Dynamic Views than it is in bridged status to the legacy topology. The *ovet_bridge* daemon is responsible for mapping APA status to *ovw* map status. The mapping between ET and the ovtopmd is controlled by a flat file called hosts.nnm. This file should not be changed by users. Resolve any descrepancies through ET discovery or through *ovw* topology database manipulation tools such as ovtopofix.

Enabling APA for the general IP environment can result in interfaces marked "normal" in *ovtopmd/ovw* that should be marked "critical." When APA attempts to match interface objects in *ovtopmd* with interface objects in the Extended Topology database, interface objects that do not directly match will be marked "normal" in the ovtopmd database and *ovw*, and a message noting this will be logged in $OV_LOG/ovet_poll.log. If an interface exists in the *ovtopmd/ovw* databases in multiple forms, only one of those interfaces will be updated.

78

If Layer-2 connectivity discovery is enabled in *netmon*, *netmon* will attempt to do connectivity discovery on bridgeMIB supporting devices, resulting in extra interfaces with the same ifNumber under some conditions. APA will only update one of these interfaces with status. Additionally, these interfaces are sometimes deleted and recreated, resulting in an inconsistency with the Extended Topology database until the next ET discovery. Similarly, some interfaces are created to connect switches or other connectors to segments in the ovtopmd database. These interfaces, which have no real interface attributes, will also be marked normal.

If Multiple IP Addresses exist on the same interface, *ovtopmd* models this as two interfaces with different IP addresses but the same ifNumber. APA and Extended Topology will treat this as a single interface with multiple IP addresses. APA will update only one of the interfaces in the *ovtopmd/ovw* database with correct status.

In general, ET re-discovery will resolve most descrepancies between the ET db's view of the topology and *ovtopmd/ovw's*.

APA aggregated port support

Newer APA events in NNM 7.5 support AgPort by mapping multiple physical ports via an ET trunk virtual port. The APA polls physical interfaces, but not logical interfaces.

Support is for Cisco PAgP in V7.5. V7.51 added support for Nortel MLT and SMLT. V7.51 supplied a white paper on the Nortel agents in:

$OV_DOC/WhitePapers/MLT.pdf

In V7.53, this documentation is rolled up into the Guide to Using Extended Topology user manual. The previous trunk support via the netmon.equivPorts configuration file is now called "redundant connection support."

Fine tune AgPort via the following ET Topology filters:

isAggregatedIF	virtual interface
isPartOfAggregatedIF	physical interface

Aggregate port scenario:
Suppose one physical port goes down on a trunk. In this case, a TrunkDegraded event issued and the trunk virtual port status changes

to minor in ET. Also, the physical interface changes to critical and the Interface Down APA event is correlated and embedded by the ConnectorDown correlation. AgPort status from ET is not propagated to the IPMAP topology and can only be observed in Dynamic Views.

AgPort status events:

OV_APA_AGGPORT_DEGRADED: the aggregate port connection between two nodes is responding to polls and some of the interfaces are down.

OV_APA_AGGPORT_DISABLED: the primary aggregated port is not responding to polls in a normal fashion. This could be because all the interfaces' ifAdminStatus are Down | Testing.

OV_APA_AGGPORT_DOWN: the aggregate port connection between two nodes is not responding to polls and all interfaces on this side of the connection may be down.

OV_APA_AGGPORT_UNREACHABLE: the aggregate port connection between two nodes is not responding to polls. The problem is due to another entity.

OV_APA_AGGPORT_CONN_DOWN: the aggregate port connection between two nodes is not responding to polls and all interfaces may be down on both sides of the connection.

OV_APA_AGGPORT_REMOVED: the SNMP query returned noSuchObj. This can occur if the port is reconfigured of if an index renumbering has occurred. It can also be a problem with the system's SNMP agent. This event was added in a patch to V7.5.

APA HSRP and VRRP status support

The NNM Advanced Routing SPI license is required to use the HSRP or VRRP ET Device agents that the APA needs to provide protocol related status. The following status events were added in a patch to V7.5 for VRRP support:

- rcVrrpTrapNewMaster
- rcVrrpTrapAuthFailure
- rcVrrpTrapStateTransition
- vrrpTrapNewMaster
- vrrpTrapAuthFailure
- snTrapVrrpIfStateChange

The following APA HSRP events were added in V7.01 and enhanced for VRRP Protocol support in a patch to V7.5:

- OV_HSRP_No_Active
- OV_HSRP_Multiple_Active
- OV_HSRP_NoStandby
- OV_HSRP_Degraded
- OV_HSRP_FailOver
- OV_HSRP_Standby_Changed
- OV_HSRP_Normal
- OV_HSRP_Multiple_Standby

New event corellations were added in V7.51 to support VRRP status. It is important to understand the poll trigger features of these corellators. More on these corellators can be found in:

$OV_DOC/WhitePapers/VRRP.pdf

In V7.53, this documentation is rolled up into the Guide to Using Extended Topology user manual. APA default configuration settings affecting HSRP status are as follows:

```
HSRPTransientWait                 60000
GenerateNoStandbyEvent            true
GenerateDegradedEvent             true
GenerateFailoverEvent             true
GenerateStandbyChangedEvent       true
```

HSRPTransientWait is milliseconds to wait for HSRP to become stable after a failover. Reducing this number increases the chance of unnecessary status events. The remaining configuration settings control the generation of intermediate status events.

APA board status support

Support for board status is rudimentary in NNM 7.5. Wider support for this feature can be expected in future versions although no additional support was added in NNM 7.51 or NNM 7.53. As of V7.53, board status is only supported for the following MIBs:

Cisco Stack MIB
Rhino MIB
C2900 MIB

Support for OLD-CISCO-CHASSIS-MIB was added in Intemediate patch 15 to NNM V7.51. The Board Down event correlation logic, as well as APA event triggered polling based on the Board Down trap, will not work with older versions of the Cisco stack MIB. Any version of the stack mib that has moduleType in var bind 1 of the module down trap, instead of moduleIndex, will not work. Confirm the appropriate version of the stack MIB through the event configuration GUI.

When a SubBoard is discovered, it is treated as a board. Boards with unreachable status imply a secondary failure.

APA board status event varbinds:

Varbind #	Description
$2	Timestamp event occurred
$3	Name of the node that contains the board
$5	Capabilities
$6	Management Address
$7	Route Distinguisher
$9	Index of the responsible board
$11	SubBoard index of the responsible board
$13	Serial Number
$14	Module Name
$15	Module Description
$16	Hardware Version
$17	Software Version

paConfig.xml: the APA configuration file

The location of this file is: $OV_CONF/nnmet/paConfig.xml.
The schema is defined in: paConfigSchema.xsd.
Changes take affect when *ovet_poll* is restarted via `ovstart`.
Remember to backup pxConfig.xml file before making changes.
Customizations need to be merged in on upgrades and patches.

paConfig.xml customization and modification best practices are:
1. Backup the paConfig.xml file, track revisions for reverting
2. Document *netmon* and APA configuration customizations
3. Use `ovet_topodump.ovpl` to test that the nodes or interfaces pass the class filter created or modified
4. Validate XML syntax using an xml editor or web browser
5. Test changes using `checkPollCfg` in support subdirectory

6. Restart *ovet_poll* process to begin using the new settings
7. verify which filter is used for node and/or interface with
   ovet_demandpoll -d nodename

Simplified paConfig.xml schema with parameterList examples:

```
<paConfig>
  <subSystemConfig>PollingEngine,StatusAnalyzer,Talker
  <globalParameters>statisticsEnable
  <configGroupList>
   <configGroup> pollingSettings;configPollSettings
   <generalParameters> GenerateDegradedEvent
   <classSpecificParameters>
     <defaultParameters>interval;snmpEnable;timeout
       <classSpecification> isRouter, isSwitch,
       <parameterList> interval;snmpEnable;timeout
```

paConfig.xml evaluation order issues

Specifications are evaluated in top to bottom order, so the first specification that passed the filter for a particular device is the one that applies.

In NNM 7.01, an IF filter would take precedence over the node level for status specifications if the IF filter appeared before the node spec.

In NNM 7.5, the above behavior was changed so that a status setting of false for a node makes that status false for every IF on that node. For the true case, however, a false IF setting changes the status of the IF on a node set to true from false.

In NNM 7.01, if a filter specifies a status for ping, but not SNMP (or vice versa), the default parameter would be applied to the missing spec and all other specs would be ignored.

In NNM 7.5, multiple filters can be evaluated and the first filter to specify a spec will be evaluated. Only after all specs have been evaluated and no spec for either ping or SNMP has been found should the default be applied.

Interface ICMP polling

Prior to NNM 7.51 Intermediate Patch 18, the APA was hard coded to mark all the IP interfaces as polled disabled and for ICMP, and this could not be changed via the paConfig.xml file. That patch introduced the isDiscoContrivedIF filter and by setting the pingEnable value to true in this filter, IP interfaces can be monitored using ICMP.

Synchronizing poll settings with configuration polls

NNM 7.5 introduced the configuration poll, so if status polling is being disabled to a node or interface in the PollingSettings config group, it may be a good idea to disable polling in the ConfigPollSettings config group as well. Configuration polls are always SNMP.

paConfig.xml polling granularity class specifications

Polling granularity in the APA is defined by classSpecifications which correspond to topology filters (discussed below) that are called within each classSpecification block.

In paConfig.xml, these settings are located under:

```
<subSystemConfig>
  <name>PollingEngine</name>
   <configGroup>
     <name>PollingSettings</name>
       <classSpecificParameters>
         <defaultParameters>
           <classSpecifications>
```

The following class specifications define the polling granularity for the APA poller in the paConfig.xml file. Details on the meanings of these specifications can be found in the APA white paper. The entries below are for NNM 7.51. They are unchanged from NNM 7.5 except for the addition of the isNewNode and isNewInterface specs. Under NNM 7.01, there was a much more limited set of specifications:

Lines in *italic* below are commented in paConfig.xml by default and will not be used unless uncommented.

Class Specification	snmpEnable	pingEnable
APANoPollNodes	*false*	*false*
isNewNode	true	true
isNewInterface	true	true
isIpPhone	false	false
ifsWithAnycastAddrs	n/a	false
isRouter	true	true
AvayaIptDevices	true	true
NotConnectedSnmpSwitch	n/a	true
isSwitch	true	false
isEndNode	false	true
WanIf	*true*	*false*
IfTypeFilter	*n/a*	*false*
isPartOfAggregatedIF	true	n/a
IFInNotConnectedSwitch	n/a	true

84

UnconnectedAdminUpOrTestRouterIf	true	true
UnconnectedAdminUpOrTestSwitchIf	false	false
UnconnectedAdminDownRouterIf	false	false
UnconnectedAdminDownSwitchIf	false	false
UnconnectedEndNode	false	true
NotConnectedIF	false	false
AllBoards	*false*	*n/a*
NoPingAddresses	*n/a*	*false*

Using ET topology filters to specify polling granularity

paConfig.xml class specifications are defined using extended topology filters. Extended topology filters are a separate entity from NNM traditional filters. To see a list of all existing filters, run: `ovet_topodump.ovpl -lfilt`

To see a dump of discovered devices that pass a given filter, run:

```
ovet_topodump.ovpl -node -filt [filtername]
```

ClassSpecification filters are evaluated in xml file order, so if a device matched both isSwitch and isRouter, the isRouter rule would apply. Extended Topology Filters are defined in:

$OV_CONF/nnmet/topology/filter/TopoFilters.xml

V7.51 provides a discussion of ET Topology Filters with examples in:

$OV_DOC/ETFilter.pdf

In V7.53, this documentation is rolled up into the Guide to Using Extended Topology user manual.

Filter assertion type attributes

Prior to V7.53, ET Filter assertion type attributes were not documented, but Kevin Smith of HP documented them in his NNM 7.51 Deployment handbook which can be found at:

http://www.fognet.com/NNM_7.51_Deployment_Handbook_v1.3.pdf

Assertions are documented in the V7.53 Using_Extended_topology.pdf user manual but are listed here for those running previous versions.

Assertions for Interface Containers, HSRP Groups and Addresses were defined in Kevin's document and may not have been supported priot ton V7.53. Use the assertions below to build custom ET filters for APA status or for Container Views:

Node Assertion Attribute Types

Attribute Type	Description
name	The internal name of the node
SysName	SysName of the node
lastUpdateTimeUTC	The last time the node was updated
description	The description of the node
IPAddress	Address on the node
sysOID	Match on SNMP System OID of the node
capability	The capability of the node
status	The overall status of the node
extensibleAttribute	An "extensible" attribute of the node
HostIDFile	Use HostName or IP Address in the file

Card Assertion Attribute Types

Attribute Type	Description
name	The nnm entity name of the card
lastUpdateTimeUTC	The last time the card was updated
index	The card index
description	The description of the card
type	MIB type field on the Card
model	MIB model field on the Card
sn	MIB serial number field on the Card
fwversion	MIB firmware version field on the Card
hwversion	MIB hardware version field on the Card
swversion	MIB software version field on the Card
componentName	SNMP System OID of the card
status	The overall status of the card
extensibleAttribute	The extensible attributes of the card
cardAdminStatus	Card adminstration status
cardOperStatus	Card Operation Status
mibType	MIB type from which card data was read

Interface Assertion Attribute Types

Attribute Type	Description
lastUpdateTimeUTC	The last time the interface was updated.
IPAddress	IPv4 address bound to the Interface
ifDescription	The description of the interface
ifDesc	The description of the interface
ifAlias	Interface Name Alias
ifName	Interface Name Alias
ifIndex	Interface Index
vlanPortType	The role of this port in VLAN config
ifAdminState	Interface adminstration state
ifOperStatus	Interface Operation Status
ifType	Interface Type
ifSpeed	Interface Speed

status	The overall status of the interface
extensibleAttribute	The extensible attributes of the interface
capability	The capability on the Interface

Interface Container Assertion Attribute Types

Attribute Type	Description
name	The nnm entity name of the If container
lastUpdateTimeUTC	The last time the If Container was updated
description	The description of the If Container
type	MIB type field on the If Container
status	The overall status of the If Container
extensibleAttribute	The extensible attributes of the If Container

HSRP Group Assertion Attribute Types

Attribute Type	Description
virtualAddress	Virtual Address of the HSRP Group

Address Assertion Attribute Types

Attribute Type	Description
IPAddress	IP Address
reachabilityState	state of the address
extensibleAttribute	The extensible attributes of the address

Filter nodes based on SNMP sysObjectID

In this example, nodes whose SNMP agent matches Bluecoat SNMP SysOID 1.3.6.1.4.1.3417.1.1.23 will be not pinged.

Add the following node filter to TopoFilters.xml:

```
<nodeAssertion name="isBlueCoat" title="isBlueCoat"
description="BlueCoat devices">
  <operator oper="NOOP">
    <attribute>
        <sysOID>1.3.6.1.4.1.3417.1.1.23</sysOID>
    </attribute>
  </operator>
</nodeAssertion>
```

Next add an interface assertion filter to match all interfaces on these nodes:

```
<interfaceAssertion name="IFInBlueCoat" title="IFInBlueCoat"
description="Interfaces in BlueCoat devices">
  <operator oper="NOOP">
    <interfaceAssociation ascType="inNode">isBlueCoat
    </interfaceAssociation>
```

```
        </operator>
      </interfaceAssertion>
```

Validate the filters with `ovet_topodump.ovpl` then add the following two class specifications near the top of paConfig.xml file:

```
      <classSpecification>
        <filterName>isBlueCoat</filterName>
        <parameterList>
            <parameter>
              <name>snmpEnable</name>
              ...
              <value>true</value>
              ...
            </parameter>
            <parameter>
              <name>pingEnable</name>
              ...
              <value>false</value>
              ...
            </parameter>
        </parameterList>
      </classSpecification>

      <classSpecification>
        <filterName>IFInBlueCoat</filterName>
        <parameterList>
            <parameter>
              <name>snmpEnable</name>
              ...
              <value>true</value>
              ...
            </parameter>
            <parameter>
              <name>pingEnable</name>
              ...
              <value>false</value>
              ...
            </parameter>
        </parameterList>
      </classSpecification>
```

Ellipses in the above xml represent sections left out that can be copied from similar definitions. Validate changes using `checkpollcfg -o <IP of node>`, then restart *ovet_poll* and then run `ovet_demandpoll.ovpl <IP of node>`.

Force a device to be polled via ICMP or SNMP only

To accomplish this, build a topology filter and a corresponding entry in paConfig.xml, perhaps by IP Address. In the paConfig.xml file, copy the configuration for a device that is currently filtering for that node, and place it above the existing entry in the file. Then modify the copied configuration and change the ICMP or SNMP polling booleans. Test the changes with `checkPollCfg` then restart the *ovet_poll* daemon.

In order to force polling via ICMP only, a quick and dirty alternative is to set an invalid SNMP community string for the device in the SNMP configuration GUI. Note that changing SNMP configuration retries and timeouts won't help, though, as the SNMP Configuration poller-related settings only apply to *netmon's* polling intervals. SNMP timeout and retry settings for APA are set in paConfig.xml in the ConfigPollSettings configuration group. Only the community string and SNMP version settings are read intot he APA from the SNMP Configuration GUI (`xnmsnmpconf`).

Filtering by ifType (APA)

Two default filters ship with paConfig.xml in NNM 7.5 and both filters are commented out by default:

- *IfTypeFilter* sets ping to false for matching types; useful to prevent polls from "waking" ISDN interfaces, etc.

- *WanIf* stops APA polling of matching types in order to suppress connection level APA status events

WanIf is defined as wanIfTypes filter anded with slowIfSpeeds filter, where slowIfSpeeds include: 9k, 16k, 56K, 64K.

To enable either of these filters, remove the comments at the end and the beginning of the filter definition; then modify the default ifTypes in TopoFilters.xml (if desired), then run: `ovstop ovet_poll` and `ovstart ovet_poll`.

For interfaces that are undesirable, netmon.interfaceNoDiscover is used by netmon to prevent discovery and it it is also used by ET to prevent discovery. More on page 55.

A complete list of ifTypes can be found at:

www.iana.org/assignments/ianaiftype-mib

Disable ICMP to a firewall (APA)

This requires establishing a new node assertion and new class specification. Here are the steps:

1. Backup paConfig.xml and TopoFilters.xml
2. Determine the SNMP sysObjectID of the firewall:
3. Neighbor View, Right Click, Details, or run:
   ```
   snmpget -T <firewallName> system.sysObjectID.0
   ```
4. In TopoFilters.xml, copy and paste an OID-based node assertion block
5. Change name, title, description and OID block to match firewall device
6. Check xml syntax and confirm filter matches the devices by running:
   ```
   ovet_topodump.ovpl -node -filt <newNodeAssertionName>
   ```
7. In paConfig.xml, copy entire isRouter ClassSpecification
8. Paste *before* isRouter ClassSpecification
9. Change the ClassSpecification name to match new nodeAssertion name
10. Change pingEnable parameter to false
11. Check xml syntax and confirm polling settings:
    ```
    $OV_SUPPORT/checkPollCfg -o <firewallName>
    ```
12. Apply changes by running ovstop/ovstart on *ovet_poll*

Switching routers and routing switches in the APA

If a node is both a switch and a router, sometime called a swouter, then APA polls it as a router by default. That is due to the fact that the isRouter class specification is above the isSwitch class specification in the paConfig.xml file. By default, a switch/router is both SNMP polled and pinged. It also means that Connected and Unconnected Admin UP interfaces would be both SNMP polled and pinged.

With the release of NNM 7.53, the following document includes an appendix which walks through a methodology for handling devices with both switch and router functionality:

$OV_DOC/whitepapers/ETandAPADeploymentGuide.pdf

If running versions prior to 7.53, Kevin Smith of HP had written the "NNM 7.51 Deployment Handbook" which contained the exact same methodology and also, coincidentely perhaps, appears in Appendix A of his document. This handbook can be downloaded from:

www.fognet.com/NNM_7.51_Deployment_Handbook_v1.3.pdf

90

Interesting switch interface filter example

The following example provided by Nils Johannessen demonstrates a typical "InterestingSwouterIF" assertion that is introduced in the section above. In this example, the list of interesting interfaces is limited to interfaces having IP addresses within a range as well as those being inside that range and also limited to the set of ifTypes given:

```
!-- added 2007-09-12 Nils A Johannessen - Manag-E Nordic->
 <interfaceAssertion  name="InterestingSwouterIF"  title=""
description="">
  <operator oper="OR">
   <attribute>
    <capability>isL2Connected</capability>
   </attribute>
   <attribute>
    <ifType>24</ifType>    <!-- 24 = loopback -->
   </attribute>
   <attribute>
    <ifType>53</ifType>    <!-- 53, 135,136 = VLAN -->
   </attribute>
   <attribute>
    <ifType>135</ifType>
   </attribute>
   <attribute>
    <ifType>136</ifType>
   </attribute>
   <attribute>
    <ifType>131</ifType>    <!-- 131 = tunnels -->
   </attribute>
   <attribute>
    <IPAddress>
     <IPv4>
      <address>10.150.*.*</address>
     </IPv4>
    </IPAddress>
   </attribute>
  </operator>
 </interfaceAssertion>
```

APA topology events

The following events are log-only by default, but can be set to log to get various details about APA decision making. Alternatively, use the ovdumpevents command to view these log-only events:

OV_TOPOLOGY_Attr_Change_Notification
Issued whenever an ET topology object's attribute changes

OV_TOPOLOGY_Life_Cycle_Notification
Issued when an ET object is created or deleted

OV_TOPOLOGY_Topology_State_Notification
Rich data pertaining to the status of ET Discovery

OV_TOPOLOGY_Status_Change_Notification
Issued for every ET topology status change

APA and important node filters

Important nodes are defined in the MyHostID.xml filter file to configure the APA to always send uncorrelated alarms associated with devices to the alarm browser. While the references to this filter in the xml files speak of bypassing the specific correlation that identifies secondary failures, in fact this filter bypasses all ECS correlations. The file accepts node names or IP addresses and has good examples of wildcard specifications. The myHostID.xml file is called by the ImportantNode filter defined in the TopoFilters.xml which is called in turn by the ImportantNodes ClassSpecification within the paConfig.xml file. The file is located in:

$OV_CONF/nnmet/topology/filter/MyHostID.xml

There is a known problem with this file in NNM 7.53 and earlier where an error is generated when MyHostID.xml has too many entries. HP recommends using IP wildcards or IP address ranges to limit the number of entries in this file. After updating this file, stop and restart the *ovet_poll* process.

APA performance improvements

APA polling statistics are available both in log-only events and through the Dynamic Views "Polling/Alanysis Summary" tab. The following performance improvement was suggested by HP with the release of V7.53: In paConfig.xml, comment out the IFInNotConnectedSwitch filter, then change the isSwitch classSpecification pingEnable from "false" to "true," and then change the UnconnectedAdminUpOrTestSwitchIF classSpecification ping setting from "false" to "true." Test the new settings with checkpollcg and restart the *ovet_poll* daemon.

Another performance improvement it to increase the APA thread counts by increasing the following parameters in paConfig.xml:

PollingEngineThreadPoolSize
statusAnalyzerThreadPoolSize

Connected vs unconnected interface APA status

Prior to NNM V7.50, the APA calculated node status based on the status of all the polled interfaces whether connected or not connected in ET. In V7.51 this changed so the APA will not propagate the failure of unconnected interfaces to the node's status.

The below paConfig.xml flag can be used to fine tune this new algorithm. If the value of this flag is true APA will propagate the status of unconnected interface to the node and vice versa. By default the value of this flag is true for all the interfaces except for all the unconnected Ethernet interfaces in connected nodes:

```
propagateStatusForUnconnectedObj
```

To revert back to NNM7.50 behavior, search for the following paConfig.xml filter and set the flag to true. Note that this may cause container view to show incorrect status of network:

```
UnconnectedEthIFInConnectedNode
```

APA memory footprint reduction

NNM v7.51 introduced this enhancement which only loads actively-polled interfaces into memory. By default, the APA loads all discovered interfaces into memory. To implement this improvement, locate the below parameter in the paConfig.xml and change its varValue from false to true, then restart *ovet_poll*:

```
loadOnlyPolledObjectsIntoMemory
```

Note that in the V7.53 document listed below, special considerations need to be taken into conseration on NNM systems running HP-UX when implementing the memory footprint reduction:

```
$OV_DOC/whitepapers/ETandAPADeploymentGuide.pdf
```

Disabling status bridge

Those who rely soley on Homebase views and are using APA can improve performance by disabling the status bridge. This means that *ovw*-based views will not have active status. Simple set the following paConfig.xml parameter to false and restart *ovet_poll* to accomplish this:

```
StatusBridgeEnabled
```

Characterizing APA polling behavior

One way to discover what filters are in effect for a particular set of nodes is to change the polling interval for a filter to a unique value. Look for that unique value in the output of the `checkPollCfg` command. For detailed tracking of what the APA is doing, enable the APA Topology events described in the section immediately above. For example, if the polling interval for the isRouter filter was changed from 300 seconds to 299 seconds, then those results from the `checkPollCfg` command that showed a polling interval of 299 seconds would indicate the isRouter filter is the filter that applies to those objects.

The "-v" and "-d" command line options for the `ovet_demandpoll` command provide, respectively, internal states of APA objects and detailed dump of the active demand poll.

Improving SNMP-based status with the APA

Default APA behavior is to fail an interface that returns an SNMP noSuchObject error if the SNMP agent re-indexes or looses track of a particular interface. V7.51 introduced a parameter which forces the APA to poll such an interface via ICMP before issuing a failure event. To implement this improvement, locate the below parameter in the paConfig.xml and change its varValue from false to true, then restart *ovet_poll*:

```
useIcmpIfSnmpNoSuchObj
```

APA and ManagementAddesss picking

SNMP preferred management addresses are initially defined through *netmon* discovery, but when an SNMP management address subsequently fails to respond to SNMP polls, by default, APA picks a new management address. This new address becomes the address used by Extended Topology as well.

If loopback addresses are enabled for most of the network devices in the managed environment, it is not necessary for the management station to pick a new address since most devices will re-assign the loopback to another working interface if the current interface fails.

For this reason, HP recommends disabling the pickManagementAddr feature if loopbacks are widely used in the environment. To do this, for V7.01 through V7.51, change the paConfig.xml file parameter `MgmtAddrInhibited` from "false" to "true" and restart ovet_poll. V7.53 introduced a new paConfig.xml parameter called `DisablePickMgmtAddress`, and setting this is set to "false" by default. Also, consider the *netmon* lrf setting `-k adjustNodeSnmpAddr=false` which is discussed in more detail on page 45.

If loopbacks are not widely used, there are three optional paConfig.xml parameters introduces with NNM 7.51 that allow the APA pickManagementAddress to be more finely tuned:

> • MgmtAddrPreferred – For a given address, if this parameter is true, the address will be considered for a new management address over an address where this parameter is false as a management address if the current management address fails. In addition, this address will be considered even if it is currently not configured to be polled. By default, this parameter is set to false.

> • MgmtAddrInhibited – For a given address, if this parameter is true, the address will never be used as a management address if the current management address fails. By default, this parameter is set to false.

> • MgmtAddrMaxSnmpQueries – When the current management address fails to respond to SNMP, the pickMgmtAddress algorithm will engage. This will cause no more than MgmtAddrMaxSnmpQueries simultaneous SNMP queries to be issued during the search for a new management address. fails. By default, this parameter is set to 10.

To get even more control, use DNS to tell NNM which address to use to as the preferred SNMP address. See page 27 and sections subsequent to that.

Troubleshooting APA

To determine a device's polling settings, run:

```
$OV_SUPPORT/NM/checkPollCfg -o <object name>
```

To print a summary of objects subject to polling, run:

```
$OV_SUPPORT/NM/checkPollCfg -l
```

The most common APA polling problems relate to mapping of isSwitch and isRouter. isSwitch and isRouter flags are assigned by *netmon* during discovery and these capabilities are used by ET topology filters. Run through these checks if certain devices are not being properly polled by the APA:

1. Check Firewalls for SNMP/ICMP blocking.
2. Force isRouter with G flag; isSwitch with B flag in oid_to_type file (see page 7)
3. Browse SNMP MIBs; check for cut tables that may prevent visibility to:

```
.1.3.6.1.2.1.1              systemTable for oid_to_type
.1.3.6.1.2.1.17.1           dot1dBaseTable, isSwitch
.1.3.6.1.2.1.4.20.1         ipAdEntTable
.1.3.6.1.2.1.2.1            ifTable, isRouter/isSwitch
.1.3.6.1.2.1.31.1.1.1.1     ifName
.1.3.6.1.2.1.31.1.1.1.18    ifAlias
.1.3.6.1.2.1.4.1.0          ipForwardingTable, isRouter
.1.3.6.1.2.1.4.21           ipRouteTable, isRouter
.1.3.6.1.2.1.4.22.1         ipNetToMediaTable, isSwitch
.1.3.6.1.2.1.3.1.           atTable
```

Sample query:

```
snmpwalk <target> 1.3.6.1.2.1.1
```

8. Traps, Events and Alarms

This section covers some basics about NNM's event infrastructure. More details about individual events are covered in the following section, Interpreting Events.

What is a trap vs. an event vs. an alarm?

In short, a trap becomes an event, and then an event becomes an alarm. "Event" is the generic term used in HP's documentation for what most often is technically an alarm.

An SNMP trap is an unsolicited, unacknowledged notification sent from an SNMP agent to an SNMP Manager. NNM wraps SNMP traps within the OV_EVENT stack of the *pmd* daemon. This adds attributes to the SNMP trap that are not otherwise defined under SNMP, such as severity, logging behavior, and event category.

Automatic actions are also added-value attributes to make the trap and event, and these attributes are added through the event configuration GUI which is a front-end to the trapd.conf configuration file.

A trap or an event passes into *pmd*, and OV events come out – they are no longer SNMP traps. *ovtrapd* is the daemon responsible for receiving traps on UDP port 162 by default and buffering them for *pmd*.

An alarm is simply a representation of an OV event in the alarm browser. Attributes that alarms have include acknowledgements, deletions, event correlation counts and embedded alarm relations. When an alarm is deleted from an NNM user's alarm browser, the underlying NNM event remains in the *eventdb*.

Configuring SNMP traps via trap macros

RFC 1215 defines the TRAP-TYPE macro and RFC 2578 defines the NOTIFICATION-TYPE macro. These macros define a way of supplying the trap definitions that devices may use within a MIB definition file. Essentially, a TRAP-TYPE macro is an SNMPv1 trap, while a NOTIFICATION-TYPE macro defines an SNMPv2 trap/notification.

When loading MIB files using the load MIB menu option within the *ovw* GUI (or by running: xnmloadmib), NNM detects macros and prompts the user for confirmation to upload embedded trap definitions if they exist.

If, when loading a MIB, no such message is displayed for the user, the MIB does not contain embedded trap definitions. The trap definitions can be manually extracted from the MIB files without uploading the MIBs. Because loaded MIBs consume memory, this may improve NNM's scalability in environments where memory is at a premium. To just load the trap definitions without loading the MIBs, run:

```
xnmloadmib -event -trapType -trapDetail 0 -load <MIBfile>
```

Note that if the MIB load utility is invoked from the command line to load a MIB (xnmloadmib -load <file>), it does not give the user the option of importing trap definitions into trapd.conf file. Running xnmloadmib with no options to invoke the GUI, however, will load the trap definitions.

Configuring events or traps via trap definition files

$OV_CONF/C/trapd.conf is the configuration file that holds the trap definitions. Some vendors provide text files that hold NNM trapd.conf compatible definitions that can be uploaded directly into NNM's event configuration. Often, the names of these files have the word "trapd" in their filenames. The commands to do this are:

```
xnmevents -load <filename>
xnmevents -replace <filename>
xnmevents -merge <filename>
```

See the man/ref pages to determine which command is best for the environment. The most common issue with loading trapd.conf-compatible files is file compatibility errors due to the file format. Often, assuring the very first line of the trapd.conf-compatible file reads "VERSION 3" resolves this issue.

Configuring events or traps manually

The third method to load NNM trap definitions is manually, via the NNM event configuration GUI. Follow these steps to do this:

1. Look at the enterprise ID. If there is not a defined enterprise matching the trap definition to be created, create a new enterprise ID using Edit > Enterprises > New. Some name must be given to the new enterprise. In some cases, and OID Alias may be specified. See the trapd.conf man/ref for more on that

2. Select the newly created enterprise then add a specific event that matches the specific number using Edit > Events > New

3. Select the "event message" tab and select the desired logging behavior, i.e. "Don't log or display" or log to a particular event category

4. If logging the event, define a severity and Event Log message. See page 102 for a list of variable binding variables that can be passed from the trap to the log message

5. Optionally test the new event configuration by formatting an event using the snmpnotify command or the script:

```
$OV_CONTRIB/NNM/sendMsg/sendMsg.ovpl
```

For more details on manually creating events, see the man/ref page for trapd.conf, and associated control commands xnmtrap and xnmevent. Always make a backup of the $OV_CONF/C/trapd.conf file when making event customizations. Note that direct edits to the trapd.conf are not supported by HP, but such edits (when carefully handled) can be a powerful way to bulk-modify whole classes of event definitions. When making manual edits to the trapd.conf file, they will not be activated in the event stack until one of the following commands is issued:

```
xnmevents -event
xnmtrap -event
```

Drop SNMP traps from particular devices

This feature appeared in V7.01. In V7.51, the ability to automatically unblock traps once the flood subsides was added. In Intermediate Patch 18, the "-c" option was added to allow a blocking time interval. Also in V7.51, Some documentation for this feature with examples appeared in:

```
$OV_DOC/WhitePapers/EventReduction.pdf
```

The $OV_CONF/ovtrapd.conf file is a list of specific IP Addresses and trap OIDs that the *ovtrapd* daemon will reject SNMP traps from. The file supports wildcards per the white paper, though the ovtrapd.conf man/ref page says that wildcards are not supported.

Important: If using the APA poller, certain traps are passed to the poller to improve status intelligence. Do not drop all traps from devices that are of concern with respect to status. See the section below for the list of traps the APA uses for status.

If the –B, –b option is set (with or without the –r option), traps would be suppressed if a storm occurs according to these rules:

With the –B option, If 1500 events come in from a device at a rate greater than 15 events per second, block the device and discard those events. After suppression starts, monitor that address it for the next 1500 events. If the rate is still greater than 15 events per second, discard the events for another interval, otherwise unblock the device and allow the events to come in. Use the –b option to change the default value of 1500 events. Use the –r option to change the default value of 15 events per second.

The –c option enables configuring a time period in seconds for the specified blocking criteria. If the number of traps coming from a particular device reaches the value configured by "-b" or "-B" in less than time duration specified by "-c", the traps will be blocked from the device. This option cannot be used with "-r" option.

Once the ovtrapd.conf file is updated, the ovtrapd daemon must be restarted using `ovstop` and `ovstart`. If running under the UNIX, the daemon can be issued a SIGINT instead of a restart as follows:

```
ps -ef|grep ovtrapd|awk '{print $2}'|xargs kill -2
```

Certain traps should not be dropped using the procedure above if polling devices using the APA, since they are passed to the poller to help dertermine device status. See page 76 for a list of these traps.

Automatically suppress SNMP trap storms

This feature seems to have appeared in V7.01 or a patch to 7.01. The –B, -b, and -r LRF options to *ovtrapd* disable SNMP traps from a device in the automatically when a trap storm occurs. These options cause automatic entries to be created in the $OV_CONF/ovtrapd.conf file.

The –B option suppresses traps if 1500 are received in a 15 second period. The –b and –r options allow the granularity of the number and rate of traps to be explicitly set for suppression. For more information, see the *ovtrapd* man/ref and see page 5 for the LRF update procedure. Here is an example ovtrapd.lrf file:

```
OVs_YES_START:pmd:-W -b 2000 -r 30:OVs_WELL_BEHAVED::
```

Note that the -W is required on Windows but not required on UNIX.

Generating ad-hoc SNMP traps or NNM events

snmpnotify is the facility for generating raw SNMP traps that can be sent to any SNMP manager. Later versions of NNM do not include the snmptrap command, which is snmpnotify's more familiar predecessor. snmpnotify output may either be an acknowledged SNMPv2C inform or an unacknowledged SNMPv1 or SNMPv2 Trap.

Another method for generating events on the NNM server is to use the ovevent command. This command provides NNM-specific data not native to SNMP traps such as severity and alarm category. Both ovevent and snmpnotify have similar syntax and provide the "-d" option for dumping ASN.1 decodes.

By default, both snmpnotify and ovevent pick up data associated with the specified target from the SNMP configuration database to pass to the command such as community strings and timeouts. The "-d" option is useful in troubleshooting SNMP configuration issues.

Examples of the ovevent command can be seen the following ovpl scripts in $OV_CONTRIB/NNM: popupMsg, ringBell, sendMsg, and setStatus.

Differences between snmpnotify and ovevent

snmpnotify uses SNMP as a the transport whereas ovevent uses TCP, which some may consider "more reliable." snmpnotify can be used to generate a trap and it can be sent to any SNMP manager. ovevent formats NNM events which can only be received by other copies of NNM.

Traps send using snmpnotify always flow into ECS, so can be correlated. Events coming from ovevent are subject to the *pmd* ov_event stack settings in pmd.lrf, so their flow either through or around ECS can be controlled.

See the *pnum* stack option in the man/ref for *ov_event* for more about ECS flow control and see page 97 for more information on the differences between traps and events,

Event variable bindings

The Event Log Message, Pop-up Window Message, and Command for Automatic Action fields in the Modify Events and Copy Events dialog boxes use special $ variables to present data that were received with the event. These special characters can help provide formatted output.

All nonprintable characters are converted to their octal (\000) equivalent for display in the event browser, or when passed to the operator initiated (manual) actions. The two exceptions are that a tab is displayed as \t in the alarm browser and as spaces in pop-up messages.

A new line is displayed as \n in the alarm browser and as a new line in pop-up messages. All nonprintable characters are passed unconverted to automatic actions executed by *ovactiond*.

Special Characters in action callbacks:

a	Alert (bell) character
b	Backspace
f	Form feed
n	Newline
r	Carriage return
t	Horizontal tab
v	Vertical tab
\	Backslash
\\	Use to separate elements in a pathname
000	Octal number, ranging from 000 to 177
Xhh	Hex number, both hh characters must be 0-9a-fA-F

Variables in action callbacks:

$1	The first sequential attribute of the event (varbind)
$#	The number of attributes in the event
$*	All attributes as: seq num, name (type): value strings
$-n	The nth attribute as: seq num, name (type): value string
$+n	The nth attribute as: name: value string
$>n	All attributes greater than n as value strings. $>0 = $*
$>-n	All attributes greater than n as seq name (type): value
$>+n	All variables greater than n as name: value strings
$x	Date event received using local date representation
$X	Time event received using local time representation

$@	Epoch time (seconds since Jan 1, 1970) using time_t
$O	The name (object identifier) of the received event
$o	The (object identifier) as a string of numbers
$V	Event type (SNMPv1, SNMPv2C, CMIP, GENERIC)
$r	The implied "source" of the event in textual form. This may not be the "true source" if proxied. See $R below
$ar	Same as $r except print the source as an IP address
$R	The "true source" of the event in textual form. If the event was forwarded, this displays the address of the remote *pmd's* machine
$aR	Same as $R except print the source as an IP address
$c	The category the event belongs in
$s	The severity of the event
$N	The name (textual alias) as defined in *trapd.conf*
$F	The textual name of remote pmd's machine if this event was forwarded, else local machine's name
$U	The NNM UUID of the event as a string of numbers
$$	Print the $ character
$C	The trap community string
$E	The trap enterprise as text string from trapd.conf
$O	The trap enterprise as text string from Loaded MIBs
$e	The trap enterprise as Object ID string of numbers
$A	The trap agent address as defined in the trap PDU If the name server can resolve, print the node name
$aA	Same as $A except print the source as an IP address
$G	The trap's generic-trap number
$S	The trap's specific-trap number
$T	The trap's sysUpTime time-stamp. This is the remote machine's time in hundredths of a second between the last re-initialization of the device and the generation of the trap. For non-SNMPv1 events this value is 0

Event logging

Events are logged to the event database. Prior to NNM 6.0, events were logged to a flat file called trapd.log. The preferred method for accessing events outside the alarm browser is to use the `ovdumpevents` command.

Pre-NNM 6.0 behavior, however, can be restored by modifying the *pmd* LRF file and adding the following switch:

```
-SOV_EVENT;t;18
```

This logs events to $OV_LOG/trapd.log and sets the logfile to roll at 8MB. See page 5 for LRF update procedure. Note that there is a significant performance hit with logging events to trapd.log.

There are three general logging modes: IGNORE, which discards the event entirely and is configured via the "Don't log or display" option in the GUI; LOGONLY, which sends the event to the event database but does not send it to the alarm browser; and Alarm Categories, which log the events to the user-customizable set of categories which can be configured via Edit->Alarm Categories in the event configuration GUI.

Sometimes, it is desirable to log all ignored SNMP traps for troubleshooting. Note once again that most of these may be OpenView enterprise alarms.

While not supported or necessarily recommended, globally searching and replacing the IGNORE flag with the LOGONLY flag can be easily done in Windows and UNIX text editors. Always make backup copies of trapd.conf before editing directly. In UNIX, use `sed`:

```
cp trapd.conf trapd.orig
sed '/^EVENT/s/"IGNORE"/"LOGONLY"/' trapd.orig >
trapd.conf
xnmtrap -events
```

Dumping the entire *eventdb*

Use the below commands to dump the raw event database. The main reason for doing this is to view events that may have fallen out of the alarm browser because the alarm browser is limited in the number of events it displays. Also, "log-only" events can only be displayed using these commands:

`ovdumpevents`	Dump entire *eventdb* to stdout
`ovdumpevents -t`	Dump entire *eventdb* to stdout, then tail output (`Ctrl-C` to stop)

These commands will show a summary of regular and correlated events. Note that `ovdumpevents` can be CPU-intensive and that the processCorrEvents tool is UNIX Only

```
ovdumpevents -s "default" > event.log
$OV_SUPPORT/processEvents event.log event-summary

ovdumpevents -c "default" > corr.log
$OV_SUPPORT/processCorrEvents corr.log corr-summary
```

Interpreting ovdumpevents output

Below is an example of an event from `ovdumpevents` output:

```
1162047602 1 Sat Oct 28 11:00:02 2006 cloudy.fognet.com    N IF lan0 Up
Capabilities: isNode  Root Cause: cloudy.fognet.com lan0;1 17.1.0.58916866 84819
```

Each event in `ovdumpevents` output is a single line of the form:

TimeStamp Cat Time EventSrc SWSrc EventMsg ; Sev EventOID OVObjId

TimeStamp is the Epoch Time that the event was received.

Cat is the numeric category as defined in trapd.conf. In the example above, it is "1" which is "LOGONLY." The default categories are:

CATEGORY 0 "IGNORE"
CATEGORY 1 "LOGONLY" "
CATEGORY 2 "Error Alarms"
CATEGORY 3 "Threshold Alarms"
CATEGORY 4 "Status Alarms"
CATEGORY 5 "Configuration Alarms"
CATEGORY 6 "Application Alert Alarms"
CATEGORY 7 "Problem Diagnosis Alarms"

Time is the human-readable translation of the Epoch Time.

EventSrc is the node that produced the event. Note that for status events whose origin is actually the OpenView server, the EventSrc will be set to the target of the event. In the above example, the EventSrc is "cloudy," which is the node OpenView detected as having Interface Lan0 come up, but the node that actually produced the event was "patchy," the management server. Use the flag that follows, SWSrc, to help determine the true source of OpenView events.

SWSrc is a single character representing the software source of the event. If the source is "-" then the event source is an SNMP trap generated by a source other than OpenView itself. In the example above, SWSrc is "N," which is *netmon*, so therefore the actual source of the event was OpenView. The possible values for SWSrc are:

C: xnmcollect	d: nmdemandpoll
D: snmpCollect	e: ECS Engine
E: xnmevents	i: ECS Circuit
F: ovtopofix	l: loadhosts
I: ipmap	m: netmon mask change
J: ovalarmsrv	n: xnmpolling
L: xnmloadmib	o: ovactiond
M: ovtopmd	p: ovspmd / ovpause / ovresume
N: netmon	r: remote pmd
P: pmd	s: xnmsnmpconf
R: ovrepld	t: xnmtrap
T: ovtrapd	6: IPV6 Polling Agent

b: nnm_bridge   -: Default
c: xnmtopoconf   ?: None of the above
a: Generic application

EventMsg is the event log message text.

Severity is a single number as follows:

Normal	1
Warning	2
Minor	3
Major	4
Critical	5

EventOID is the SNMP Object Idenfier of the event.

OvObjId is the OpenView Object ID, or 0 if not available.

Dumping parts of *eventdb*

Use the -l (ell) option to the ovdumpevents command to dump events
between the number of minutes specified and the time the command is
run. For example, to dump all events logged in the last day, run:

```
ovdumpevents -l 1440
```

The following script provides a template that can be customized to
select specific events from the *eventdb*. By default, the script dumps
events generated "today" into files separated by severity, e.g.
severity.Critical.qry.out:

```
$OV_CONTRIB/NNM/event/EventsBySeverity.ovpl
```

Ad hoc queries of the *eventdb*

ovdwquery allows direct access to the data warehouse via SQL. The
following example outputs all events received today:

```
ovdwquery -u ovdb -password -ovdb -file a.qry
```

The file a.qry's contents might look like this:

```
select message from nnm_event_detail
where $BEGIN_TODAY <= event_timestamp
and event_timestamp < $NOW;
```

Dump nodes from topology:

```
echo "select ip_hostname from nnm_nodes;" |ovdwquery
```

Trap and event forwarding

Forwarding raw SNMP traps to other SNMP managers is problematic and unsupported by NNM. NNM events may be forwarded to other copies of NNM, however. Individual events can be forwarded through the event configuration GUI (*xnmtrap*). Forwarding all events is problematic, but a script to insert the proper forwarding data into the record for every logged event defined in trapd.conf is not too difficult to write (make a backup copy of trapd.conf first). The problem is that traps subsequently added via macros in MIBs will not have the forwarding information added automatically. Note that NNM-forwarded events use TCP port 162, not UDP port 162, and only copies of NNM, OVO or IBM's Tivoli NetView can receive them.

An alternative to using NNM's event forwarding facility is to set up an automated action that creates an SNMP trap using the snmptrap or the snmpnotify command. Another alternative is to use NNM's SNMP API or CSOV to build an application that copies the event stream and generates SNMP traps to send to the target application. See page 182 on using NNM's APIs or CSOV.

Many third party products exist that can forward raw SNMP traps or NNM events. Tavve (www.tavve.com) provides a free toolkit that is a popular method for bulk-forwarding NNM events as SNMP traps to remote destinations. Bytesphere's SNMP Trap Manager is another free tool that can manage SNMP traps forwarding, and is available from the following url:

www.oidview.com/trap_fault_management.html

OpenView Operations product has an agent-based trap receiver which is capable of receiving traps from NNM in the ov_event format from the *pmd* daemon directly. OVO SNMP trap templates are then used to filter the feed of all messages from NNM to OVO.

When forwarding events from NNM running under Windows, there is a known problem in that the forwarded events do not have the original event's AGENT-ADDR properly encoded in the forwarded trap. Search for HP Doucment ID OV-EN000876 for details on the work-around, which is basically to set the –W LRF switch for the *ovtrapd* daemon. More on setting LRF switches on page 5.

OpenView enterprise and NNM-generated events

Events generated under the OpenView enterprise are those generated by NNM itself. For OpenView generated events that concern a managed node, such as status events, the source of the event is always used as the source of the event in the alarm browser, even though the true source is the NNM server itself. This is carried through the special varbind .1.3.6.1.4.1.11.2.17.2.2.0. Most NNM status events also carry the source as regular varbind. For *netmon*-based status events it's $2 and for APA-based status events it's $3.

NNM also uses events for inter-process communication. Most of these events are configured to "don't log or display" (ignore), but they can useful for troubleshooting NNM and for other purposes. In event dumps, the 5th attribute is the OpenView daemon that generated the event. The OV_EVENT man/ref shows what daemons correspond to what code letter in the dump, where M is *ovtopmd*, N is *netmon*, etc. This is instructive in interpreting events. All external traps should show *ovtrapd* (T) as the source.

It is also instructive to note that *netmon*-based interface status events are from *netmon*, but node-level events are from *ovtopmd*. Understanding that node status events are generated as the result of a set of topology conditions rather than from actual status is very important. A node up event is generated "when all interfaces are up" and doesn't always correspond to a node down event and vice versa. *netmon* provides status for interface-level entities only. The APA, on the other hand, provides direct status at four separate levels.

Alarm and icon status color defaults

Color defaults can be changed within $APP_DEFS/OVw. See page 9 for more on $APP_DEFS.

Operational Status Colors:

Blue	Unknown
Green	Normal/Up
Cyan	Warning
Yellow	Minor/Marginal
Orange	Major
Red	Critical/Down

Administrative Status Colors:

Beige/Off White	Unmanged
Tan	Testing

Salmon	Restricted
Dark Brown	Disabled

Meaning of an Acknowledged alarm:
- Alarm shows as acknowledged (Checked) in all browsers
- Alarm does not change status color propagation to category

Meaning of a Deleted alarm:
- Alarm shows as deleted (removed) in all browsers
- Alarm changes status color propagation to category
- Underlying event is not deleted from *eventdb*

ovalarmsrv **LRF settings**

Performance tuning parameters:

-a <*num*>	Max events to hold in ovalarmsrv internal cache
-d <*num*>	Num. of alarms to delete after max alarms reached
-s <*secs*>	How often (in seconds) to save browser state info

User control parameters:

-Baucsd	Default user control behavior
-Ba	User can acknowledge alarms
-Bu	User can un-acknowledge alarms
-Bc	User can change an alarm's category
-Bs	User can change an alarm's severity
-Bd	User can delete an alarm
-BX	Exclusive: User has none of these capabilities
-BA	Exclusive: User has all capabilities (-Baucsd)

Alarm browser settings (XNmevent app-defaults)

To modify alarm browser app-defaults settings:

UNIX:	Edit or add the keyword in $APP_DEFS/XNmevents.
Windows:	Edit the following registry key:
	MKEY_LOCAL_MACHINE:SOFTWARE\Hewlett-Packard\OpenView\Network Node Manager\xnmevents

Some of the more useful of the settings include:

maxEvents:	Num. alarms viewable in browser (3500)
warnOnDelete:	"false" turns off confirmation on deletes
maxDisplayMsgs:	Max Num. pop ups to display (unset)
filterByMap:	Display events only for nodes in map (false)
readOnly:	Disable any/all –Bauscd settings (false)

Additional actions

Additional actions are available from the alarm browser menu bar. These can be extended and configured.

To Configure Actions:

Use the commands Actions: Additional Actions to configure actions that are registered through the LRF process (page 5).

To launch custom URL's from Actions: Views:

Edit and add URL's in xnmeventsExt.conf, close alarm browser, run: `ovstop ovalarmsrv; ovstart ovalarmsrv`, Open alarm browser.

9. Interpreting Events

SNMP agents are typically very quiet by default in terms of trap generation. Most events that are typically seen in the NNM alarm browser are generated by NNM itself. These are the OpenView enterprise events. Mostly, these are NNM's poller results.

Note that all poller results in the alarm browser show the node affected as the source, but all poll results are in fact generated by the OpenView server itself. This can be misleading as there is no way to know that the actual source of the event was the OpenView server versus the node source displayed in the alarm browser.

NNM's handling of generic and specific traps

The SNMPv1 protocol defines seven Generic SNMP traps as follows:

0	Cold Start
1	Warm Start
2	Link Up
3	Link Down
4	EGP Neighbor Loss
5	Authentication Failure
6	Enterprise

The Enterprise generic is special because it allows for the use of the "specific" trap field to accommodate vendor extensions via variable bindings (varbinds), so the OpenView Enterprise Node_down event, which is generated by NNM, is conveyed with the following SNMP data:

Enterprise:	.1.3.6.1.4.1.11.2.17.1
Generic:	6
Specific:	58916865
Varbinds:	1,2,3...n

Generic traps and origin event OIDs

SNMPv2 introduced the concept of an event OID, so generic traps (like authentication failures or link up/down traps) would fall under enterprise .1.3.6.1.6.3.1.1.5.1 in the MIB tree. The old method was for vendors to define private versions of the generics within their enterprise MIB subtrees. In order to accommodate the new handling of generics with the old method, NNM automatically prepends the trap's enterprise followed by the generic trap number + 1 to the enterprise whenever an agent sends a generic trap along with a private enterprise.

This was set up this way so a link down from a Cisco router, for example could be differentiated from a link down from a Nortel router. After NNM v5, the event configuration GUI lists generic traps under the .1.3.6.1.6.3.1.1.5 enterprise. Previously, link down events, for example, would have been listed under generic 3. So a Cisco Link Down, for example, would be configured in the event configuration (trap.conf) with an id of:

.1.3.6.1.6.3.1.1.5.3.1.3.6.1.4.1.9

Taking this apart, this is the SNMPv2 snmpTraps enterprise (.1.3.6.1.6.3.1.1.5) followed by the generic trap number (3) and then the Cisco enterprise OID (.1.3.6.1.4.1.9.) The alarm browser is coded to display any such an alarm as a generic link down, i.e. as being from .1.3.6.1.6.3.1.1.5.3.

This gives NNM users the flexibility to create custom event definitions more generically for what was formerly a monolithic generic event. So, for any distinct SNMP agent OID, a distinct event definition can be created. For example, link down traps for Catalyst 3550's would have the OID:

.1.3.6.1.6.3.1.1.5.3.1.3.6.1.4.1.9.1.431.

Similarly, the definitions can be made higher up the OID tree. For example, a custom event definition can be made for link downs for all Cisco OIDs (1.3.6.1.6.3.1.1.5.3.1.3.6.1.4.1.9), or all link down events from all enterprises (.1.3.6.1.6.3.1.1.5.3). The OID that would cover all generic events from all enterprises would be .1.3.6.1.6.3.1.1.5.

Note that all generic traps under enterprise .1.3.6.1.6.3.1.1.5 are set to LOG-ONLY by default, so none of the traps described above will be seen in the event browser unless they are explicitly set to log.

"Received event X, No format in trapd.conf"

This default event is generated by HP OpenView and it represents an SNMP trap that has been received for which the NNM event system has no translation defined in NNM. It is captured by the default enterprise OID .1.3.6.1.4.1.

Events that are caught by this trap definition need to have event configurations added for them using one of the three methods described at the beginning of this section. But before simply defining an enterprise to accommodate it, it is important to determine if the trap is meaningful and desirable in the first place.

First, determine the trap source. Look at the source's name or IP. Is it in the NNM Topology (it doesn't have to be)? Is the source an SNMP agent known to NNM by SNMP OID in *oid_to_type* (see page 7)? Is the MIB for the trap's enterprise loaded? Browse the MIB using the MIB Browser or use the `snmpwalk` command.

Try to control SNMP traps from the agents directly first. Every device manufacturer provides a different methodology for configuring the SNMP agent and enabling and disabling SNMP traps (no standard configuration interface or conventions exist for SNMP agent administration or customization). Typically, these parameters are set through the device's IOS.

Lots of popular SNMP MIBs can be found in the $OV_SNMP_MIBS directory, and some of these hold trap macros. To determine if a particular MIB holds trap macros, look (grep) for the keyword "NOTIFICATION-TYPE" inside the MIB file. If that fails, try the vendor's web site, a general web search or a public MIB repository. Page 147 lists several good MIB repositories.

All private enterprise SNMP agent's OIDs are of the form:

.1.3.6.1.4.1.*number...*

Number is the IANA-assigned vendor ID. Any dotted numbers beyond the number immediately following .1.3.6.1.4.1 are vendor-specific designations. The master list of enterprises' number assignments can be found at:

www.iana.org/assignments/enterprise-numbers

113

Note that the vendor ID may often be misleading due to the mergers and acquisitions the high tech industry is subject to. Cisco is 9, HP is 11, Bay Networks is 18, etc.

If there are lots of Cicso OID traps coming through with no format, i.e., the OID starts with 1.3.6.1.4.1.9, then see the procedure for formatting traps on page 113. It may be easiest to log into cisco.com's CCO, and search for the NNM Integration Utility and install it. This may not only solve this problem, but might also provide custom symbols for Cisco devices as well.

Finally, it may be desirable to *not* format unformatted traps. One reason may be that it's too time consuming to track down or build the trap definitions. Another reason may be that the unformatted traps convey enough information in their varbinds that a formatted trap definition isn't necessary.

In highly-scaled environments, trap definitions consume memory and CPU and it may even become desirable to delete existing trap definitions, forcing them into the enterprise default. In either case, if "no format" events are frequent and expected, change the event message to simple pass the event data (for example, $*) so the events don't convey that there is something wrong with NNM's configuration.

Agent in distress; "spinning in ifTable or ipAddrTable"

This happens when an SNMP agent reports bad or corrupt information. Generally the agent vendor may need to be contacted for advice. "Spinning in ifTable" means that the SNMP agent has reported fewer interfaces present in the variable ifNumber than present in the router tables.

This is a known problem with some Cisco PIX routers that was fixed by newer code. If this is happening, it could cause performance problems on the device the agent is running on and should be immediately addressed. In other words, the agent really is in distress and may be running loops that consume CPU and/or memory.

"Spinning in ipAddrTable" means that the SNMP agent is reporting the same IP Address for the same interface (ifIndex) more than once in the table. There may be other reasons these alerts are being generated, but almost always, it is because there is a problem on the target agent, not with NNM.

OV_PhysAddr_Mismatch

This event is generated by HP OpenView. One common reason to see this event is due to proxy-ARP from the routers and/or the default routing config on end-nodes, which NNM has trouble with. Proxy-ARP is an alternative to defining large routing tables on edge devices, and more can be learned about it by reading RFC 1027. In the case of a host with a default route, its ARP cache has the router's MAC address as the MAC address for every non-local host it has communicated with.

The ARP-cache of the router to which the non-local hosts are connected will have the appropriate *real* entries, as will the actual hosts. When OV sees the apparent discrepancy, it generates this event. If Proxy-ARP is in use, it is completely reasonable to change this event from an error alarm to log-only or to IGNORE. The same can be said for the OV_ARPChgNewPhysAddr event.

Inconsistent subnet mask

Most commonly, the device's configured mask is actually incorrect. Sometimes, the first device discovered in a new network is an improperly-configured netmask, so subsequently-discovered devices with proper netmasks generate a flood of these events. This event is also generated because NNM applies a classful mask because it doesn't have enough information to properly determine the correct mask. In this case, NNM is the culprit.

For example, suppose the first device discovered in the entire NNM topology that has a 10 address is 10.1.142.5. *netmon* asks the device for its mask with ICMP mask request, but perhaps the device doesn't support that or filters that query out. *netmon* then queries the device via SNMP but the device doesn't answer that either.

In this case, NNM creates a network object called 10.0.0.0/8, based on the classfulness of the 10 network, and places the new node in this new network in the topology. *netmon* subsequently discovers 10.1.142.10 and asks it for the network mask which answers 255.255.255.0, which NNM then calls inconsistent because it believes it should be 255.0.0.0. If a name for the corresponding subnet number isn't found in

/etc/networks, then NNM names the network symbol as the subnet number. NNM removes trailing zeros from the name.

Therefore, 11/8, 11.0/16, 11.0.0/24 and 11.0.0.0/30 might all look like "11" when named per this method. If nodes exist in both the 11.0 and 11.0.0 networks, inconsistent subnet mask events would then be generated for the nodes in the network that were discovered later; after the mask was set for the "11" network.

The solution is simply to add /etc/netmask entries, delete, than rediscover the nodes. The netmasks file on Windows resides in the OS directory under system32\drivers\etc. Finally, `loadhosts` may be used to force the masks for networks to be created when they don't yet exist in the topology. DNS can also be used to configure networks with corresponding netnames and netmasks, which gives better control over the netmasks.

Another common reason this event is generated is when using variable-length subnet masks (VLSM), which NNM normally handles fine. NNM support for VLSM was added prior to NNM 6.0. As discussed above, it's possible to have more than one subnet mask for a class A network. For example, if one used a 16 bit mask (e.g., 10.1/16) and another used a 24 bit mask (e.g., 10.2.1/24). This is OK - however, it would be "illegal" or wrong to have an interface with a 24 bit mask that fell in the 10.1.x.x pattern, because it would be inconsistent according to NNM.

To fix this, validate the correct mask for the network and check if it is consistent with what NNM reports by right-clicking on the network icon and displaying the object properties; the IP Map attributes show the netmask that NNM has assigned upon discovery.

If this is incorrect, `ovtopofix -r 10` can sometimes fix the problem. If not, shutdown *netmon* using `ovstop netmon`, delete the network symbol from all submaps, and from all defined maps, then rediscover the core device in the network using `loadhosts` with the `-m <mask>` option (page 44). Restart *netmon*, confirm the proper netmask is assigned to the network symbol, and issue a demand poll to the device.

In extranet environments, the same sort of thing can happen to CIDR-based subnets. If `rnetstat -I` on the offending device returns different netmasks for itself and its route, the network settings could be CIDR compliant but not RFC 950 compliant.

In general, NNM is very strict on RFC 950 compliance and if there are nodes with interfaces that have subnet masks "less" than the class of network in question, then NNM will generate inconsistent subnet mask events.

For example, `rnetstat -r <node>` output shows:

```
Interface IP address     Network Mask    Network Address
Loopback  10.177.104.9    255.255.255.252 10.177.104.8
BRI0      10.177.104.154  255.255.255.248 10.177.104.152
```

To fix it, delete the incorrect interface from NNM and re-add it using the proper subnet mask. Use `loadhosts` (see page 47) or manually add the interface using map operations. Remember that CIDR is Classless Inter-Domain *Routing*, not classless *Addressing*.

RFC 1518 says that it specifically does not address "procedures for assigning host IP addresses." It is a mistake to take routing policies and concepts and try to apply them to interfaces. If there is not an entry in the netmasks file or if the netmask is not specified when nodes are added using `loadhosts`, NNM uses the default netmask for the class of network, and inconsistent subnet mask messages may result.

OV_Duplicate_IP_Address

There are several reasons these may be generated other than a mis-configuration in the managed environment. The most common reason is the presense of HSRP or VRRP devices which have migrating IP addresses. The most recent versions of NNM detect HSRP interfaces and treat them appropriately via ET and the APA, but *netmon* may still complain. To stop this complaining, these interfaces can be added to the netmon.noDiscover file and then deleted from the topology.

In many cases, backup duplicate interfaces are flagged as administratively down in the MIB tables, so sometimes managing these via SNMP may work if polling is via *netmon*. If desired, the OV_Duplicate_IP_Address event can be suppressed for this class of device using the "-I" LRF switch for *netmon* (see page 5 for updating LRFs).

When an IP address is moved from one device to another, NNM may generate OV_Duplicate_IP_Address events if the move wasn't "complete." In most cases, deleting the objects and rediscovering them solves the problem using the procedure on page 203. It may not solve the problem, though, if for example DNS wasn't properly updated, or if the interface was set to administratively down instead of being removed from the source device.

OV_DuplicateIfAlias

Duplicate ifAlias messages may appear after an upgrade to NNM 6.31 or above. NNM uses ifAlias by default for naming interfaces because they are a more stable way of tracking interfaces than using ifName (because ifName may change due to index remapping by the SNMP Agent). Some agents, however, automatically set the ifAlias to "testing" if the ifAdminStatus is set to "testing."

To eliminate these messages, configure the offending interfaces with different ifAliases if it's not too much trouble. Some devices' SNMP agents, however, may not permit a change in the ifAlias. To force NNM to revert to the legacy behavior of using ifName, set the following *netmon* LRF switch using the procedure on page 5:

```
-k useIfAlias=false
```

Another approach is to modify the OV_DuplicateAlias event and set its logging behavior to "Ignore."

If using the APA poller, the paConfig.xml file provides much more sophisticated methods for handling ifAliases.

Observe that some physical interfaces show up in the interface tables as several interfaces, and on the device it is only possible to configure the SNMP ifDescr on one of them. In this case, the OV_DuplicatIfAlias alarm may be generated since the ifAlias may be identical on the primary interface and sub-interfaces. This behavior is common with ISDN BRI interfaces on Cisco devices. You may want to use netmon.interfaceNoDiscover for such subinterfaces.

Authentication failures

These generic SNMP traps are generated by SNMP agents in response to a failure to properly authenticate an incoming SNMP request. For example, an SNMP get request with the improper community string.

Such a request could very likely be generated by agents that are being contacted by the NNM server itself, since in general, it issues a lot of SNMP requests.

Therefore, these traps typically indicate the need to set the proper SNMP community string in NNM's SNMP Configuration GUI. To determine the string NNM is using to contact an SNMP agent, run:

```
xnmsnmpconf -resolve <target>
```

Most SNMP agents do not provide a facility to identify the source of the failed SNMP requests. Determining the source of bad SNMP requests can be accomplished using a sniffer (page 180) to pull the source from SNMP PDU of the offending requests. Detailed *pmd* tracing (page 137) will dump SNMP PDU data as well.

A few devices do provide this data in proprietary traps, however, and NNM's syslog facility may also be of use in this case. Remember, it's sometimes hard to explicitly determine the cause of an AuthFail trap because it is a rather limited response from an agent node to another node's attempt to access its SNMP agent. To toggle SNMP authentication failures off at the source, use the SNMP agent vendor's implementation-specific methods. Or, if the "write" community string is known for the agent, use:

```
snmpset <node> snmp.snmpEnableAuthenTraps.0 integer 2
```

By default, the Authentication Failure event in NNM is set to "log-only." Consider logging them as a security or scalability precaution. At the very least, the event should be set to log a status on occasion to validate that AuthFail traps aren't causing potential performance issues.

Run `ovdumpevents` to view log-only events. It may not be a bad idea to set up a scheduled script that greps AuthFails from the event log and reports summary findings. In larger environments where certain volumes of AuthFail traps are expected, set the logging behavior to "IGNORE" to improve performance of the NNM server.

In the trap description for the AuthFail trap, there is a note that claims:

"HP-UX only: On HP-UX agents, the valid community names can be found in the /etc/snmpd.conf file. The IP address that caused the authentication failure can be determined by either looking in the log file (snmpd.log), or by doing a snmpwalk on the SNMP variable:

> .iso.org.dod.internet.private.enterprises.hp.nm.snmp.
> authfail.authFailTable.authFailEntry"

Neither the snmpd.log nor the stated MIB variable is ever updated after bad requests to HP-UX instances of NNM. Still, the trap description continues to claim this to be so (erroneously).

Unknown or unrecognized ASN.1 type # messages

These may show up embedded in SNMP trap varbind fields or in the pmd.log0 file and may cause *pmd* and/or other daemons to crash. The cause of these errors is usually malformed SNMP traps. *pmd* stack tracing (see page 137) may be required to determine the trap source.

One solution is to disable the transmission of these particular traps from the source and/or to seek updated agent code from the vendor of the trap source equipment. It may also be possible to format a trap definition (see page 98) that doesn't use the offending varbinds.

Eliminating events from undesirable systems

Regardless of whether a node is in NNM topology or not, SNMP traps may be received from devices that aren't "managed." This is because there agents are configured with the NNM server as a trap destination.

Often this can be reset at the agent. On systems that support popular operating systems, this is usually set in the snmpd.conf file. Stopping undesirable traps at the source is ideal.

If running V7.01 or above, the ovtrapd.conf file can be used to suppress traps from particular devices. See page 99 for more information on ovtrapd.conf. If running an older version, there are several considerations offered below.

Sometimes a device is generating undesirable traps for a specific enterprise. Within NNM, a trap definition for that particular enterprise can be defined in the event configuration and then configured to "Ignore" all events.

To force the NNM server to reject all traps from all enterprises for a particular node, assign an incorrect community string to the target node in the SNMP Configuration GUI. Similarly, an SNMP proxy could be configured with a bad community string, for example 127.0.0.1, so the NNM server no longer issues requests to it. These tricks will cause additional timeouts and retries and may affect server performance. Again, the most desirable approach is to address each offending node individually by configuring its agent not to produce the traps in the first place.

10. Event Correlation

The ECS runtime engine was added to NNM in version 6.0 to support the suppression of cascade failure events. ECS circuits were supplied by HP, and the Correlation Manager was provided as a front-end to adjust basic settings and to turn correlations on or off. Until NNM 6.31, there was no facility in NNM for enhancing ECS correlation logic other than purchasing the expensive ECS Designer product.

The Correlation Composer, however, was added in NNM 6.31 and it provides an interface for creating advanced logic sets that are analogous to ECS circuits, but it does not provide the full circuit development capabilities of the Designer. The Composer is actually a front-end interface to a "super-circuit" in terms of ECS runtime and the ECS Designer. The composer is actually implemented as a regular ECS circuit.

What is event correlation?

Event correlation is used as a generic term to describe the ability to preemptively act on a stream of events in order to add intelligence to and control over that stream.

One implication of event correlation in this context is that past events are related to current events in order to reduce the overall amount of events generated. To accomplish this, event correlation tools must be "state aware," that is, they keep track of events over time.

Many modern event correlation products deploy finite difference engines internally to maintain state, and a set of logical constructions can be manipulated to form specific logic sets (circuits) that then act on "streams" of messages, interrupting or re-directing their flow through the event management system at various stages with great efficiency and scalability.

When discussing event correlation in terms of NNM, it refers to a set of subsystems which are heavily integrated into the NNM product. These subsystems include the ECS runtime engine, the correlation manager, the correlation composer, various configuration entry points within the NNM GUI and various configuration files.

Correlation Manager

This is the legacy interface to event correlations built in to NNM starting with version 6.01. It provides a JAVA-based GUI for changing parameters associated with NNM's built-in ECS circuits. Access the Correlation Manager through the NNM menus:

Options -> Event Configuration -> Edit -> Event Correlation

Or, the manager can be invoked by URL:

http://host.fqdn/OvDocs/C/ecs/ecscmg.html (Windows)
http://host.fqdn:3443/OvDocs/C/ecs/ecscmg.html (UNIX)

On UNIX installations, the port number (:3443) must be appended to the NNM Server hostname in the URL above.

Correlation Composer

The Correlation Composer is accessed via the Correlation Manager. The Composer can be launched by selecting "modify" after highlighting the "Composer" circuit in the Correlation Manager. Alternatively, in UNIX, the Correlation Composer can be started with the ovcomposer command. In Windows, the composer can be started with:

```
ovcomposer -m o        operator mode (read-only)
ovcomposer -m d        developer mode
```

The Composer is a front-end interface to a "super circuit," which is to say that it is a single ECS circuit that can be used to create a fairly wide range of correlation logics specifically for NNM.

It provides a way to add correlations for specific SNMP events, and is bundled with NNM 6.31 and higher. In essence, the Composer is a fancy interface to create and manipulate very fancy external ECS fact stores.

The Composer provides a few correlations that serve as examples as to the sorts of logic that can be created with this GUI.

The path to the correlator store is $OV_CONF/ecs/CIB and the NNM-provided correlators with V7.5 include:

NNMBasic

> OV_Connector_IntermittentStatus
> OV_Chassis_Cisco
> OV_Multiple_Reboots

NodeIf

> OV_NodeIf_NodeDown
> OV_NodeIf_PrimaryIFUnknown
> OV_NodeIf_NodeNotCorrelator

Poller

> OV_Connector_IntermittentStatus

PollerPlus

> OV_Link_Intermittent
> OV_Conn_IntermittentStatus
> OV_Addr_IntermittentStatus
> OV_Interface_IntermittentStatus
> OV_Node_IntermittentStatus

For creating custom correlations, the Composer provides the following correlator templates:

Enhance:
> Trigger the creation of a new output alarm
> Modify the information for an existing alarm

Multi-Source:
> Discard, modify, consolidate or create new output alarm(s) based on a set of multiple input alarms

Rate:
> Count like input alarms and emit all or none plus a new alarm indicating the threshold was breached

Repeated:
> Mode 1: Discard duplicates in window of first alarm
> Mode 2: Replace/embed latest alarm in browser
> Same logic as DeDup correlation with more control

Suppress:

Discard alarms matching conditions

Transient:
Monitor rate and/or consolidate status-oriented alarms
Same logic as PairWise correlation with more control

User-Defined:
Alarms meeting advanced filter or simple alarm signatures invoke an
input function such as a C or Perl script.

ECS Designer

The Designer provides a full and robust interface for ECS circuit development. The correlations provided with NNM were themselves developed with this tool (except for the Composer). With the introduction of the Composer, the ECS Designer is longer needed to develop most correlations that mirror the form and function of the existing correlations. For more advanced correlations, however, the ECS Designer is a must.

The Designer provides the interface for compiling ECS raw circuit files (.ecs files) into compiled circuits (.eco files) that can then be loaded into the ECS runtime engine.

The ECS Designer is not required to load compiled ECS circuits (.eco files) into the runtime engine. This implies that circuits developed by someone else can be shared (or, as is sometimes the case, sold) to be loaded into an environment where the ECS Designer is not installed.

Instances and streams

Inside the ECS runtime engine, events are separated into streams, or flows of events. All of the default ECS circuits and Correlation Composer instances are configured to run on the default stream. It is very unusual to use multiple streams in most environments.

Even when events are coming from different sources, for example via *pmd* through NNM, and via *opcmsg* through OVO, the events all flow through the default stream. Only in this way can events from different sources such as this be related to each other. Only when events come from sources that must be completely separated should separate streams be employed.

An ECS instance is like a copy of the runtime ECS engine that is dedicated to a particular set of event sources. Multiple instances of

ECS runtime can and do run on single server and each are separate in their input and output. Circuits operating in separate instances do not interact with each other even though they may all be configured to use the same stream at the same time.

The default instance is "1" and it is used for NNM's embedded ECS runtime. It gets its feed from *pmd*. `ecsmgr` commands are directed to the default instance unless the specific instance is specified with the "–i" option. So, for example, the following two commands are equivalent:

```
escmgr -i 1 -info
escmgr -info
```

Two other instances that may be of interest are instance 11 and instance 12. Instance 11 is reserved for the OVO management server and instance 12 is reserved for the OVO agent. A UNIX OVO management server, then, may have three operative instances of ECS runtime, but they won't be operative by default, since there are no out-of-box correlations for OVO server or OVO agent.

Special correlations

The DeDuplication correlator (DeDup) is special because it is a post-processing correlator. This is required in order to interact with the alarm browser in such a way as to "move" existing alarms from their time-based position in browser. To accomplish this, the correlation externally communicates directly with the *ovalarmsrv* process. The only configuration entry point for this circuit is:

$OV_CONF/dedup.conf

Connector down event correlation circuit

This correlation is managed by the Correlation Manager. NNM's first correlator, this ECS logic was introduced in V6.0. Connector Down affects both *netmon* & APA status. Both *netmon* and APA internally distinguish between primary and secondary failures, and pass this data to the correlation by way of varbinds. What this circuit does, however, is very different at a functional level with respect to *netmon* versus APA behavior.

For *netmon*-based events, the circuit performs three layers of correlation which can be seen in the event browser as an event with embedded events which themselves have embedded events (see

Figure 10-1). At the top layer are node events with interface-level events embedded below.

For each interface event, secondary interface alarms are subsequently embedded, representing cascade failures beyond the primary interface

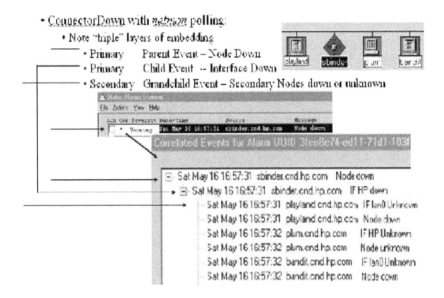

Figure 10-1

in terms of network path. *netmon* builds and maintains path data on daemon start for every interface in the topology. Only with later versions does *netmon* issue dynamic polls based on connector status. For all versions after V6.0, though, *netmon* doubles (by default) scheduled polls to secondary interfaces.

For APA-based events, all secondary alarms are suppressed, so the circuit is instead used to correlate the three layers of event based on Address events, Interface events, and Node events (see Figure 10-2). Like *netmon*-based correlation, the node level is the top layer, with interface events embedded below and address level events embedded below that. Note that APA-based primary/secondary determination is performed by *ovet_pathengine*, not *ovet_poll*. In ET Dynamic views, secondary status in the topology is set to unknown and in IPMAP, the status is unchanged.

For *netmon*-based correlation, an Important Node filter defines nodes that will always be considered primary. This is defined using NNM's standard filter definition language. The *genannosrvr* process feeds important node filter data to ECS. For APA-based correlation, important nodes are configured in the paConfig.xml file. Important nodes always get a status change when a device in the path to them becomes unreachable.

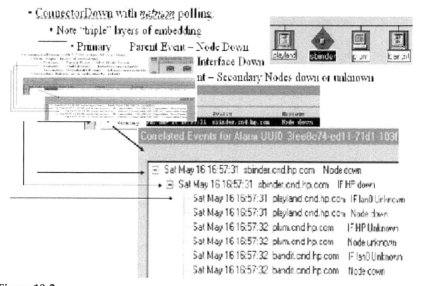

Figure 10-2

NodeIf event correlation

This correlation is managed by the Correlation Composer, and affects *netmon* status only. It was introduced in V6.31. Also called "Router/Switch Health," this correlator supplements the Connector Down circuit.

NodeIf suppresses simple node downs and is central to the major shift introduced in V6.31 from node-centric status events to Interface-centric status events for *netmon*. NodeIf also correlates the dynamic *netmon* polls for neighbor interfaces also introduced in V6.31 (see page 58).

NodeIf's effect is that OV_IF_Unknown and OV_IF_Down status alarms from interfaces within routers or switches are suppressed and embedded if a corresponding node-level status alarm (OV_Node_Unknown; OV_Node_Down) is received within the specified time window.

NodeIf suppresses interface status alarms from devices other than routers or switches so that these alarms never appear. *The assumption is that end-node status alarms are not desirable.*

NodeIf suppresses interface status alarms from unused (unconnected) ports within routers or switches.

NodeIf addresses the following failure scenarios that ConnectorDown doesn't:

- If fewer than all the interfaces on a router or switch fail, displays the interface status alarms

- If all the interfaces on a router or switch fail, display the OV_Node_Down alarm with the interface alarms nested underneath

- If a router or switch failure is a secondary failure, then all secondary events are embedded, unless they pass the Important Node filter

Repeated event correlation circuit

This correlation is managed by the Correlation Manager. The functionality of this correlator, which should be considered a legacy circuit, is superseded by introduction of DeDup correlation in NNM 6.4. The repeated event circuit embeds subsequent matches under original event in alarm browser, incrementing the correlated message count. Contrast this to DeDup, which deletes and embeds original alarm, effectively "moving" the original alarm to the head of alarm list.

This correlator is useful for suppressing informational messages, and is employed on the *netmon*-based Node_up event. The Node_up event occurs when "all interfaces are normal or unknown," so in the case where one interface goes down and comes up again, a Node_up event may be repeatedly generated.

This circuit is useful for indicating the condition without moving the message in the alarm browser each time the condition repeats, which is what the DeDup correlator would do.

PairWise event correlation circuit

This correlation is managed by the Correlation Manager and it applied to most status events generated by either *netmon* or the APA. The behavior of PairWise is very dependent on the version of NNM and substantially changes between V6.31, V6.41, and again in V7.01. The behavior of PairWise is also loosely coupled to DeDup correlation behavior.

NNM V6.0, V6.1, V6.2:
Status alarms are *acknowledged* if the parent event received within 10 minutes (PairedTimeWindow). Child events are released immediately to browser and associated actions are immediately launched. There is no reduction in the number of alarms, as the parent events not embedded (suppressed).

NNM V6.31, V6.41:
Status alarms are *deleted* if the parent event is received within 10 minutes (PairedTimeWindow). Child events are *held* (not released immediately), and should not be seen in the alarm browser at all. Actions are launched only if the PairedTimeWindow expires or the parent event is detected. No alarms are seen at all if parent event is received within the window and if the PairedTimeWindow expires, the child event is released with the *original* time stamp to the alarm browser. Subsequently, the parent event is embedded, and should be subject to being deleted by the DeDup circuit (see below).

NNM V7.01+:
Child events are released immediately to the alarm browser and associated actions are immediately launched. Status alarms subsequently deleted if parent received within 10m. Parent event received after window is sent to alarm browser, and are not embedded.

DeDup event correlation

This correlator is managed by the Correlation Composer and affects *netmon* & APA status. It was introduced in V6.41+. It is an improvement on the Repeated Event in that it uses post-processing logic that takes feed from event database as opposed to the event stream via *pmd*. DeDup deletes and embeds the existing matching alarm, "replacing" it with the latest alarm.

DeDup was coupled to PairWise circuit in NNM 7.0+. Any child event defined in DeDup *and* PairWise should be deleted by the receipt of the parent alarm, even after PairWise PairedTimeWindow expires. The affected "down" status alarms are always deleted from the alarm browser when matched with their corresponding "up" alarm.

This correlator is configured via an external file, $OV_CONF/dedup.conf. Uncomment the following line to entirely disable this correlation:

DEDUPLICATION=OFF

Intermittent Status event correlation

This correlation is managed by the Correlation Composer, was introduced in V6.31, and affects *netmon* status only. This correlation is also called "Router/Switch Intermittent Status" or "OV_Connector_IntermittentStatus." Intermittent Status shows flapping interfaces whose status would otherwise be suppressed by the PairWise correlation's behavior. This logic only applies to connector interfaces, and it generates a new event, OV_IF_Intermittent (OpenView enterprise 58982423) to indicate the flapping condition. The new event is generated when the input event occurs RATE_COUNT times within RATE_PERIOD, where by default:

RATE_COUNT = 4 in V6.31
RATE_COUNT = 5 in V6.4
RATE_COUNT = 4 in V7.0+
RATE_PERIOD = 30 minutes

OV poller plus event correlation

This correlation is managed by the Correlation Composer, was introduced in V6.41, and affects APA status only. This correlator is unloaded by default. This correlator has the same functionality as IntermittentStatus, but applies to the LinkDown event and to APA status events affected by PairWise correlation.

The correlator comprises five individual logic sets for APA connection, interface, address, node events and LinkDown traps. The new event generated when a flapping condition is detected is of the form:

OV_APA_[INTERFACE | NODE | ADDR | CONN]_Intermittent

This alarm is generated when like alarms processed by PairWise correlation repeat RATE_COUNT times within RATE_PERIOD, where:

RATE_COUNT: Default is 2 in V7.01
RATE_PERIOD Default is 30 minutes

To enable this correlator (disabled by default), add the following entry to the $OV_CONF/ecs/CIB/NameSpace.conf file, then redeploy the correlators within the Correlation Composer window:

OV_Poller_Plus=PollerPlus.fs

Multiple reboots event correlation

This correlation is managed by the Correlation Composer and is not tied to OpenView status events. This correlator creates a new alarm when 4 (by default) or more coldStart or warmStart traps are received within 5 (by default) minutes from a specific SNMP-agent/IP-address pair. This correlator is yet another repeat of the functionally of Intermittent Status (see above). Introduced in V6.31, this correlator was designed to detect multiple reboots which would otherwise never been seen per the PairWise 6.31 behavior (see above).

Cisco chassis event correlation

This correlation is managed by the Correlation Composer and it monitors the following CISCO-STACK-MIB traps and generates one of three new OpenView enterprise alarms if the condition persists for 10 minutes:

.1.3.6.1.4.1.9.5.5
.1.3.6.1.4.1.9.5.6

The OpenView traps generated are:

OV_Chassis_Temperature (specific 8982424)
OV_Chassis_FanFailure (specific 58982425)
OV_Chassis_PowerSupply (specific 58982426)

The circuit requires that the Stack MIB is loaded on the management server and that the traps are enabled for each Cisco device (they are disabled by default). See page 195 for instructions on how to enable these traps.

Summary of event correlations affecting status

Figure 10-3 shows some of the interactions between NNM and the event correlation engine. Events flow into the *ovevent* stack within *pmd*. There, events are directed on parallel tracks to daemon that register with *pmd*. The daemons register for raw, correlated, or all output from the *ovevent* stack. ECS is one of the daemons that register for this feed, but it is special in that it is able to feed its output back into the *ovevent* stack as input.

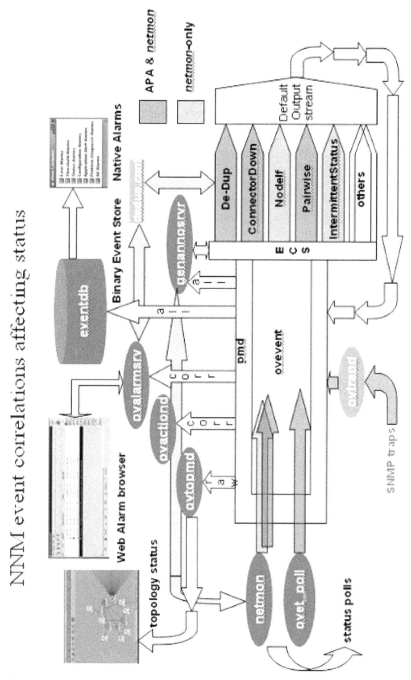

Figure 10-3

Useful ECS manager commands

The following commands display Engine Status and details:

```
ecsmgr -info
ecsmgr -stats
ecsmgr -stats verbose
ecsmgr -snapshot <output_file>
```

The `ecsmgr -stats` command shows which ECS circuits are doing what with each event they process. If there is a count associated with the undecided stat, this gives the number of events that are currently being held by the circuit in some sort of time window.

The `ecsmgr -snapshot` command dumps detailed information about the states of operating circuits. It will also show details about the events that are currently being held by each ECS circuit.

To externally disable/enable ECS circuit:

```
ecsmgr -disable PairWise
ecsmgr -enable PairWise
```

To externally change ECS Circuit, modify the .ds file, then:

```
ecsmgr -disable PairWise
ecsmgr -circuit_reload PairWise
ecsmgr -enable PairWise
```

Configuring ECS circuits

When NNM-supplied ECS circuits are configured using the Correlation Manager to change parameters such as time windows, etc., the following files should get updated automatically. Sometimes, errors are produced after changing parameters. If so, check these files:

```
$OV_CONF/ecs/circuits/<circuit_name>.ds
$OV_CONF/ecs/circuits/C/<circuit_name>.param
```

Disable or enable ECS

ECS runtime and default ECS correlators are enabled by default when NNM is installed. To permanently disable ECS, add the following switch to pmd.lrf (procedure on page 5):

```
-SOV_EVENT;p0
```

Disable ECS on the running pmd: `pmdmgr -SOV_EVENT\;p0`

To re-enable ECS after removing the `-SOV_EVENT;p0 LRF` flag, run: `pmdmgr -SOV_EVENT\;p1`

To disable all ECS circuits on the NNM instance until the system reboots or the `ovstart` is issued, run: `ecsmgr -reset`

To re-enable all circuits after a reset: For each .ds file in:

> $OV_CONF/ECS/circuits: `ecsmgr -enable <circuit_name>`

Or, manually toggle the correlations back on in the GUI.

Logging incoming ECS events

To capture all events entering the ECS engine:

Turn on logging	`ecsmgr -log_events input on`
Turn off logging:	`ecsmgr -log_events input off`
Change log size:	`ecsmgr -max_log_size event <Kbytes>`

The log file name is ecsin.evt0. It is a rolling log, and is 512k by default. It is located in:

> $OV_LOG/ecs/1/ecsin.evt0 and
> $OV_LOG/ecs/1/ecsin.evt1

Logging output and correlated events

To capture events (including ECS-created events) output or discarded by the currently enabled correlators:

```
ecsmgr -log_events stream on
ecsmgr -log_events stream off
ecsmgr -max_log_size event <Kbytes>
```

The log file is named default_xxx.evt0. It is a rolling log, it is 512K by default, and is located in:

> $OV_LOG/ecs/1/default_sout.evt0
> $OV_LOG/ecs/1/default_sout.evt1

Events which are discarded by the stream (or suppressed by a circuit) are written to:

> $OV_LOG/ecs/1/default_sdis.evt0
> $OV_LOG/ecs/1/default_sdis.evt1

Simulate events for testing ECS logic

`ecsevgen` and `ecsevout` in $OV_CONTRIB/ECS can be used to replay event logs for testing the effects of ECS circuit changes. For more info, see TroubleshootingEventCorrelation.txt in that directory.

ECS tracing

ECS tracing can be extremely verbose, but certain development activities can't be sufficiently troubleshot without it. To enable full ECS tracing:

```
ecsmgr -i 1 -trace 65536
pmdmgr -D0xffffffff -SECSS\;T0xffffffff
```

The traces are then written to $OV_LOG /pmd.trc0.

Stack tracing via pmdmgr

To turn on the tracing of the OV_EVENT stack:

```
pmdmgr -SOV_EVENT\;T0xffffffff
```

This should produce entries in $OV_LOG/pmd.trc0. To turn on *pmd* debugging to trace all stacks (SNMP, etc):

```
pmdmgr -D0xffffffff       or
pmdmgr -D0xffffffff -SECSS\;T0xffffffff
```

To make sure *pmd* problems are not related to ECS, before starting *pmd*, rename or move the ECSS stack configuration file:

/etc/opt/OV/share/conf/stacks/pmd/ECSS.cfg

To turn tracing off, simply restart OV, or run:

```
pmdmgr  -SOV_EVENT\;T0x0
```

Monitoring *pmd* bottlenecks (NNM 6.1 only)

This version only showed *pmd* performance in ovstatus output. This reporting was later removed, as it was a development debugging switch that was accidentally left on. Running 'ovstatus pmd' would report:

```
pmd RUNNING Statistics: cce=3, rqts=0, memory unfreed=6
```

"rqts" is number of pending operations in the *pmd* event processing queue. A value above 50 could mean bottlenecks.

Correlation Composer tracing

Follow these steps to enable Composer tracing.

1. Enable tracing within the Composer GUI
2. cd $OV_CONTRIB/ecs/CO
3. Run: ecsmgr -fact_update Composer CompTraceOn.fs
4. Run: pmdmgr -SECSS\;T0xffffffff
5. Tracing output is written to $OV_LOG/pmd.trc0

To disable Composer tracing:

1. Run: pmdmgr -SECSS\;T0x0
2. Run: ecsmgr -fact_update Composer CompTraceOff.fs
3. Disable tracing within the Composer GUI

11. SNMP Functions

Upon installation, NNM implements a proprietary SNMP agent infrastructure (Emanate) designed to accommodate multiple SNMP agents on a single server (the NNM management station). This allows NNM's special agent to co-exist with OS-oriented agents, therefore allowing for extensibility. The Emanate master and subagents are OEM'd from SNMP Research, Inc. as part of the NNM package. SNMP Research is also the provider of the SNMP Security Pack that is required for NNM to support SNMPv3 agents. SNMPv3 provides strong security support, among other advanced SNMP features.

As of NNM 7.5, the SNMP Security Pack comes bundled with the AE version, but only the Emanate agent is installed by default. The Security Pack includes an application to remotely configure SNMPv3 user credentials, access rights, and keys on the managed nodes. The SNMP Security Pack requires licensing through SNMP Research and it is available for all platforms and versions supported by NNM. NNM 7.5/Security Pack integration also provides support for ET discovery via SNMPv3. Installation of the SNMP Security Pack replaces the Emanate agent with SNMP Research's more advanced Brass agent.

SNMP versions and history

SNMPv1 and V3 are full IETF standards. SNMPv2 never achieved standard status. There are three versions of non-standard SNMPv2 that have been implemented by a variety of vendors: V2C, V2U, and V2*. SNMPv2C is supported natively in NNM. SNMPv1 appeared in 1988 under RFC's 1065, 1066, and 1067. It is still widely used but has been criticized for its use of client authorization via cleartext community strings. SNMPv2, sometimes also referred to as SNMPv2P, was initially introduced through RFC's 1441 and 1452. It offered improvements of SNMPv1 and implemented a party-based security system which some viewed as overly complex. SNMPv2C (as proposed in RFC's 1901 though 1908) introduced a community-based security model which comprised SNMPv2 without the controversial new SNMPv2 security model, using instead the familiar community-based security scheme of SNMPv1.

SNMPv2U (as proposed in RFC 1909) attempted to offer greater security than SNMPv1, but without incurring the high complexity of SNMPv2. A variant of this was commercialized as SNMPv2* and the mechanism was eventually adopted as one of two security frameworks in SNMPv3. SNMPv3 as defined in RFC's 3411 and 3418 achieved full standard status in 2004. It encompasses strong security, provides remote configuration, has advanced scalability and distribution features, and is compatible with deployed previous SNMP versions.

Configuring SNMP community strings on NNM agent

Community strings for NNM's custom SNMP agent (Emanate) are configured in the snmpd.conf file.

On UNIX, this file is in:	/etc/SnmpAgent.d
On Windows , this file is in:	%OV_CONF%\SNMPAgent

Note that Emanate does not allow the write and read communities to be set to the same string.

Configuring SNMP versions

NNM supports SNMPv1 and SNMPv2C, and SNMPv3 with the SNMP Security Pack. To specify SNMPv2C as the protocol to use for a particular agent, use `xnmsnmpconf` with the `-setV` option. To determine the version, use:

```
xnmsnmpconf -getV <target>
```

Multiple protocols can be specified, for example:

```
xnmsnmpconf -setV <target> 1,2C
```

Configuring multiple SNMP agents on a single node

Some devices (e.g. servers) can support multiple SNMP agents if those agents are bound to non-conflicting ports. NNM supports only one SNMP port per IP Hostname, though. If the target system had multiple adapters, or if virtual IP addresses were assigned to an interface, separate SNMP agents could work if each address were assigned a separate DNS name so that NNM could discover them as though they were two nodes. This is actually how SNMP agent simulators like Gambit's MIMIC work. If the system is the NNM server, the Emanate extension agent can be used to add SNMP agents. On Windows, *wpaagt* loads extension agents. The adapter reads this registry key to find the extension agent DLLs to load:

HKLM\SYSTEM\CurrentControlSet\Services\Paramters\ExtensionAgents

On UNIX, the extension agent is *naaagt* and is configured via the file:

/etc/SnmpAgent.d/naa.cnf.

More info in can be found in the agent's respective man/ref pages. A creative way to support multiple monolithic agents: is to configure some extensible agent that is bound to port 161 to proxy requests to the agents that are bound to other ports. For more on extensible agents, see page 152.

SNMP master agent switches

To enable tracing on UNIX platforms, first stop the daemon using:

/sbin/SnmpAgtStart.d/K03SnmpMaster

To enable tracing on Windows platforms, first stop the NT master agent Service. For both platforms, once the agent has been stopped, run:
```
snmpdm -apall -start
```

The trace file should be either /var/adm/snmpd.log or /tmp/snmpd.log. For SNMP Packet dumping, see the -hexdump - vbdump options. To re-install, run:

```
snmpdm -stop -remove
snmpdm -install
```

SNMPv3 configuration using SNMP security pack

Once the SNMP Security Pack is properly installed, configure the SNMPv3 agents through the standard SNMP Configuration GUI (xnmsnmpconf) and enter the authentication data using the keyword as part of the community string, e.g:

```
"3A;AuthPassword/AuthUser"
```

SNMPv3 offers three levels of security where Authorization (Auth) equates to user authentication and Privacy (Priv) equates to data encryption. The Security Pack security mode prefixes (like that used in the example above) correspond to the levels as follows:

3N;	noAuth/noPriv:	supply username only, e.g. "guest"
3A;	Auth/noPriv:	supply pass phrase (user/pass)
3P;	Auth/Priv:	supply pass phrase (user/pass)

SNMPv3 Security Pack installation

Follow these steps to install the SNMPv3 Security Pack:

1. Install the Pack (UNIX target is /opt/Snmpri/SecurityPack)
2. Make sure the process *brassd* is running: `ovstatus -c brassd`
3. Edit the configuration files for the *brassd* daemon:
   /etc/srconf/agt   for agent
   /etc/srconf/mgr   for the manager side of SNMPv3 process
4. Configure the username/password for SNMPv3
5. Configure the devices to allow SNMPv3 protocol

Note that the Pack replaces the Emanate Agent with *brassd*.

Log file:	/opt/Snmpri/SecurityPack/log
Commands dir:	/opt/Snmpri/SecurityPack/brass/bin
MIB directory:	/opt/Snmpri/SecurityPack/mib

Examples of SNMPv3 queries:

```
snmpwalk -v 3 -l authNoPriv -a MD5 -u usr -A pwd <node>
snmpwalk -c 3A;authPassword/authUser <target>
```

Configuring and controlling trap destinations

The NNM server attempts to set itself as the trap destination for any device it discovers. Most SNMP agents are fairly quiet with respect to the amount of SNMP traps they generate, but there are definitely exceptions. HP network printers, for example, can be very chatty by default. To globally prevent NNM from setting itself as an agent's trap destination, use the "-N" LRF flag to *netmon* (see LRF Procedure on page 5). To prevent NNM from setting itself as an agent's trap destination for a class of devices, disable SNMP discovery using the "-I" flag in the *oid_to_type* file (see page 7).

Prior to V6.0, *netmon* used (according the *netmon* man/ref page) a mechanism that "bypassed normal SNMP authentication measures." After V6.0, *netmon* uses the set community string provided in the SNMP configuration (`xnmsnmpconf`) to attempt to set the management server's IP address as the trap destination for any discovered SNMP agent.

SNMPv3 and VLAN information

There is a known problem with NNM 7.53 and earlier versions of NNM where if only SNMPv3 queries are made to the device (via ET's hook into the BRASS agent), in most cases, the VLAN tables of such a device can not be queried due to the fact that the special character (@) that ET internally appends to the configured community string does not work for the special community string configuration entries needed for use by the BRASS agent.

Controlling the NNM server SNMP address

Control over which interface on the NNM server is set for trap destinations and outgoing SNMP requests can be changed using the $OV_CONF/ov.conf file. See the ov.conf man/ref page for details.

Controlling an agent's SNMP address

The SNMP address used for an agent is determined during *netmon* discovery using the algorithm listed on page 27. By default, *netmon* tests other addresses if the discovered address fails to respond. This behavior is controlled by the -k pickSnmpAddrPolls option as discussed on page 45.

For APA polling, the SNMP Address is initially determined by *netmon* discovery and is affected by -k pickSnmpAddrPolls as mentioned above, then futher refined through paConfig.xml confiruration settings. To force a node to use an SNMP Address other than the one picked by *netmon* discovery, see the procedure on page 46.To control the preferred management address options in the APA, see page 94.

Community string discovery

This is a useful feature, but it is also a possible source of performance degradation if it is used too generally in highly scaled installations. Configure community string discovery using:

$OV_CONF/netmon.cmstr

Prior to V 7.53 Intermediate Patch 19, the hash character (#) was an invalid character in community strings. After that patchm that character is allowed, but it must be contained within double quotes.

Try to limit the use of wildcards, particularly in highly-scaled environments. See page 54 for information about setting SNMP timeouts and retries. In the following example, public1 is used for devices in the 10.2 network, and public2 is tried if public1 times out:

```
"public1", "public2" : 10.2.*.* : : :
```

CERT advisory CA-2002-03, SNMP vulnerabilities

In 2002, OUSPG ran tests and found issues with SNMP request handling and with SNMP trap handling in both agents and managers. In essence, the advisory said what everybody everywhere all ready knew: that SNMPv1 is insecure and its use can expose system to exploitation. It further found specific vulnerabilities for a limited set of SNMP agents that could lead to DOS attacks, buffer underrun exploits, and other nastiness. The source of these was found to be in the vendor-specific functions written to parse ASN.1 formatted MIB definitions, but fortunately not in ASN.1 itself. These vulnerabilities were immediately addressed by most vendors and by HP through patches to NNM 6.2 and other HP products. More info on this at:

www.cert.org/advisories/CA-2002-03.html
www.cert.org/tech_tips/snmp_faq.html

SNMP PDU size limitations

This is a concern when using data collections. When there are many collections configured, there may be excessive fragmentations attributable to NNM SNMP operations. RFC1157 states that "An implementation of this [SNMP] protocol need not accept messages whose length exceeds 484 octets. However, it is recommended that implementations support larger datagrams whenever feasible." NNM has no such limitations, but some agents may adhere to this lower limit. In practice, this is an exception and not the rule.

Accounting for IP and UDP encapsulation, the theoretical maximum SNMP PDU size is 65467 bytes (max UDP datagram size - max IP header length - UDP header length). It is very likely, however, that such an IP packet is fragmented, increasing the chance of losing the entire PDU, since many MTUs for IP are set at 1500 bytes. In this case, the max PDU would be cut into over 40 fragments, the loss of one of which due to a collision, for example, means the loss of the entire PDU. For this reason, it is recommended that SNMP PDUs be limited to just under the minimum MTUs in the route between the server and target.

In NNM, PDU size can be dictated through the "-m" LRF (see page 5) option to *snmpCollect* and monitored via the `ovstatus -v snmpCollect` command. Also, there was a known security problem with invalidly-formed traps whose PDU sizes exceeded 4.5k bytes with NNM version 6.2 and prior. That specific issue was addressed via patches. More on this CERT advisory-related issue can be found below. Note that SNMPv3 addressed some of the above-mentioned limitations directly.

ovtrapd daemon not starting (Windows)

There is known problem with NNM 6.x version on Windows which is caused by the fact that Windows services start in random order, and *ovtrapd* is dependent on WinSNMP service. The error that intermittently occurs on system boot up is:

```
ovtrapd is not running.  Error message is:
winsnmp snmpregister() failed: 100. exit 1
```

To resolve the problem, configure *ovtrapd* to listen for traps directly on port 162/udp and 0xc900f/ipx and not register with the Windows SNMP trap service. Do this by configuring *ovtrapd* to use the "-W" LRF switch (see page 5).

NNM with SMS or other SNMP tools (Windows)

SMS (and several other tools with SNMP management capabilities) replaces wsnmp32.dll with their own versions or installs the Microsoft version of wsnmp32.dll. When NNM is installed, it installs a custom version of wsnmp32.dll. If there is a conflict, let the newer application use its preferred version of wsnmp32.dll and use the `-W` LRF switch to ovtrapd.lrf. See page 5 for LRF procedure.

Binding SNMP trap reception to ports other than 162

ovtrapd can be made to listen to other ports for SNMP traps. In the services file (/etc/services on UNIX, or on Windows: ..\windows32\drivers\etc\services), there is an SNMP trap entry set to port 162 (UDP), and this can be changed to a different UDP port. *ovtrapd* daemon follows the port binding of SNMP. *pmd*, however, uses port 162 (TCP) for talking to other copies of NNM, so changing the SNMP trap receiving port to any other value can break the remote *pmd* communications in environments using DIM or NNM to NNM event forwarding.

SNMP manager command line utilities

All the commands below are tied to NNM libraries, so they will only work on the NNM server:

snmpget	Query a single MIB variable
snmpwalk	Query an entire MIB table
snmpset	Set or change a writeable MIB variable
snmpbulk	Query a MIB table via SNMPv2 GetBulk
snmpnotify	Issue an SNMP trap or inform request
snmptrap	(deprecated by snmpnotify)
xnmsnmpconf	SNMP configuration utility
snmpcollect	Data collector background daemon
xnmbrowser	MIB browser
xnmtrap	Event configuration utility
xnmloadmib	MIB loader utility
xnmevents	Native event browser
xnmgraph	MIB graphing utility
mibtable	SNMP table data display utility
rnetstat	SNMP network statistics utility

Note that many SNMP manager packages use the same names for these programs. For example, Red Hat Linux AS 2.1 includes the ucd-snmp package which includes several utilities named the same. If running NNM under AS 2.1, the ucd-snmp utilities with the same names as the NNM utilities will run before the NNM supplied commands because /usr/bin is appears in the path definition before /opt/OV/bin. Simple update the $PATH variable so /opt/OV/bin is before /usr/bin to get around this issue. It may be necessary to alo update the $MANPATH variable in a similar fashion.

Strip OID and type data from SNMP query output

This works on both UNIX and Windows platforms. Normally, SNMP queries return a lot of garbage, e.g.:

```
C:\>snmpget patchy ifEntry.ifDescr.2
interface interfaces.ifTable.ifEntry.ifDescr.2 : DISPLAY
STRING- (ascii):  3Com 3C920 Integrated Fast Ethernet
Controller (3C905C-TX Compatible)
```

The following command strips the OID and datatype data:

```
C:\>snmpget patchy ifEntry.ifDescr.2 |
   %OV_BIN%\bin\perl\bin\perl -p -e "s /.*: //g;"
3Com 3C920 Integrated Fast Ethernet Controller (3C905C-
TX Compatible)
```

146

Perl script: output a node's IP address table via SNMP

This is useful for feeding other tools or for troubleshooting DNS issues. It is also a good template for using Perl and NNM's SNMP query tools for building reports, etc.:

```perl
#! /usr/bin/perl
$host = $ARGV[0];
$mib2 = '.iso.org.dod.internet.mgmt.mib-2';
$ipt = 'ip.ipAddrTable.ipAddrEntry.ipAdEntIfIndex';
@cmd = `/opt/OV/bin/snmpwalk $host $mib2.$ipt`;
foreach $line (@cmd) {
 $line =~ /^$ipt\.(\d{1,3}\.\d{1,3}\.\d{1,3}\.\d{1,3})/;
 $ip_addr = $1;
 print "$ip_addr\n";
}
exit;
```

Script output example:
```
peasoup # ./snmpIPtable.pl sunny
127.0.0.1
192.168.1.107
192.168.1.108
peasoup #
```

SNMP web resources

General SNMP Info:	www.snmplink.org
Many MIBS:	www.oidview.com/mibs/detail.html
Many MIBS:	www.mibdepot.com
Many MIBS:	assure24.com/databases/snmp-mib/private
SNMP OID Registry:	www.iana.org
All OIDS:	www.iana.org/assignments/enterprise-numbers
OID translation:	jaguar.ir.miami.edu/~marcus/snmptrans.html

Cisco specific info:
    www.cico.com/warp/public/477/SNMP/mibcompilers.html
NNM device and protocol support:
    www.openview.hp.com/products/nnmet/support/device_support.html
NNM device support:
    openview.hp.com/products/nnmet/support/device_requirements.html

12. Systems Management

Several facilities exist within NNM to help manage system resources such as disk space and system performance metrics, but NNM is not a substitute for a full function distributed systems management tool.

Syslog integration facility

Any system or device that uses the syslog facility (RFC 3164, 3195) can provide a feed to this light-weight version of HP's OpenView Operations (OVO) logfile encapsulator agent. This feature was integrated into AE versions of NNM starting with version 7.0 and it is only supported on NNM running on UNIX platforms. If a syslog consolidator is required for Windows environments, several third party products are available. Kiwi is a popular choice.

The syslog integration feature is covered in detail in Section 6 (Section 7 for V7.53) of the Guide to Using Extended Topology user manual. The V7.53 documentation is more extensive than previous coverage. Also, help is available at the following URL:

http://<nnmserver>:3443/OvCgi/OvWebHelp.exe?Content=slgref

If APA is enabled, certain event correlation logics will use syslog events to increase the intelligence of the APA. Investigate what syslog events affect the APA by launching the correlation composer using the command `ovcomposer -m o`. Examine the `OV_Poller*` correlators. These correlations can be extended by adding additional syslog events to them in order to trigger APA polls, etc.

The agent converts syslog messages to NNM events and uses the same proprietary configurable message pattern matching expression anchoring language used in OVO. To activate the NNM syslog facility in "NNM Deployment Mode", which means the syslog facility will work independently of a peer OVO installation, the following generalized steps are required:

1. If running HP-UX 11.0, make sure DCE is installed.
2. If running NIS, add opc_op user and opcgrp group on the NIS server.
3. Otherwise, add opc_op and opcgrp locally
4. Use `$OV_BIN/ovsyslogcfg` to configure trap mappings
5. Run: `setupSyslog.ovpl -standalone -deploy`
6. Test

For example:
Solaris:
```
logger -p user.err %LINEPROTO-5-UPDOWN: Line
protocol on IF test2, changed state to down
```
HP-UX:
```
logger %LINEPROTO-5-UPDOWN: Line protocol on
Interface test2, changed state to down
```

Use the logfile to troubleshoot syslog configuration or installation:

$OV_PRIV_LOG/setupSyslog.log

To configure a Cisco device to log to the NNM server:

```
(set) logging server <nnmserver ip>
(set) logging server enable
(set) logging level 5 all
```

Cisco logging levels:

```
0   emergencies
1   alerts
2   critical
3   errors
4   warnings
5   notification
6   informational
7   debugging
```

In some cases, messages may be logged to a different filename such as local7log instead of being logged to the syslog or messages file. If this is the case, modify syslog.conf to point local7 to syslog, and the do a `kill -HUP <PID>` on the syslogd PID.

The following file is written to by the syslogTrap facility and this file can grow without bounds:

/var/opt/OV/tmp/OpC/msgagtdf

To limit the size of that file and the other queue files as well, enable OpC message queue buffering by adding the below entries to the opcinfo configuration file in /opt/OV/bin/OpC/install:

```
OPC_BUFLIMIT_ENABLE TRUE
OPC_BUFLIMIT_SIZE 10000
OPC_BUFLIMIT_SEVERITY critical
```

Managing systems with HOST RESOURCES MIB

There are HOST-RESOURCES-compliant (RFC 2790) agents that are available both commercially and for free. Some support extensions that do neat things like logfile scraping. Vendors include HP, SNMP Research, and Concord (CA). www.net-snmp.org provides a complete agent as well as SNMP management tools for free.

For HOST-RESOURCES MIB support on the NNM server itself, the purchase of SNMP Research's CIAgent is required because the agent has to be a subagent to the Emanate Master agent for that one particular host. An alternative is to configure an SNMP agent that supports HOST-RESOURCES to use a port other than UDP 162. Be sure to specify the designated port when making queries to this agent using the GUI or command line tools.

Monitoring processes using HOST RESOURCES MIB

Once an SNMP agent is in place that supports HOST-RESOURCES, one can set up a data collection on the NNM server. For each instance of hrSWRunName that corresponds to the process (as reported in the corresponding instance of hrSWRunStatus), configure the collection using the following parameters: don't store, check thresholds, and configure a threshold event that reports if the value is > 1. The OID for hrSWRunName is:

.1.3.6.1.2.1.25.4.2.1.2.

Monitoring disks using HOST RESOURCES MIB

Once an SNMP agent is in place that supports HOST-RESOURCES, on NNM, set up a MIB Expression (see page 155) per below and then set up a data collection (page 153) using that expression.

```
FreeDiskMB \
"( hrStorageSize-hrStorageUsed) times \
   hrStrorageAllocationUnits\
   divided by 1024*1024          " \
   1.3.6.1.2.1.25.2.3.1.5  \
   1.3.6.1.2.1.25.2.3.1.6 - \
   1.3.6.1.2.1.25.2.3.1.4 * 1048576 /
```

Managing systems using RDMI (Windows)

Windows versions of NNM support RDMI management through the *ovcapsd* daemon. RDMI is HP's proprietary extension to access DMI management information remotely. Only some of HP's hardware lines support RDMI. When NNM discovers any device, it tests for RDMI capability and sets the isRDMISupported capability flag. Use the search function to list RDMI supported devices that have been discovered. The embedded DMI browser can then be used on those boxes. DMI as compared to SNMP:

- The DMI Client is roughly equivalent to an SNMP Manager
- The DMI Service Provider is equivalent to the SNMP Agent
- The DMI MIF is equivalent to the SNMP MIB
- A DMI Event is equivalent to an SNMP Trap

Forwarding Windows events to NNM as SNMP traps

The Windows command line utility `evntcmd` (or its GUI-based equivalent `evntwin`) can be used to configure events to be forwarded to NNM via SNMP. The traps come to NNM under the enterprise 1.3.6.1.4.1.311.1.13.1. Best bet is to manually create a new enterprise for these traps rather than try to chase down any MIBs that might exist (they don't).

Forwarding NNM events to Windows event log

Use the following Perl code snippet as part of an action callback script that passes NNM event data to a Windows Event Log:

```
Use Win32::EventLog;
my $ELog;
my %event=(
    'EventID',100,
    'EventType',EVENTLOG_WARNING_TYPE,
    'Category',NULL,
    'Strings','This is a String',
    'Data','THIS IS DATA',
);
$ELog = new Win32::EventLog( 'MyScript' )||die $!;
$ELog->Report(\%event) || die $!;
```

Managing systems using Solstice enterprise agents (SEA)

Default installations of Solaris do not have SNMP agents enabled. SEA ships free with most versions of SUN's operating systems and implements a SNMP master/subagent architecture similar to Emanate that supports MIBII, DMI, and an SNMP-DMI cross mapper. For more information, or to download see:

151

www.sun.com/software/entagents/features.xml

Accessing WMI data via SNMP

The third party SNMP Informant shareware product provides a WMI to SNMP agent that installs proprietary MIB extensions on Windows systems. It requires that the Microsoft SNMP agent is installed and that the SNMP Informant MIB is loaded on the NNM server. The basic agent with visibility to around 60 metrics is free, and extensions for more detailed WMI objects are available through the fully licensed version.

NNM server system management via SNMP (UNIX)

The Emanate SNMP master agent and included subagents shipped with NNM for HP-UX and Solaris provide HP proprietary systems management extensions. Access to these can be found via the *ovw* performance menu as "CPU Load" and "Disk space."

Extensible SNMP agents

These agents provide a platform for developing custom SNMP objects and MIB trees. Some of these agents provide facilities and features that go beyond simple SNMP agent development. HP sells such an agent as do other NMS vendors. The Net-SNMP agent (www.net-snmp.org) is very popular as well and also provides SNMP get, set, and trap generation commands. SNMP Research's CIA Agent is also a popular and comprehensive solution, as is Concord's SystemEdge solution.

13. Data Collection and Thresholds

SNMP agents are designed to hold very simple data types. This allows the agents to be very efficient, but makes the job of the SNMP manager very hard. Except in the case of RMON, SNMP agents do not track trends or keep history of data. Interface traffic, for example, is held in the SNMP agents as counter values that simply increment when traffic passes through.

When the counter fills up, it resets to zero. NNM's *snmpCollect* background daemon polls MIB values, determines the difference between the current value and the last polled value, discards any counter wraps or resets, then records the delta in the *snmpCollect* database on the management server.

Interface utilization, perhaps the most commonly used NNM performance metric, is not available from direct SNMP agents. To report this, SNMP managers must poll ifInOctets, ifOutOctets, and ifSpeed, then add the counter values and multiply by 8 to get the total number of bits before dividing by ifSpeed, and then multiply the result by 100 to obtain a percentage, as follows:

$$\frac{(ifInOctets + ifOutOctets) \times 8}{ifSpeed} \times 100$$

Math that combines MIB variables is performed in NNM by the MIB Expression feature and is configured in the mibExpr.conf file. Note that SNMP values for interface link speed may not be accurate. Also, the formula expressed above is fine for half duplex Ethernet interfaces, but others, like frame relay and serial lines or full duplex FastEthernet or GigabitEthernet interfaces carry full duplex traffic. ifType can tell them apart, but *snmpCollect* isn't smart enough to distinguish half duplex from full duplex lines.

Some of this confusion was mitigated by the addition of the ovexprguru in V6.01. This wrapper for MIB data and MIB expression data performs

153

queries to determine what MIB variables are supported before the data collector actually goes off and collects them, and it has some limited abilities to distinguish collections by ifType.

xnmgraph is the foreground process that displays SNMP data from history, real time feeds, or both. It is designed to read raw data from the *snmpCollect* database. Data from *snmpCollect* is exported to the data warehouse for trend reports.

Data collection best practices

Review the data collections that are set by default when NNM is installed. Depending on the version, some collections may be very intensive for certain devices. The NNM versions closer to V6.0 had the most liberal settings for these collections.

In general, the default collections are in place to support the reporting function. Disabling SNMP data collections directly in the data collections and thresholds configuration GUI can affect certain reports. Conversely, disabling reports using the reporter GUI doesn't necessarily disable the underlying data collections. When setting thresholds, a number greater than two is recommended as the value of "for X consecutive samples." Most SNMP-based data tends to be "spiky" by nature and this guarantees that only sustained threshold violations generate threshold alarms.

Do not set the polling intervals too tight. Generally, 15 minute, 30 minute, and 1 hour sampling intervals are best. While tighter polling intervals tend to more accurately gauge actual trends by more accurately capturing data around counter wraps and better isolating data spikes, the best practice is to use tighter intervals on only a small set of collections which are intended to be temporary where the focus is on specific problems.

Too many collections with tight intervals lead to performance issues that ultimately degrade all collections' integrity due to increased failed data collection points from timeouts, etc.

If%util (or other % expression) is greater that 100%

Typically, this is because the interface being monitored is running at full duplex. The If%util MIB expression is designed for half duplex lines only. The next most common cause of this is that ifSpeed is set incorrectly at the agent. To verify the speed as reported by SNMP, select the node and select the Configuration->Network Configuration->Interface Properties menu item in *ovw*. Another cause may be that the router is compressing data before sending it over WAN links. In this last case, the SNMP agent is recording the incoming data before compression and/or the outgoing data after decompression.

Utilization may exceed 100% might be due to the presence of 64-bit counters in the MIB. See section below on exhausted 32-bit counters in the presence of 64-bit counters.

On frame relay links, the ifSpeed is typically the line CIR, which is usually less than the maximum burst rate for the link, so it is not impossible to have utilizations that exceed 100% on these types of interfaces.

Yet another possibility is that inbound traffic and outbound traffic are not sampled simultaneously. This is due to numerous factors affecting the snmpCollect poller and the difference could be several seconds, particularly when line utilizations approach 100%. The underlying MIB data is accurate, but inaccuracy is introduced because the time intervals used to calculate the deltas are fixed, yet the actual sampled data doesn't correspond exactly to those intervals.

Typically, however, these timing issues only account for minor differences in the reported utilization. Also, opening up the polling interval reduces the chance for this sort of error. Finally, some people are determined to somehow combine inbound and outbound utilization on full duplex links. While setting up an expression that sums the two rates and then divides by two should never exceed 100%, but this is a poor practice and can hide real problems.

For example, if inbound is pegged at 100%, and outbound is averaging 20%, it would never be detected since the expression would report 60% "average" utilization. The best practice is to separate the inbound and outbound collections on Full Duplex links. The best solution when dealing with mixed duplex/half duplex interface environments to use NNM's newer `ovexprguru` feature, which is covered in more detail below.

MIB expressions using mibExpr.conf and mib.coerce

As illustrated above, simple SNMP queries have to be combined to make useful graphs. $OV_CONF/mibExpr.conf allows the creation of

MIB expressions. Math in these formulas uses RPN (Postfix notation). See the man/ref for mibExpr.conf

One requirement of creating MIB expressions is that MIB values used in those expressions must be of the same data type. If an expression seeks to combine a gauge type variable with an integer type variable, an error results. *mib.coerce* is provided to coerce MIB variable to a specific type so they can be used in expressions.

MIB expression guru (ovexprguru)

Introduced in NNM 6.01, `ovexprguru` is an NNM command that is used to pre-select the appropriate MIB expression (*mibExpr.conf*) to use to graph certain generic collections based on the collected object's capabilities. Its use can be seen in the ARF files for NNM menu bar performance and fault graphs. The command takes the following generic keywords and attempts to apply the appropriate mibExpr from the mibExpr.conf file:

```
utilization            datarate
packetrate             percentdiscards
averagepacketsize      framerate
thruput                framedatarate
errorrate              framecongestion
percenterrors          frameerrors
discardrate            frameeligiblediscards
```

In the case of utilization (and several others of the above arguments) *ovexprguru* polls the ifType table and compares the results to a table of interface types that are hard-coded in the command. If the instance is a full duplex interface then the in and out utilization are graphed separately. For a half duplex interface the in and out are combined. For more info, see the *ovexprguru* man/ref.

Default Data collections based on MIB expression such as If%util do not use the MIB expression guru by default. In order replace an existing collection for If%util, follow these steps:

1.   Add a new MIB Expression in the $OV_CONF/MibExpr.conf file, e.g.:

     BetterIf%Util \
     "Interface Utilization that applies the appropriate expression\n\
      Based on the ifType of the interface being monitored."\
     INDIRECT : utilization : COMBINED

2.   In the Data Collections and Thresholds , select the If%Util Object and Edit -> MIB Object -> Copy, then select the new expression from the list of expressions.

3. Suspend the If%Util collection and save. Run: `ovstop snmpCollect`
    `ovstart snmpCollect`

NNM V7.51 Intermediate patch 18 introduced an undocumented option to enable it to dump SNMP packets. The option is "-d."

Understanding and manipulating statistical thresholds

Statistical thresholding was introduced in NNM V6.2. This feature uses standard deviations on collected data that is exported to the Data Warehouse. Previously, only fixed thresholds were available. When configuring a data collection object, "Fixed", "Both Statistical and Fixed", or "Either Statistical or Fixed" can be selected under Threshold Parameters.

Standard deviation calculations require the MIB variables be stored in the snmpcollect DB and exports of trend data to datawarehouse are enabled. The default time intervals for statistics are as follows:

The data points are sorted into 3 buckets: Workhours (8am-5pm weekdays), WeekDayOffHours (5pm-8am weekdays), and Weekends.

These buckets can be changed using the following configuration file which does not exist by default:

$OV_CONF/ `statTimeRanges.conf`

There is a man/ref page for this file which describes how to configure it in detail. The stats that are exported from the Data Warehouse to build the standard deviations are stored in a flat file:

$OV_DB/`snmpCollect/snmpColStats.txt`

snmpCollect commands

To dump configuration data to $OV_LOG/snmpCol.trace, run:

```
snmpCollect -S
```

To delete snmpCollect data older than 90 days (2160 hours):

```
ovcoltosql -N -D 2160
```

To remove all collected data for the *snmpCollect* database:

```
rm -r $OV_DB/snmpCollect/
```

157

pingResponseTime, pingPercentRetry threshold events

These threshold events come from default data collections that ship with some versions of NNM like 6.x (but not 7). They indicate potential problems with *netmon* polling or with SNMP data collections. They can be turned off or configured from "Data Collections and Thresholds" from the "Options" menu.

These are actually "external" MIB expressions, and that means they are MIB expressions that are defined externally to the mibExpr.conf file, so are not exposed to users. See the man/ref for mibExpr.conf for more information.

Data collection and device naming/IP address issues

The *snmpCollect* daemon stores data by IP address. When *xnmgraph* is invoked to read the database, it performs a lookup to determine which IP address to use to recall data. There are several cases where *xnmgraph* fails to extract the appropriate data from the *snmpCollect* db. These examples include:

> Targets that use round-robin DNS
> Targets that use HSRP
> Cluster nodes
> Targets that have been renamed or re-IP addressed

The data for the aged-out IP addresses can be retrieved by using the explicit IP address. A good tip is to use loopback for management and reporting for routers (see page 27.)

OpenView specifics reserved for custom events

The standard threshold and rearm events are designed to be copied to create custom events that provide more meaning and facilitate custom actions. The following specific event identifiers have been reserved for use for this purpose:

> 1001-9999 odd   For threshold crossed or error events.
> 1002-10000 even Custom rearm or return to normal events

Data collection and high speed links

Most SNMP standard MIB counters are 32-bit. A DS3 line at full bandwidth causes a counter like ifInOctets to wrap in about 12 minutes. An FDDI line wraps in less than 6 minutes. With a 64-bit counter, however, a 1 tbs (terabits per second) link would take nearly 5 years to wrap at full bandwidth.

A counter wrap during a polling interval results in an ignored value in collected data. One way to improve graph accuracy in this case is to poll high speed links more frequently to reduce the number of ignored data points, but this can very quickly cause adverse performance problems (see page 154). 64-bit counters were introduced along with SNMPv2 to resolve these issues and thus are only found in agents that support SNMPv2 or greater.

The 64-bit counters that correspond to the standard interface table MIB can be found in the ifMib table, and echo their 32-bit counterpart's name save for "HC" for High Capacity inserted into their names, so for example: ifHCInOctets is found at 1.3.6.1.2.1.31.1.1.1.6. See the support matrix on page 304 for information on NNM's support for various versions of SNMP.

Exhausted 32-bit counters when 64-bit is supported

If the MIB supports 64-bit counters, RFC 2233 (ifMib) mandates support of the corresponding 32-bit counters for backward compatibility and states that these counters do NOT reset between $2^{32} - 1$ and $2^{64} - 1$. Here is the actual verbiage:

```
When 64-bit counters are in use, the 32-bit counters
must still be available.  They will report the low 32-
bits of the associated 64-bit count (e.g., ifInOctets
will    report    the    least    significant    32    bits    of
ifHCInOctets).
```

Most vendors that supply HC counters comply with this RFC. To test this, poll both the 32-bit counters and the 64-bit counters (e.g. ifInOctets and ifHCInOctets, etc.) See if the 32-bit counters are incrementing when the values for the 64-bit counters are greater than $2^{32} - 1$. If the 32-bit counters are not incrementing that could explain any undesirable results. Modify the collections to use the HC MIB variables. For those systems in the collection that do not support the HC counters, separate them out and apply the traditional collections. Note that *ovexprguru* is able to test for 64 vs. 32-bit counter support.

Printing graphs (UNIX)

The default output format for graphs is *xwd*. To convert this output into more familiar image formats, use the conversion utility at $OV_CONTRIB/NNM/ImageMagik. To print to an attached or network printer, for example, a color LaserJet, comment out the default data for the .printcommand listed in $APP_DEFS/XNmgraph and replace with:

```
*.printcommand: xpr -device pjetxl -rv -header
"$OVTITLE" | lp -d <colourPrinterName>
```

For more information of modifying app-defaults settings, see page 9.

Insufficient memory when launching graphs (Solaris)

This specific error message relates to maxMallocPercent resource and occurs mostly on Solaris 2.7 servers. The error is caused by a too small of a stack size, which can been seen with the command: ULIMIT -a. To resolve, run: ULIMIT -s unlimited

Exporting graphs to other image formats (UNIX)

NNM graphs can be saved by default in xwd format. An excellent (and free) utility to convert from xwd to a variety of popular formats is netpbm which can be found at:

http://netpbm.sourceforge.net/

Data collections on VLANs

SPAN or port mirroring can be used to monitor VLAN traffic. Typically, a whole VLAN is mirrored to a single port to be monitored. Try not to oversubscribe the destination port, i.e., mirroring a 1000MB VLAN to a 100mb port.

xnmgraph command examples

All NNM's menu-bar performance, fault and configuration graphs are direct invocations of the xnmgraph command line utility. The command invocations can be seen in the $OV_REGISTRATION/C directory. For more info on ARF, see page 6. Registration files for graphs produced using the MIB Application Builder are placed in the ovmib subdirectory.

Graph serial interface utilization using duplex MIB expressions ("2" is the ifIndex of the target interface):

```
xnmgraph -title "Duplex Interface Utilization" -mib
IfInFDplxUtilization::2:::::::,IfOutFDplxUtilization::2::
::::: <target>
```

<target> is the ip address of the device and the '2' in between all of the colons is the ifIndex of the interface to graph. To graph Cisco port bit rates, including real time and collected data (+browse):

```
xnmgraph +browse -title "Cisco Port Bit Rates" -mib
.1.3.6.1.4.9.2.1.1.1.6:label:3::::::
.1.3.6.1.4.9.2.2.1.1.8:label:3::::::: <target>
```

SNMP data collection terminology

PDU. Packaged Data Unit. A term for a message of a given protocol comprising payload and protocol-specific control information, typically contained in a header. PDUs exist between the OSI layers of protocols, and are not specific to any particular layer. PDU is often used incorrectly to describe an SNMP Message.

Packet. A discreet unit of data sent across a packet switching network, e.g. IP, Frame Relay, etc. Per RFC 1594: "'Packet' is a generic term used to describe unit of data at all levels of the protocol stack, but it is most correctly used to describe application data units." Packets contain data and a header containing an ID number, source and destination addresses, and error-control data and can be of fixed or variable size. Used interchangeably with datagram.

Datagram. Per RFC 1594, "a self-contained, independent entity of data carrying sufficient information to be routed from the source to the destination computer without reliance on earlier exchanges between this source and destination computer and the transporting network." The differentiator between a datagram and a packet centers on this concept of self-sufficiency. Because of this, there is an implication that datagrams are UDP (connection-less) vs. TCP, which is connection-oriented, but this is not always true.

MTU. The Maximum Transmission Unit is the largest packet that a given network medium can carry. Ethernet, for example, has a fixed MTU of 1500 bytes, ATM has a fixed MTU of 48 bytes, and PPP has a negotiated MTU that is usually between 500 and 2000 bytes.

Octet. Eight contiguous bits of data. A byte is often 8 bits of data, but not always. An Octet is always 8 bits of data.

Frame. In generic terms, a frame is a basic logical unit in which bit-oriented data is transmitted. An Ethernet Frame is equivalent to a packet. A Frame Relay frame is a data unit containing a start-of-frame (SOF) delimiter, header, payload, cyclic redundancy check (CRC), and an end-of-frame (EOF) delimiter. The payload can be 0-2112 bytes, and the CRC is 4 bytes.

Fragment. A piece of a packet, also called a runt. When a router is forwarding an IP packet to a network that has a maximum packet size smaller than the transmitted packet size, it is forced to break up that packet into multiple fragments. These fragments should be reassembled by the IP layer at the destination host.

Payload. The Payload is the part that represents application information and application overhead information in a set of data being processed or transported.

System Insight (Compaq Insight) Manager MIBs

The CIM/SIM MIBs are loaded by installing the SIM/NNM integration package (URL for this package is on page 308). To manually load the MIBs when not using the integration package, load in the following order:

1. cpqhost.mib	5. cpqstdeq.mib
2. cpqhealth.mib	6. cpqstsys.mib
3. cpqsinfo.mib	7. cpqthrsh.mib
4. cpqsrvmn.mib	8. cpqups.mib

SNMP data collection vs. RMON

RMON (RFC1757) and RMON-II (RFC2021) are used interchangeably below. The difference between SNMP and RMON is that the "M" in SNMP stands for management whereas the "M" in RMON stands for monitoring. RMON data is aggregated by RMON probes, or agents, and these are implemented as SNMP MIBs. While RMON provides a much more efficient way to monitor traffic at or nearer to the source, for the most part, vendors are moving away from supporting RMON and relying more on SNMP and packet capturing tools to provide the monitoring functions. Note that NNM, however, does not provide any packet capturing capabilities out of the box.

There are different "layers" of RMON, and different capabilities that a node may implement. Most RMON implementations do not conform to RFC standards, relying on proprietary extensions to the standard MIBs to provide better monitoring. Examples of RMON use range from gathering simple statistics about the network like utilization and collisions, to actually capturing packets which are then retrieved remotely. There is also SMON, which is RMON for switched networks created by Lucent, but few vendors other than Lucent have implemented it. In fact, few vendors who support RMON bother to fully implement the standard parts of it. They often only include the first few RMON groups and leave the full packet capturing capabilities to their proprietary extensions. That said, some useful troubleshooting data can be mined from RMON. Look into the statistics group to determine if abnormal traffic is flowing over a particular port. Details may include frame+ size distributions, unicast/multicast/broadcast and framing error types such as runts and giants.

Calculate epoch time for snmpColDump, etc.

Time stamps for NNM database records for *snmpCollect* data and for events are kept as epoch time (seconds since January 1, 1970). Place the epoch time to translate where is says "c" below:

```
%OV_BIN%\Perl\bin\perl -e "print scalar localtime(c)"
$OV_BIN/Perl/bin/perl -e 'print scalar localtime(c)'
```

14. Notifications

Notifications from NNM are generated as action callbacks defined within the event subsystem. There are no actions associated with SNMP Traps, so all actions are defined from the manager. Note that most NNM events are generated by NNM itself as the results of status polls or other anomalies detected by NNM's discovery and polling engines. The *ovactiond* daemon is responsible for running actions assigned to events, and actions are configured in the event configuration GUI (*xnmtrap*). Actions associated with events are called 'action callbacks'.

Configuring an action callback

Follow these general steps when setting up an automatic action based on an NNM event:

1. Configure and test the script/tool outside of NNM from the command line (UNIX: By default, the actions run with UID and GID of user bin)
2. Select useful variable bindings to pass. The variable bindings are often listed in the event description. For most OpenView enterprise events, $2 represents the event source. Additional variables are listed below under Selected Special Variables
3. Configure trustedCmds.conf (see below)
4. Optional step.   Test the command using the OpenView event OV_application_alert in conjunction with the $OV_CONTRIB/NNM/sendMsg/sendMsg.ovpl script

Using trustedCmds.conf file

In NNM 6.2+, only commands listed in a file in the following directory can be executed by *ovactiond*:

> $OV_CONF/trustedCmds.conf/

Changes to files in trustedCmds.conf must be signaled to *ovactiond* by running the `xnmevents -event` command from the command line. trustedCmds.conf is documented in the man/ref page for *ovactiond*.

Any file placed in that directory is parsed for valid command names (with absolute path) and aliases, for example, suppose a file called ringbell in $OV_CONF/trustedCmds.conf contains:

```
ringBell=/opt/OV/contrib/NNM/ringBell/ringBell.ovpl
```

In the "Command for Automatic Action" field (action callback), use "ringBell".

Override the trusted commands feature by creating a file named ALLOW_ALL in the $OV_CONF/trustedCmds.conf directory. If this file, which should be empty, is found then *ovactiond* does not check whether a command being executed is trusted.

General action callback usage considerations

Exit codes. *ovactiond* listens for the exit codes returned from scripts or programs and reports a failed action if it detects a non-zero exit code. UNIX UID for *ovactiond*: *ovactiond* executes commands as user bin, and thus is not environment or path aware. To change the user that *ovactiond* executes as, add the -u <user> LRF switch in ovactiond.lrf. See page 5 for the LRF procedure. UNIX UID and ping: If the action callback executes (or launches a script that executes) ping, the command may produce a failure to open socket. ping must be executed as the root user because it opens a raw socket and only root on UNIX can open raw sockets. Use the -u root option discussed above.

Scalability: When scripting or calling programs, it may be necessary to consider issues which may arise from multiple successive calls to *ovactiond*. Consider configuring actions to fork, spawn or exec so the children do the work and the parents exit, allowing *ovactiond* to launch the next buffered program calls. Semaphore locking may also be a useful way to deal with overrun issues associated with event floods. In this case, the first process gets the lock and does the work. The second process fails to get the lock because someone else is already handling the issue, and exits. Also consider event correlation. The correlation to handle duplicate events can be added very easily using the dedup.conf (see page 130), and prevent multiple pages, for example. For some correlations like PairWise (page 130), release of the action may be delayed pending the receipt of an event (which may clear the initial condition). See page 166 below for some more notes on interactions of ECS with notifications.

Metacharacters in action callbacks

Action callbacks do not support Regular Expressions. The caret (^), for example, is used to quote. The list of metacharacters is:

```
;   &   |   <   >   new-line
```

In addition, any command substitution in the varbinds is also quoted. Any string enclosed in ' ' or $() is considered a command substitution.

Selected special variables in action callbacks

This is a partial list of some of the more useful variables:

$#	The number of attributes in the event.
$*	All attributes as "seq name (type): value" strings.
$n	nth attribute as a value string. Must be 1 to 99.
$x	Date event received using the local date representation.
$X	Time event received using the local time representation.
$V	Type: SNMPv1, SNMPv2C, CMIP, or GENERIC.
$ar	The implied source as an IP address.
$c	The category the event belongs in.
$s	The severity of the event.
$$	The $ character.
$E	The trap enterprise as a text string if possible.
$A	The trap agent address as defined in the trap PDU.
$aA	Same as $A except the source as an IP address.
$G	The trap's generic-trap number.
$S	The trap's specific-trap number.
$T	sysUptime in hundredths of a second since agent up

These characters can be specified directly in the action callback:

a	Alert (bell) character
b	Backspace
f	Form feed
n	Newline
r	Carriage return
t	Horizontal tab
v	Vertical tab
\	Shell escape (\\ indicates Windows pathnames.)
ooo	Octal number in range 000-177
xhh	Hex number in range x00-xFF

Notification interactions with event correlation

After NNM 6.31, certain status events may be "held" by the NodeIf and/or Pairwise event correlations pending related events. Automatic actions are held as well, and the related events could cause the child event and its action to be discarded.

All prior versions of NNM always released automatic actions immediately. Following that, certain ECS circuits may affect the timing of the release of automatic actions. In particular, the PairWise and NodeIf correlations may or may not affect the timing of the release of automatic actions, depending on the version of NNM. To force automatic actions to run immediately, regardless of event correlation settings affecting actions, add the -f RAW flag to the *ovactiond* daemon via the LRF process.

ovactiond LRF settings

See page 5 for general instructions on modifying LRF flags.

-u *username*	(UNIX only) set UID and GID for *ovactiond* Note: default is bin:bin
-t	Trace execution of *ovactiond*
-v	More verbose logging
-l	Use logfile other than $OV_LOG/ovactiond.log
-w *maxwait*	Seconds to wait for non-zero exit code before giving up and killing execution. 0 indicates never give up; 300 is default
-f *flowtype*	RAW, CORR, or ALL; see Interactions with Event Correlation (above)
-s *maxlog*	Maximum size of logfile; defaults to 500K

Limiting Action callbacks to a subset of objects

To set up an action that runs only a subset of event sources, make a copy of the target event, give it a unique name, and specify sources using "add from map." See page 98 for more basics on manual event configuration.

"Find" is a powerful tool for building lists of node sources based on common attributes. Once a set of objects is highlighted on the map as the result of a "find" operation, use "View - Select Highlighted" to select objects across multiple submaps, then "add from map" within the Event Configuration GUI.

Selection names can be wildcarded in the event source specification. For example, *soup* would match selections peasoup and soupy. IP

Addresses can also be used as event sources, and * or - wildcards can be specified as well, for example: 10.10.0.* or 10.10.0.2-252.

See the section below on using an external file to specify

External File to specify action callback sources

To use an external list of sources, enter the full path to a text file containing valid selection names or IP addresses, one per line, in the sources area of the Event Configuration GUI. Use *xnmevents –event* to force a re-read of the file after making updates.

Wildcards cannot be used in this external file for either selection names or IP Addresses. Wildcards can, however, be used directly in the event source specification (see section above).

Using Perl for actions callbacks

NNM is shipped with an embedded version of Perl located at $OV_BIN/Perl/bin/perl. Taking advantage of this is fine for relatively simple scripts, but it is inadequate for scripts that call for additional Perl Modules because NNM's Perl doesn't incorporate all the libraries necessary for extensibility. Install or use a full-blown Perl distribution if calling perl modules in scripts. For Windows platforms, ActiveState Perl comes highly recommended. To use NNM's embedded Perl on any platform, simply use the ".ovpl" file extension for the script. On UNIX, call Perl at the top of the script using:

```
#!/opt/OV/bin/Perl/bin/perl
```

When making action callbacks to Perl scripts in UNIX, enclose the arguments to be passed in double quotes, for example:

```
/opt/OV/bin/myperl.ovpl "$x $X $r $R $*"
```

When making action callbacks to Perl scripts in Windows, either alias Perl using trustedCmds.conf, use the registered .ovpl if using the NNM-embedded version of Perl, or call the full path to an alternate Perl executable, as in:

```
cmd /c start /min c:\\perl\\bin\\perl.exe c:\\perl.pl $2
```

Action callbacks on Windows platforms

The most common issue with calling scripts on Windows platforms is difficulties in interpreting path names with embedded spaces and in handling special characters. Use double quotes in this case as in the following action callback example:

```
d:\\"Program Files"\\"HP OpenView"\\bin\\perl\\bin\\perl
d:\\"Program Files"\\"HP OpenView"\\scripts\\pager.ovpl $r
```

The simplest way to avoid such trouble is to use aliases for commands via trustedCmds.conf (see the *ovactiond* man/ref). OVSHELL and OVHIDESHELL are special keywords available under NNM on Windows to display action results in a new window or to suppress the popup of a command shell. OVSHELL is the default. These keywords also work with aliases defined in trustedCmds.conf. Example:

```
OVSHELL notepad file.txt (same as "notepad file.txt")
OVHIDESHELL cmd.exe /s file.bat
OVHIDESHELL telalert -i phil -m "$2 down"
```

In the first example, the popup window is forced. In the second example, an explicit callback is issued that would require the ALLOW_ALL file exists in trustedCmds.conf. In the third example, the full path to the telalert executable is defined in trustedCmds.conf and aliased to "telalert." The equivalent to OVHIDESHELL can be accomplished with:

```
cmd /c start /min command c:\\bmail -s smtp@d.com -t
test@d.com -f from@d.com -a "$2 down" -b "Body text"
```

Or, for fans of Window Scripting Host, pop-ups can be suppressed with this example:

```
Set WshShell = CreateObject("WScript.Shell") RetVal =
WshShell.Run("CMD.EXE /C dir/w",0,TRUE)
```

Sometimes, it is desirable to keep the command window up, as in when input is required by the calling program, for example:

```
start /wait c:\\shutdown\\shutdown.exe
```

There is a problem with using pipes ($|$) or redirects (>) in action callbacks on Windows. These are supported on the Windows command line, but just don't work in NNM action callbacks.

Email notifications using native tools (Windows)

IIS is installed with NNM. IIS has SMTP capabilities, which can be configured from the IIS properties page. Once configured, IIS attempts to deliver files with the proper format that are dropped in the following directory via SMTP:

C:\Inetpub\mailroot\Pickup

A Perl script snippet that can be used as an action callback to send an email to a paging service using Microsoft's IIS's built-in SMTP server is shown here:

```
$node = $ARGV[0];   # $r.
open OUT, ">c:\\page.txt";
print OUT "From: openview\@domain.com\n";
print OUT "To: 12345678910\@archwireless.net\n";
print OUT "Subject: Node $node Down\n";
print OUT "\n";
print OUT "Node $node Down\n";
close OUT;
`copy c:\\page.txt c:\\inetpub\\mailroot\\pickup`;
`del c:\\page.txt`;
exit;
```

MAPISEND is part of the Exchange Resource Kit. It is on the TechNet CDs. To configure this, install Outlook on the monitoring server and configure a profile using the service account that is being used for NNM. Here is an example MAPISEND command action callback:

```
MAPISEND.EXE -u <outlook profile name> -p <service account
password> -r user@domain.com -s $2 Down -m "Node $2 is down"
```

Email notifications using native tools (UNIX)

`mailx` and `elm` are native to both HP-UX and Solaris OS. Both use very similar syntax when invoking from the command line. In the following examples, the `elm` and `mailx` commands could be interchanged:

```
echo "$r Up" | mailx -s "$r Up" user@domain.com
elm -s "$2 down" user@domain.com < /tmp/body.txt
```

`sendmail` can also be used, for example:

```
echo 'Subject: Openview Trap object $r for event $N $1
$3\n' | /usr/lib/sendmail 'usera@d.com userb@d.com'
```

And yet another way for Solaris systems, demonstrating how to pass null as the file handle where one is required:

```
/usr/ucb/mail -s "$2 down" user@d.com </dev/null
```

Email notifications and DNS issues (UNIX)

Some enterprise email servers do not forward email along unless the sending system formats the originating address as an FQDN. The preffered method to do this is by properly configuring the

/etc/resolv.conf file on the management server with a line that contains: "search domain.com". Another method which may accomplish this, if for example NIS is being used, is to set the "Dj" setting in the *sendmail.cf* file.

Audio notifications (UNIX)

Use `$OV_CONTRIB/NNM/ringBell/ringBell.ovpl` to ring the bell on the NNM server. To modify the volume and duration of the sound, edit the $APP_DEFS/XNmevents file and find section on ringing the bell. Remove the "!" comment, set as desired (try the maximum first - bellpercent 100).

To ring the bell of any remote system that accepts X display redirects, including PC's running X windows software, first create a script "beep.sh" that looks like this:

```
#!/bin/sh
echo "This window beeps then closes in 1 second"
echo "$1 down" #args passed in order from callback
echo ^G #Use real control-G (in vi): CRTL-V CRTL-G
sleep 1
```

Next add the action callback like this:

```
/usr/bin/X11/xterm -display <IPAddr>:0 -e /beep.sh
```

To play an audio file (Solaris only), try:

```
cat crash.au > /dev/audio
```

It may be required to change the permissions for /dev/sound to 666 in the /etc/logindevperms file for this to work.

To enable PC's running Exceed X-windows emulation, edit win.ini and add the following:

```
[exceed]
DefaultSystemBeep=1
```

Sound notifications (Windows)

Install Windows Media Player, or some other default WAV file player that can be invoked from the command line. For the action callback, use:
```
mplay32 c:\\<path>\\file.wav
```

Example notification setups

Example using BLAT (Windows):

171

1. Create $OV_CONF\trustedCmds.conf\testmail containing:
   ```
   testmail=c:\\testmail.bat
   ```
2. Run `xnmevents -event` from a command shell
3. C:\testmail.bat contains:
   ```
   C:\blat - -subject "%1 is down" -to user@domain.com -
   body "%1 is down at %2 on %3 "
   ```
4. Action callback for OpenView OV_Node_Down event:
   ```
   OVHIDESHELL testmail $2 $X $x
   ```

Example using Telalert with ALLOW_ALL (Windows):

1. Create empty file:
   $OV_CONF\trustedCmds.conf\ALLOW_ALL
2. Run: `xnmevents -event` from a command shell
3. Action callback for OpenView OV_Node_Down event:
   ```
   cmd /c start /min d:\\vytek\\telalertc -i mypager -m "$2
   down"
   ```

Example Perl script that spawns so *ovactiond* returns:

1. Create empty file:
   $OV_CONF\trustedCmds.conf\ALLOW_ALL
2. Run: `xnmevents -event` from a command shell
3. Action callback for OpenView OV_Node_Down event:
   ```
   /usr/bin/perl do_my_thing.pl $A $1 &
   ```

Popular notification and paging tools

The following products are often mentioned by NNM end-users:

Commercial Products:

Vendor	Product	URL	Platform(s)
Calamp	Telalert	www.calamp.com	Unix/Windows
Semotus	Hiplink	www.semotus.com	Unix/Windows
Invoq	Alarmpoint	www.alarmpoint.com	Unix/Windows
iTechTool	EtherPage	www.ppt.com	Unix
Inventive	PowerPage	inventivelabs.com	Windows
PageGate	NotePage	notepager.net	Windows
Spatch	Spatch	www.spatch.com	Unix/Windows
Sysman	SMS Server	www.sysman.no	Windows

Freeware/ Shareware/GPL/Open Source:

Product	URL	Platform(s)
Sendpage	sendpage.cpoint.net	Unix

sendpage	www.sendpage.org	Perl (Both)
Blat	www.blat.net	Windows
Bmail	beyondlogic.org/solutions	Windows
qpage	www.qpage.org	Unix
Postie	infradig.com	Windows

Useful link for Tap Modem Phone numbers:
> http://www.notepager.net/tap-phone-numbers-a.htm

Scrolling message displays that accept pager input:
> http://www.ams-i.com

Configuring an attached modem on UNIX servers

While somewhat of a challenge, setting up a directly-attached modem for pager notifications can increase the reliability of notification systems that may rely on the services (email) they are monitoring as a transport for those notifications, thus eliminating the possibility that pages are missed if a dependent service (such as a network connection to the email server) fails. cu (call unix) can be used to initiate pages to directly-attached modems. To use cu, configure uucp to the port the modem is attached to as follows:

Solaris:

> Set serial port on Solaris /dev/cua/a for a modem to dial up:
> ```
> chmod +x /devices/sbus@1f,0/zs@f,1100000:a,cu
> ```

HP-UX:

> SAM – peripherals – terminals & modems, modem
> Edit /etc/uucp/Devices
> Add the following line to the end of the file:
> ```
> Direct cul0p2 - 19200 direct
> ```
> Note: The actual cu device corresponds to the tty returned by SAM

The following command can be used on Solaris to invoke kermit to send a page to a locally attached modem:
```
kermit -l /dev/cua/a -m hayes -b 9600 -C \"set dial
timeout 15,dial {$pager_number,,,$message_string
#},hangup,exit\"
```

$OV_CONTRIB/NNM/beep95_lx/beep95_lx.sh is a front-end to the cu script, but it was removed from later versions of NNM distributions. A copy can be found in some search engines. A Perl script can be constructed to interact with cu using the open2 Perl Module, for example in the following snippet:

```
use IPC::Open2;
use Symbol;
$WTR = gensym();
$RDR = gensym();
```

173

```
$pid = open2($RDR, $WTR, "cu -s 9600 -b 7 -t -e -l
/dev/cua/b");
 (code goes here to dial and communicate)
print $WTR "~.";  # terminate cu
close ($WTR);
close ($RDR);
```

15. Fault Analysis Tools

This section focuses on tools which are part of NNM (and some which are not) that are used to troubleshoot network faults.

Problem diagnostics (PD)

PD is included with NNM AE v7.0+ and is enabled along with ET via setupExtTopo.ovpl. On initialization, it installs a probe on the NNM server. Additional probes can be installed from one of the files probeHP.tra, probeSUN.tar or probeWIN.zip, found in the $OV_Install_Dir/pdAE/bin directory. V7.53 included improved documentation for PD in the Guide to Using Extended Topology user manual.

Problem Diagnostics probes network flows between critical devices, automatically base lining path performance. It sends events if performance deviates from the norm, and detects path blackouts, brownouts, routing loops, flapping paths and other instability. PD uses traceroute to determine Level 3 paths and uses ET topology data to place Level 2 devices in paths.

To start/stop the probe:
UNIX:

```
$OV_MAIN_PATH/pdAE/bin/pdcentral.sh -start|stop
```

DO NOT use the `kill -9` command on the Java process! Irrecoverable data corruption may occur.

Windows:

From the Services applet, select NetPath and click Start (or Stop).

DO NOT use the Windows Task Manager to terminate the Java process! Irrecoverable data corruption may occur.

To disable a probe:
UNIX:

Move the file from the rc3.d directory.

Windows:
>> Use the Services applet to stop the NetPath service, and run:
>> `pdcentral.bat -uninstall`

To uninstall probe and server:

UNIX: `pdpuninstall.sh`
Windows: `pdpuninstall.vbs`

To link the probe to multiple servers:
Edit npprobe.conf on the probe system, modify existing lines, then stop and restart the probe. A probe uses the same port to talk to all servers.

Logs (located in $OV_MAIN_PATH/pdAE/logs):
pd.log   messages from the PD Central application
npprobe.log   messages from the probe on this system

Troubleshooting PD:
- If the GUI applet is not working check java console within browser for exceptions
- If PD Central doesn't start via `ovstart`, try using `ovstop pd`, then running PD manually via `pdcentral.sh -start` or `pdcentral.bat -start`.
- Use "<DEBUG>true</DEBUG>" in the pdconfig.xml file to generate debug output in the pd.log file. This option should only be used briefly because it can generate large amounts of data
- Use `pdcentral.sh -dbmgr` (or `pdcentral.bat -dbmgr`) to launch a UI that allows SQL queries on the PD database

Smart path (access path view)

Smart path is a contributed application added in V7.51. Smart path has two functions: the first is to graphically show the Layer 2 and Layer 3 access path between two nodes and the second is to find a rougue MAC addesss. The first function shows up as a new dynamic view called Access Path view. The second function is a command line tool. Access path view is not enable by default.

Enabling and disabling SmartPath will stop and restart the *ovas* process To enable SmartPath, run the following command:

>> $OV_CONTRIB/NNM/SmartPath/ovAccessPath.ovpl –enable

The new Dynamic View is available in the drop down menu of NNM's HomeBase. This view accepts two endpoints as input. SmartPath consults the NNM Extended Topology and makes a number of SNMP queries which may take several minutes.

If multiple MAC addresses are forwarded on the last port of the last switch, an "Unknown" device is added to the path. This happens when a hub or L2 device has not been discovered by ET.

Find rouge MAC addresses

To find the switch that a MAC address is connected to:

```
$OV_CONTRIB/NNM/SmartPath/ovAccessPath.ovpl –mac <MAC> –file <file>
$OV_CONTRIB/NNM/SmartPath/ovAccessPath.ovpl –mac <MAC> –router <ip>
```

<MAC> is the MAC Address in quotes, for example: "00 AA BB CC DD EE". If the -file parameter is used, the L2 devices specified in the file are examined to find the MAC address. The file contents are expected to be one line per IP address. If the -router parameter is specified, ET is queried for the L2 neighbors of the router, which are then examined to find the MAC address.

The output is an XML document that shows which switches the MAC is forwarded on as well as the board/port. For each switch, a flag is included that indicates if more than one MAC is being forwarded on the port. The switch port which only forwards the specified MAC is likely to be the switch that the MAC is wired to.

The ping tools

The Fault-Ping menu option used to call the native OS Ping utility, but after NNM 6.2, the `natping` wrapper was added to convert the private IP into the public IP address when pinging into NAT environments. This also changed the tool from using a continuous ping to one that only issues 5 ICMP requests then stops. This is controlled by the "-n 5" option in the `natping` script in $OV_BIN. Remove the option in that file to restore continuous pings. Also, to allow the user to stop the ping while it is running, change the following line:

```
"system ("$pingExe $PublicIP $pingArgs")"
```
to:
```
"exec ("$pingExe $PublicIP $pingArgs").
```

In addition, add the `-followOutput` parameter to the `xnmappmon` call to `natping` in the NNM-IP.tbl registration file in $OV_REGISTRATION/C/ipmap. This allows the end of the output to continuously display so the user doesn't have to scroll down to see the results. See page 6 for more info on modifying ARF files.

Isolating local network issues

The following commands can help isolate network performance issues related to the NNM server, its network stack, and the locally-attached NIC. Check for UDP-related socket overflows:

```
netstat -p udp
```

Overflows can indicate SNMP traffic is overwhelming the IP stack. This can be because of over aggressive data collections, or too many devices being polled. On UNIX, use ndd to tune the network stack. Note this command replaces the older nettune command used under HP-UX.

rnetstat

rnetstat is an NNM-supplied SNMP-based version of the familiar netstat command for pulling basic network stack data via SNMP. rnetstat is also the front-end to some of the configuration, fault and performance menu-bar items in the NNM GUI. Some of the following rnetstat switches are not documented or supported by HP:

List route table:	rnetstat -rn <target>
List connected and listening ports:	rnetstat -a <target>
If names, addrs, mask, net addrs:	rnetstat -In <target>
If names, status, type, cap., alias:	rnetstat -o ifsum <target>

rnetstat -a is a very powerful tool for retrieving connected port info, and works by cross-referencing the returned MAC addresses to the $OV_CONF/physAddr.conf file. This file can be customized, but is over-written by NNM upgrades, so take appropriate precautions. Sometimes users prefer not have the MAC addresses translated by the rnetstat command. In this case, simply comment out particular entries in the physAddr.conf file or rename the physAddr.conf file entirely.

Display port address mappings

There is a menu-bar item under tools-Port-Address Mapping Table which displays port connections for all devices connected to the selected node. The URL for this tool is:

http://<server>:3443/OvCgi/connectedNodes?node=<node>

...where <node> is the FQDN of the target node and <server> is the name of the NNM server. This tool is a front-end for the `rnetstat` command discussed immediately above.

netcheck

`netcheck` is a handy but poorly documented NNM tool that is the guts behind the menu item: Fault ->Test IP/TCP/SNMP. It can be issued from the command line to test one or more of the three protocols just mentioned. Two examples follow:

```
netcheck -e -o tcpPort=telnet <target>
netcheck -e -o tcpPort=21 <target>
```

Note if the name of the service specified, as in the first example above, the tool cross-references the service port with the services file.

mibtable

This command dumps table views of SNMP MIB subtrees in text formatted output, and like `rnetstat`, is a very powerful and popular tool for NNM administrators. For example, to display port connection table entries:

```
mibtable -table ".1.3.6.1.2.1.4.22.1" -fields
"Index=1:3,PhysAddress=2:18,IPaddress=3:15" -node <node>
```

On UNIX systems, this example produces `mibtable` output that is nicely formatted:

```
mibtable -table ".1.3.6.1.2.1.4.22.1" -fields
"IPAddress=3,Physaddress=2" -node somenode | nawk
'$0~/^[1..9]/ {printf ("%-15s %s-%s-%s-%s-%s-
%s\n",$1,$2,$3,$4,$5,$6,$7)}'
```

tracert and traceroute

These native commands, which are used in NNM's Fault menu, show the network hops a packet takes to the destination. The path need not always be the same, nor may the return path. Both commands are native OS commands. NNM Windows ships with a copy of `tracert.exe` in %OV_BIN%, but it is no different that the native one.

Windows `tracert` differs from UNIX `traceroute` in that it is limited to using ICMP exclusively (`traceroute` uses UDP datagrams or optionally, ICMP). Windows also has native utility called `pathping` which provides broader protocol support than Windows' `tracert`. With NNM 7.0+, Problem Diagnosis is built into NNM. This tool provides more comprehensive pathing and status data if PD probes are properly configured. See the beginning of this section for more on Problem Diagnosis.

Packet sniffers

NNM does not contain a built-in tool for packet sniffing. However, some NNM daemon tracing facilities can produce detailed packet dumps, for example `pmdmgr` (see page 137). There are some commercial and freely available packet sniffers that are widely used to supplement the NNM users troubleshooting toolset. Following is a short list of selected sniffers that are used by some NNM administrators.

Network Monitor (`netmon.exe`) is a packet sniffer provided by Microsoft that is available in Microsoft Resource CDs. `nettl`/`netfmt` is a UNIX native packet dumping facility that is somewhat difficult to work with, but examples may be found below. `snoop` is native to Solaris, and its packet capture format is the basis of RFC 1761. To capture UDP datagrams:

```
snoop -x 0 udp <target>
```

Use `debug` on Cisco routers to sniff out specific protocol issues.

Ethereal from www.ethereal.com is free and ported to all platforms, and is very popular. Nmap, which is available for Windows as NmapWin is from www.insecure.org. Tcpdump, www.tcpdump.org, is ported to Windows as WinDump.

Using nettl

`nettl` is a native tracing utility on UNIX systems. An example command to initialize a `nettl` trace is:

```
nettl -tn pduin pduout -e <entity> -f /tmp/net
```

where `<entity>` is the name of the Ethernet entity (driver) being used. Get a list of these entities with `nettl -ss`. Typically it is BTLAN. A list of the drivers actually used on the system can also be obtained using:

```
ioscan -kf
```

The `nettl` command produces trace files named /tmp/net.TRC000 and /tmp/net.TRC001 (circular files). In the case where a wrong entity is selected, the trace file stays with a size of 128 bytes. Stop the tracing with:

```
nettl -tf -e <entity>
```

The binary trace files can be formatted with:

```
netfmt -l -N -f /tmp/net.TRC00[0,1]
```

To reduce the output, define filters (see netfmt man page) on a file and use it on the netfmt command line with -c <file>.

16. Third Party Tools

NNM gained popularity as an SNMP management platform in large part because of its APIs. Ten years ago, device-specific vendors weren't interested in developing standard SNMP manager features, and HP wasn't interested in developing device-specific management features. That formula worked well for many years, but it has changed more recently. More recently, device makers are less and less interested in providing management tools for even their own products and HP has responded by added devices-specific management support to NNM. HP maintains a catalog of certified NNM-integrated solutions at:

http://openview.hp.com/partner/isv/index.jsp

Using NNM APIs via the NNM Developer Kit provides access to the NNM SNMP event streams, allows customized topologies to be automatically constructed, and provides programmatic access to certain NNM legacy database data via C++ and JAVA programming interfaces. All these same programmatic interfaces are also available in Chip Sutton's CS-OV PERL Module available at: www.cs-net.com. Below are selected third party solutions, some of which are certified by HP, and some of which are not. This is a small list that represents those solutions that are most often mentioned by NNM users on the OpenView Forum user group listserv.

Environmental monitoring and contact management

Tools for monitoring room temperature or for interfacing with other analog devices and then conveying that information to NNM include:

www.imci.net	www.omnitronix.com
www.netbotz.com	www.sensorsoft.com
www.uptimedevices.com	www.akcp.com

Freeware utilities for UNIX

Assorted tools used often by other NNM administrators include:

Expect	expect.nist.gov
Swatch	swatch.sourceforge.net
Putty (SSH)	www.chiark.greenend.org.uk/~sgtatham/putty

VNC, only better	www.tightvnc.org
Web Load tester	www.wpidalamar.com/projects/123loadtest
I2Trace	www.geocities.com/milicsasa/Tools/l2trace

Emulating X windows on Windows machines

Reflections and Exceed are the most popular commercial tools for emulating X windows under Microsoft Windows systems. Freeware tools that accomplish this include Xming and Cygwin/X. Users report Xming is easier to install and that Cygwin with X11 packages is more highly configurable.

Event correlation tools

Tools that supplement or replace the functionality of NNM's built-in event correlation engine, OpenView ECS include:

ECS-based solution provider	www.logec.com
SEC – Simple Event Correlator	kodu.neti.ee/~risto/sec
InCharge	www.smarts.com
NerveCenter	www.openservice.com

SNMP and network management tools

Tools that supplement or replace the functionality of NNM's built-in SNMP manager features include:

SolarWinds SNMP tools	www.solarwinds.net
OpenNMS	www.opennms.org
Nagios	www.nagios.org
SNMP Toolkit	www.taave.com
Big Brother	www.bb4.org
Windows Extension agents	www.snmp-informant.com
TrapBlaster	www.realops.com
Net-SNMP agent	www.net-snmp.org
MIB Browser	www.innerdive.com
Badger TrapServer	www.badgerac.com

Topology and network modeling tools

Tools that aid in topology mapping and modeling include:

Edge enPortal and nVision	www.edge-technologies.com
Mimic SNMP Simulator	www.gambitcomm.com
Amerigo and other tools	www.taave.com
Opnet	www.opnet.com

Reporting and graphing tools

Tools that supplement or replace the functionality of NNM's built-in data collections and reporting features include:

| RRDtool | www.rrdtool.com |

NMIS	www.sins.com.au/nmis
Ploticus	ploticus.sourceforge.net
Cricket	cricket.sourceforge.net
OverTime and PingTime	www.netic.com.au
StatSeeker	www.statseeker.com
Kardinia	www.kardinia.com
Concord eHealth	www.concord.com
MRTG	people.ee.ethz.ch/~oetiker/webtools/mrtg

17. Cisco Devices

This section covers managing Cisco devices with NNM.

Cisco MIBs

The primary reason to load Cisco MIBs is that they contain embedded translations for SNMP traps that appear in the alarm browser. The easiest way to integrate Cisco MIBs into NNM is to load the appropriate CiscoWorks-NNM integration package. This also provides custom symbol mappings for some Cisco devices. If only the MIB files are of interest, they can be extracted from the integration package and loaded. Look for a file named:

> AllCiscoMIBs.my

If the integration package is not available, most top level Cisco MIBs ship with NNM. They can be found in the $OV_SNMP_MIBS/Vendor/Cisco directory. Load them in descending order as follows:

1. SNMPv2-SMI
2. SNMPv2-TC
3. SNMPv2-TM
4. SNMPv2-CONF
5. SNMP-FRAMEWORK-MIB
6. CISCO-SMI
7. CISCO-PRODUCTS-MIB.my
8. CISCO-TC.my
9. ENTITY-MIB
10. CISCO-ENTITY-ASSET-MIB

The most updated Cisco MIB's can be found at

> ftp://ftp.cisco.com/pub/mibs/v2/v2.tar.gz and
> ftp://ftp.cisco.com/pub/mibs/v1/v1.tar.gz

CiscoWorks and NNM

For years, CiscoWorks (CW2K) required the presence of a network management platform such as NNM. CiscoWorks then became a standalone product with a separate integration package for sharing data with NNM.

Similar to NNM, CW2K is a collection of integrated toolsets. It is comprised of Cisco RME (Resource Manager Essentials) and CWSI Campus (Campus Manager), which combines CiscoView, Traffic Director (formerly NetScout RMON), and ATM Director. In 2007, a number of other point products have been added to the Cisco Works suite. Also a number of Cisco network management software products for use outside the CiscoWorks suite have been released.

Cisco's "Third Party Integration Kit" provides the NNM integration elements. This package adds CiscoView and Campus Manager to the NNM menus, and is intended to be used for integrating NNM and CW2K when both sit on *separate* platforms. Both Cisco and HP provide CW2K integration package downloads for NNM. They are supposed to be identical but there are indeed differences. Field consultants report fewer problems with the Cisco-originated integration package and claim the site is kept more up to date.

The internal integration utility that ships with CW2K is intended to be used for integrating NNM and CW2K when both products sit on the same platform. Both products contain un-integratable embedded databases and CW2K is memory-intensive, so it is recommended to run CW2K on a separate platform from NNM.

If both are to be installed on the same platform, set up separate disk partitions for each product. The products formerly used incompatible versions of JAVA for user interface, but in 2006, a patch was released so CW2K supports JRE 1.4. Once CW2K and NNM are integrated, the recommendation is to turn off CW2K Availability Polling and setup NNM to forward traps to DFM. IE browsers behave best with CW2K.

See Page 23 for details on handling multiple version of JAVA clients when running CiscoWorks and NNM on the same client or server.

CiscoWorks, NNM, JPI and Internet Explorer

CiscoWorks 2000 requires Java Plug-In 1.3.1, and when a JPI 1.4.1 applet is started from the same instance of Internet Explorer, you can get Internet Explorer errors. If you start CiscoWorks 2000 from *ovw*, the system will try to use the same browser window that was last launched. If that browser was running Home Base (and hence JPI 1.4.1), Internet Explorer will throw a runtime error. If you first start CiscoWorks 2000, then launch Home Base, you will see a dialog box, "Attachment to a running Virtual Machine failed", followed by an Internet Explorer crash.

The workaround is to start CiscoWorks 2000 in a separate Internet Explorer instance. Start a new Internet Explorer (from the start menu, not using File: New) and browse to http://<machine>:1741. This will start CiscoWorks 2000. Start another new Internet Explorer window, then start Home Base from the ovw menu. This will use the new IE window, and leave the CiscoWorks 2000 applet in the old window. Alternatively, you can start a new IE window after starting Home Base, so that CiscoWorks 2000 will start in its own instance of Internet Explorer.

NNM and handling Cisco VLANs

By default, Cisco switches store the CAM table for VLAN1 in the dot1dTpFdbTable, which is the table NNM's discovery uses to build level 2 topologies. If there is nothing in that table, i.e. dot1dBaseNumPorts returns 0, then NNM maps it as a "flat" topology. This can be overcome by discovering the device with the community string appended with @vlan_no where vlan_no is a VLAN in use on the switch.

This can cause trouble for discovery if querying an NNM unsupported device. Be sure to use the latest Cisco Agents for the NNM version used. See Page 227 for the URL to check ET device agents.

Cisco builds separate bridge tables for each VLAN. To view MIB data for VLANs, issue snmpget or snmpwalk requests with the VLAN number added to the community string, followed by the @ character. For example, the community public@200 gives info on VLAN 200's MIB data. Note that VLAN 1004 is present on every Cisco switch (default VLAN for FDDI). To get a list of VLANs try one or the other of:

```
snmpwalk vtpVlanState.1.1 <node>
snmpwalk.1.3.6.1.4.1.9.9.46.1.3.1.1 <node>
```

187

To get more granular VLAN traffic reports from Catalyst 6000 switches, setup NDE with a netflow collector and configure bridged features such as bridged flow stats. NDE details can be found at:

www.cisco.com/univercd/cc/td/doc/product/
lan/cat6000/sw_7_6/confg_gd/nde.htm

Another approach is mining the vlan.dat database file from the switch. This file contains data pertaining to IDs, names, port membership, trunks, VTP, etc. This is only configuration data, however. If running a version of IOS less than 12.1(18.4)E or 12.2(20.4)S there was a bug where if the VLAN table was empty, the device would generate authentication traps. ET will poll for VLANs.

NNM's Cisco discovery configuration feature

NNM V7.51 introduced the Cisco Discovery Configuration (CDC) feature to help control and improve the speed of ET Discovery. This powerful scalability feature allows the data pulled from these devices to be controlled with respect to the IP Address and/or the SNMP OID.

Discovery of the following entities can be controlled with CDC:

- Forwarding Database (FDB) Tables
- Per-Module (Per-Board) Information for Multiple Boards
- Interface to Board Mapping
- VLAN Membership Information
- Port Aggregation

The CDP Agent comes with an msi-file for Windows installation. Enable CDC by copying the CiscoSwitchSnmp.user.cfg file from $OV_NEW_CONF/HPOvCiscoAgt/conf/nnmet/agents/ to the $OV_CONF/nnmet/agents directory and modify the new copy.

Before enabling CDC, note that while CDC can improve performance, it may do so at the expense of accurate topology data and CFA data that is used by the APA. It may be beneficial to disable the Forwarding Database (FDB) tables on strategic devices. Doing so will force reliance on only on CDP for connectivity, but connectivity to non-CDP devices from Cisco devices will then not be discovered. For example, if you have a Cisco switch that is connected to a Windows server, you will not discover the connection to the server even though the server is monitored by NNM. If disabling the FDB tables is not practical, see the section below on setting ET to give CDP priority over FDB.

188

HP recommends experimenting on a few test devices before disabling FDB tables more widely. They suggest monitoring the "Number of L2 links" stat in the "View Topology Status" tab under "Discovery Status" after applying changes that affect CDC. When configuring CDC, it is very important to read and understand the HP White Paper on CDC:

$OV_DOC/WhitePapers/CiscoDiscoveryConfiguration.pdf

In V7.53, this documentation is rolled up into the Guide to Using Extended Topology user manual.

Setting ET to prefer CDP over FDB connection data

If ET is enabled, ET will create multiple connections on an interface when a connection is reported both in CDP and FDB for the same interface. NNM V7.51 Intermediate Patch 18 introduced a method to force ET to prefer a CDP connection over an FDB connection in case multiple connections are being reported from the same interface on a Cisco device. To enable this behavior, configure the m_UseInferenceLogic flag with a value of 17 in the following file:

$OV_CONF/nnmet/DiscoSchema.cfg file.

Useful Cisco IOS SNMP commands

To disable Cisco TCP connection reset traps generated when a telnet session to a Cisco device is reset:

```
snmp-server disable traps tty
```

See "Configuring Cisco IOS Traps" below for more on this. To force a Cisco device to TFTP its config file, use snmpset on writeNet (.1.3.6.1.4.1.9.2.1.55); it is equivalent to being logged on the Cisco device and issuing a 'write network'. For example:

```
snmpset -c <WriteCommunityString> <RouterName>
.1.3.6.1.4.1.9.2.1.55.192.168.1.1 octetstringascii
<TargetFilename>
```

The target directory must exist and have proper file permissions. To set the source address of SNMP traps to be the loopback IF:

```
snmp-server trap-source loopback 0
```

189

The command to send a test SNMP trap, for example, the chassisAlarmOn trap (trap number 6, specific number 5):

```
test snmp trap 6 5
```

Here are the commands to set router to check avgBusy1 every 60 seconds and sends traps on rising/falling thresholds of 70/60 percent:

```
rmon event 1 trap RM7net description "High CPU Util"
rmon event 2 trap RM7net description "Low CPU Util"
rmon alarm 1 lsystem.57.0 60 absolute rising-threshold 70
1 falling-threshold 60 2 owner <system>
```

To disable link up/link down from non-IP interfaces on a switch:

```
conf t
int gi 1/1
no snmp trap link-status
```

Assign or change ifAlias for an interface. Generally, ifDescr and ifName are not writable. Note that Cisco CAT OS doesn't support ifAlias, and writes instead to the port name in the port table under the Cisco Stack MIB.

```
conf t
int fa0/1
description <newname>
```

ifAlias MIB is: mib-2.ifMib.ifMibObjects.ifXtable.ifXentry.ifAlias

Advanced Board status via the APA

The APA poller provides board entity status and generates special events relating to boards if properly configured. See page 81 for more information on this feature.

Command to create cut SNMP views

The example would cut the routing table from being viewed by a server named hpov. This would keep NNM from consuming too much CPU on routers with very large route tables, like edge routers. This can also be accomplished by setting the "-R" lrf option on *netmon* (see the section on limiting discovery on page 41). More on this in the paper referred to below on the undocumented CPU priority switch.

```
snmp-server view hpov internet included
snmp-server view hpov ip.21 excluded
snmp-server community <comm-string> view internet RO
```

Hex target IP for Cisco ping MIB

Use the following PERL code to covert an IP Address to hexadecimal notation for setting the CiscoPingAdress octetstringhex using the MIB Browser or using `snmpset` commands:

```
#! /opt/OV/bin/Perl/bin/perl
# convert IP address to hex
@i = split ('\.',$ARGV[0]);
$hip .=  sprintf("%02X", $_) foreach (@i);
print "$hip\n";
```

Undocumented IOS commands

The undocumented snmp-server command is used to set SNMP CPU priority:

```
snmp-server priority {low | normal | high}
```

The "Q" column of "`show process`" shows current priority
This does not affect SNMP trap process. For more, see:

www.cisco.com/warp/public/477/SNMP/ipsnmphighcpu.shml

Use the following undocumented event logging control command for toggling syslog event messages:

```
logging event {link-status | subif-link-status}
```

The "no" form of the `logging event link-status <interface>` command is used to turn off sending up, down and change messages for an interface to the syslog. This is very useful on live systems since these systems generate so many of these messages. This is a companion command to the documented command which prevents sending the associated snmp trap: `no snmp trap link-status`.

Weird trap OIDs (.1.3.6.1.6.3.1.1.5.4.1.3.6.1.4.1.9)

This is an SNMPv2 origin event OID. To resolve, create an OID alias in trapd.conf. For a full explanation, see the section on origin event OIDs on page 111.

Unknown trap 1.3.6.1.2.1.0.1&2 from Catalyst 2950

The Cisco 2950 Catalyst switch IOS has a bug that causes the unknown trap. Upgrade the IOS. Here is the text of the Release Notes for IOS 12.1_(9)EA1:

"When enabling traps on a catalyst 2950, messages are received at the NMS with erroneous object identifiers (.1.3.6.1.2.1.0.2 and .1.3.6.1.2.1.0.1)"

Cisco linkDown trap configuration

Sometimes, the TRAP macros for Cisco MIBs don't properly define the Cisco OID_ALIAS properly, so Cisco Link down traps show up in the alarm browser with a message like:

```
linkDown trap received from enterprise cisco.1.469 with 4
arguments
```

The solution is to add an enterprise identification using the event configuration GUI for the .1.3.6.1.4.1.9.1.469 enterprise. Alternatively, manually add the enterprise to the $OV_CONF/C/trapd.conf file in OID_ALIAS section, for example:

```
OID_ALIAS ciscoProductsC2621 .1.3.6.1.4.1.9.1.469
```

Run xnmevents -event after applying direct trapd.conf edits.

Controlling Cisco link down trap variable bindings

With IOS version 12.1, Cisco added support for RFC 2233 conformance. This added support gives end-users a choice for what sort of data is being passed with the linkDown and LinkUp traps. RFC 2233 defines linkUp and linkDown traps in the Interfaces Group MIB module (IF-MIB.my) as follows:

```
linkDown NOTIFICATION-TYPE
OBJECTS { ifIndex, ifAdminStatus, ifOperStatus }
::= { snmpTraps 3 }

linkUp NOTIFICATION-TYPE
OBJECTS { ifIndex, ifAdminStatus, ifOperStatus }
::= { snmpTraps 4 }
```

Prior to this change, Cisco's link down/up traps conformed with RFC 1573, as defined in the Cisco Interface Capability MIB module (CISCO-IF-CAPABILITY.my) as follows:

```
VARIATION linkUp -- TRAP-TYPE
-- OBJECTS { ifIndex, ifDescr, ifType, locIfReason }

VARIATION linkDown -- TRAP-TYPE
-- OBJECTS { ifIndex, ifDescr, ifType, locIfReason }
```

The advantage of RFC 2233 conformance is that SNMP is supported for sub-interfaces. The disadvantage is that the ifDescr, locIfReason, and ifType are not included. Those objects may be more desirable data to have in the event message (for notifications, etc.). Note that if using the older behavior, `locIfReason` should be an arbitrary value for sub-interfaces. The Cisco IOS commands to control this behavior are below:

Set RFC 2233 conformance:	`snmp-server trap link ietf`
Set the older behavior:	`no snmp-server trap link ietf`

Interface index remapping

NNM's more recent versions have features to detect interface index remapping that may occur after device reboots, etc. These rely on use of ifAlias, which requires consistent interface naming practices. ET and the APA also have facilities to handle index re-mappings, but these algorithms are not perfect. The following Cisco IOS command locks out index remappings and at a minimum should be run on devices that are being polled by NNM's data collector to facilitate consistent reporting:

```
snmp-server ifindex persist
```

ifSpeed and polling issues with data collections

Cisco's locIf*BitsSec are gauge variables, being a 5 minute exponentially decaying average computed as:

$$\frac{\text{(previous minute rate) + (the previous 5 minute rate)}}{2}$$

Unlike variables like ifInOctets, which are pure counter values, the polling interval has no effect on the values stored by snmpCollect. ifSpeed is a MIB-2 variable, and may not always contain accurate data for the interface for Cisco devices. Unless the speed is manually configured in the router, it should be the default, which is T1/E1 for any serial connection, 10M for eth, 100 for fa, etc. If there are subinterfaces configured, they inherit the speed of the underlying physical port. With Frame Relay, if the router is connected to a switch, the router takes clocking from the switch, ignoring any configured speed setting. An incorrect ifSpeed configuration won't affect transmission in this case, but it may cause errors for the routing protocol in use.

193

From an NNM perspective, most utilization collections and performance graphs may show false data since some of them use ifSpeed to calculate utilization.

Interesting Cisco MIBS, OIDs and MibExprs

Use CISCO-CONFIG-MAN-MIB.my to track config changes
Use CISCO-ISDN-MIB.my for basic rate ISDN on access router
Use CISCO-VPDN-MGMT-MIB-V1SMI.my for VPDN Per-user

Cisco MIB's for Layer 2, CDP, and VLAN:

```
cisco-stack.mib:
    portIfIndex, vlanPortModule, vlanPortVlan
cisco-cdp.mib:
    cdpCacheAddressType, cdpCacheAddress
    cdpCacheDevicePort
cisco-vtp.mib:
    vlanTrunkPortManagementDomain
cisco-vlan-membership.mib:
    vmVlan
```

Cisco system stats are mostly found under the lsystem MIB tree.

CPU busy percentage in the last 5 second period. Note that these measurements are based on the last 5 second period in the scheduler, not the last 5 realtime seconds. This makes them better indicators of potential issues that arise from CPU consumption:

```
.1.3.6.1.4.1.9.2.1.56      --busyPer
.1.3.6.1.4.1.9.9.109.1.1.1.1.3
```

1 minute exponentially-decayed moving average of the CPU busy percentage:

```
.1.3.6.1.4.1.9.2.1.57      --avgBusy1
.1.3.6.1.4.1.9.9.109.1.1.1.1.4
```

5 minute exponentially-decayed moving average of the CPU busy percentage:

```
.1.3.6.1.4.1.9.2.1.58      --avgBusy5
.1.3.6.1.4.1.9.9.109.1.1.1.1.5
```

mem%util "Percent available Memory on a Cisco Device Computed by: ((TotalDRAM – freeMem)/TotalDRAM) * 100"\

```
.1.3.6.1.4.1.9.3.6.6.0 \
.1.3.6.1.4.1.9.9.48.1.1.1.5.2 \
+ .1.3.6.1.4.1.9.9.48.1.1.1.6.2 \
+ .1.3.6.1.4.1.9.2.1.8.0 \
```

```
.1.3.6.1.4.1.9.3.6.6.0 \
- .1.3.6.1.4.1.9.9.48.1.1.1.5.2 \
+ .1.3.6.1.4.1.9.9.48.1.1.1.6.2 + / 100 *
```

PIX Firewall failover status:

.1.3.6.1.4.1.9.9.147.1.2.1.1.1.3 cfwHardwareStatusValue variable from CISCO-FIREWALL-MIB. It could be active(9) or standby(10), depending on the primary unit's status.

What is exponentially-decayed moving average?

Common in stock charting as well as performance monitoring, this type of correlated statistical averaging is also known as exponentially weighted or exponentially damped moving averages (EWMA), and is commonly deployed in Cisco SNMP agents. This statistical model allows for good compensation for lost data points or wild spikes combined with the need to keep very few past samples in memory. In essence, this model gives the highest weights to the most recent data points, providing a good indication of general volatility. A concise and straightforward explanation of how Cisco implements it can be found at: www.cisco.com/warp/public/66/3.html

Cisco temperature probes

Not all Cisco devices have variables that pertain to environmental monitors are instrumented the same. For Catalyst 6000 series switches, load the following MIBs: CISCO-ENTITY-SENSOR-MIB, ENTITY-MIB-V1SMI. The OID for entSensorValue is: .1.3.6.1.4.1.9.9.91.1.1.1.1.4.

Each entSensorValue instance in the above variable maps to an entPhysicalIndex (1.3.6.1.2.1.47.1.1.1.1.2) for which an entPhysicalDescr (1.3.6.1.2.1.47.1.1.1.1.2) is needed. Some Cisco devices use the ENVMON MIB, including Catalyst 5000's, 7x00 routers 12000 routers, etc.

```
ciscoEnvMonTemperatureStatusIndex:
1.3.6.1.4.1.9.9.13.1.3.1.1

ciscoEnvMonTemperatureStatusDescr:
1.3.6.1.4.1.9.9.13.1.3.1.2

ciscoEnvMonTemperatureStatsValue:
1.3.6.1.4.1.9.9.13.1.3.1.3

ciscoEnvMonTemperatureThreshold:
1.3.6.1.4.1.9.9.13.1.3.1.4

ciscoEnvMonTemperatureLastShutdown:
1.3.6.1.4.1.9.9.13.1.3.1.5
```

```
ciscoEnvMonTemperatureState:
1.3.6.1.4.1.9.9.13.1.3.1.6
```

Note that 3600 routers only report ciscoEnvMonTemperatureState.

Directly integrating Cisco syslog messages

A lightweight version of HP's OpenView Operations (OVO) logfile encapsulator agent was integrated into UNIX-only AE versions of NNM 7.0 and later. This facility provides a robust syslog encapsulation tool for passing syslog entries to NNM alarm browser.

This facility is intended only for "occasional" use, for example for traversing firewalls for few critical devices where SNMP cannot pass. Because of the added system overhead, it is not recommended for use as a replacement for SNMP traps, which are much more efficient and scalable. See page 148 for details on the NNM syslog facility.

Cisco-specific event correlation circuits in NNM

The Event Classifier circuit classifies Cisco events into meaningful categories grouped by device. The chassis failure circuit monitors Cisco traps for temperature, fan failure and power supply faults, consolidating a set of environmental traps into new OpenView Enterprise events.

Cisco links

MIBs: www.cisco.com/public/sw-center/netmgmt/cmtk/mibs.shtml

Mibs via FTP: ftp://ftp.cisco.com/pub/mibs/oid/

Mib Repository and trap translator:
        www.cisco.com/cgi-bin/Support/Mibbrowser/unity.pl

Configuring Cisco IOS Traps:
        www.cisco.com/en/US/tech/tk648/tk362/technologies_tech_note
        09186a0080094a05.shtml

Mib supported by VPN 3000 concentrator:
        ftp://ftp.cisco.com/pub/mibs/supportlists/vpn3000/vpn3000-
        supportlist.html

Configuring VPN3000 concentrator to send events as SNMP traps:
        www.cisco.com/univercd/cc/td/doc/product/vpn/vpn3000/3_6
        /config/events.htm

Syslog How-to:
> www.cisco.com/en/US/products/sw/cscowork/ps2073/products
> _tech_note09186a00800a7275.shtml

OSPF Configuration Management with SNMP:
> www.cisco.com/en/US/tech/tk869/tk769/technologies_white_pa
> per09186a00801177ff.shtml

RANCID (Really Awesome New Cisco config Differ):
> (freeware for automated login to Cisco devices)
> www.shrubbery.net/rancid/

DFM White Paper:
> www.cisco.com/warp/partner/synchronicd/cc/pd/wr2k/dvftm
> n/prodlit/digdf_wp.htm

CiscoWorks links

CiscoWorks Documentation
> www.cisco.com/univercd/cc/td/doc/product/rtrmgmt/cw2000/

HP-based NNM Integration Adapter:
> www.openview.hp.com/downloads/try_nnm_0001.html

Cisco-based NNM Integration Adapter (CCO login required):
> www.cisco.com/kobayashi/sw-center/cw2000/cmc3rd.shtml
> and www.cisco.com/cgi-bin/tablebuild.pl/cw2000-utility

CiscoWorks in Large-Scale environments White Paper:
> cisco.com/warp/public/cc/pd/wr2k/prodlit/ckspp_wp.htm

Extended SAA agent support for MPLS/VPNs:
> www.cisco.com/en/US/products/sw/iosswrel/ps1839/products_
> feature_guide09186a0080087b0a.html#wp1037443

18. *ovw* Map Operations

ovw is the foreground process that launches the NNM static map. Under UNIX, it is sometimes called the Motif GUI. It may be referred to as the legacy GUI in future versions since HP plans to deprecate that older interface in favor of Homebase, or JAVA-based dynamic views.

IPMAP is the program that runs to build the *ovw* 5-tiered topology based on OSI layer 3. *ovtopmd* is the background process that feeds status to IPMAP. IPMAP is the application that is registered with the *ovw* APIs to produce the familiar level 3 topology-based view that is broken into a hierarchy of five submap layers: Root, Internet, Network, Segment, and Node.

Containment realms add virtual layers at the Internet and Network levels to allow users to logically customize their topologies. IPMAP reads data from the map database and synchronizes it with data in the topology database via *ovtopmd*. *netmon* provides direct status to interfaces at the node level and the APA provides direct status via the status bridge *ovet_bridge* to *ovtopmd*.

Map operations – selecting, cutting and pasting objects

Selecting multiple objects can be tricky for map operations for cutting, copying and pasting. If care is not taken, inadvertent copy/paste or cut/paste operations can be irreversible and unrecoverable. Sometimes, in order to recover certain map customizations, database wipes and network rediscovery may be necessary. The following keyboard operations are supported:

Multiple select:	Control key and click on objects
Multiple select:	Rubber band select
Multiple select:	Rubber band and control-click deselect
Move selected:	Left click and drag
Cut/copy – paste:	Right click popup menu
Cut/copy – paste:	Hotkeys ctrl-x/c/v – use with care

Tips for using the find operation

Most find operations key off of NNM object database field values. To peruse the available field values for a particular object, Right-click over a node in the *ovw* GUI and select object properties. Any of the object properties such as capability flags can be used in search operations.

Find operations can also be made based on symbol properties, so all nodes that map to a certain symbol type can be selected.

A very handy way to select a bunch of objects that are in multiple submaps (to copy and paste to a container, for example), is to apply a find operation which highlights to search results then select Edit->Select Highlighted.

Exact match of the string entered in the find field is the default behavior for find operations. Note the exact match radio button in the find window.

Regular expressions (RegExp) are supported in find operations:

```
  .       Any printable character
  *       Zero or more of the preceding character
  ^       If first, following chars match beginning
  $       If last, following chars match string at end
  \       Escape special characters
  [ ]     Ranges of characters
```

Examples of find strings:

```
192\.168\.[1-4]\.[0-255]   All IPs in subnets 192.168.1
                           through 192.168.4
^.*\.bc\.ca                Any node in the domain: bc.ca
```

Setting unset capability fields

Capability fields are useful for find operations, for filtering operations, and for building reports using `ovtopodump` or `ovobjprint`. Capabilities that are unset are not displayed.

Change this behavior by modifying the $APP_DEFUALTS OVw (see page 9) setting and changing the value of the below keyword to TRUE:

showUnsetCapabilitiesFields TRUE

Map object visual cues

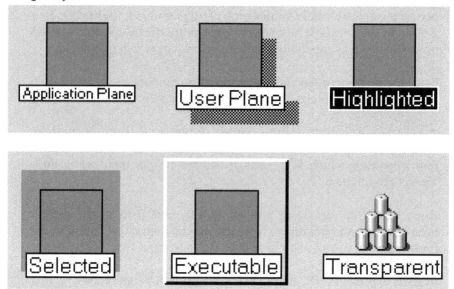

Figure 18-1.

Application Plane:	The IPMAP application placed the object
User Plane:	Object can't be placed logically in IPMAP
Highlighted:	The results of a Find operation
Selected:	The objects can be passed to actions
Executable:	Double click on the object launches an action as opposed to opening an underlying submap
Transparent:	Object has bitmap, but no "box." This is a developer feature used by third parties

Summary of *ovw* submap properties

The following attributes can be set for a submap:

- Show Connection Labels
- Submap persistence
- Background Graphics
- Layout (auto, bus, star, ring, row/column, PTP, etc.)
- Window Geometry (size and placement of submap)
- Overlay (on | off, explode into same or new window)

New objects do not show up in maps

When using `loadhosts` (see page 47) or when new objects show up in the object database, as seen via `ovobjprint`, they sometimes cannot be found in any maps. A common reason this occurs could be that the network or the segment that the node is a part of is unmanaged. Use find on the device's subnet to confirm that the network or segment exists and is managed.

Two devices combine into a single node

There are several reasons for this, and several things to check when this happens. First, confirm that the DNS names assigned to all interfaces on the two nodes have no overlaps. And, if using DNS, also check if there is anything in /etc/hosts, since it may be looking there after failing to find an entry in DNS. Next, check that the devices do not have any interfaces that have the same IP address assigned. If this were the case, a duplicate IP address alarm should have been generated.

Duplicate IP addresses are not supported unless they meet the requirements discussed under OAD on page 254. If an IP address had been first assigned to one node, then re-assigned to the other nodes, there could be shadow data that NNM is picking up that causes it to merge the nodes. Improper subnet masks on the interfaces could cause the devices and NNM trouble in attempting to learn the new assignment data.

In order to resolve this situation, delete the nodes from the topology and open any closed NNM maps. Run: `xnmsnmpconf -clearC`. Search the NNM database using all the names associated with both nodes. Use menu bar Find-Object by Selection Name.

Highlight and delete any returned results and let NNM rediscover the nodes. See page 47 for information on using `loadhosts`. If objects persist and continue to turn up in object find results, run: `ovtopofix` as described in the the procedure on page 20. Run: `snmpwalk` on the interface tables of the devices.

On Cisco devices, walk the IpAdEntAddr table. In some cases, devices will retain old IP addresses where they shouldn't and report these long after an interface has been re-IP'd. Using the IOS global command "clear interface name/number" will in most circumstances clear the IP address. If it is a deleted virtual interface, reconfigure the interface,

201

assign an unused IP address, clear the interface, and then delete the interface again. If none of these methods work, a router reboot will in most cases clear the stale entries from the SNMP tables.

Controlling trunked or meshed connections in *ovw*

Multiple connections between objects on a map are represented as metaconnections, which are connections that explode to view the underlying multiple connections. If it is preferable to represent these as a single connection via user-specified specific ports, this can be accomplished using the $OV_CONF/netmon.equivPorts configuration file.

Note that prior to V7.51 Intermediate Patch 18, netmon couldn't support multiple port equivalence records for a single host, but that patch resolved that and multiple entries can now be made in the file.

Understanding symbol and object delete operations

The key distinction to help understand delete operations is that from the GUI perspective, symbols are deleted, not objects. From the database perspective, objects are only deleted if all symbols representing that object are removed from all maps.

Objects deleted from one map will not be removed from the object database if there are symbols representing that object in another map. The "synchronizing" message that appears when a map is opened is the operation that keeps the map database and the topology database in sync.

This operation reconciles objects that are marked for removal in the object database with symbols representing them in that map's map database. If there are no more symbols left corresponding to the underlying object, it is removed from the object database.

"Delete From This Submap" only deletes symbols from that one submap. For example, a gateway object may exist in multiple segment's submaps. "Delete From All Submaps" marks for deletion every instance of that symbol from all submaps, and all symbols that are contained if the symbol is a container object.

The right-click menu delete is equivalent of "Delete from all Submaps."

Finally, the following command externally deletes an object:

```
ovtopofix -r <node name>
```

Fatal IPMAP or ovwinit failed errors

These errors typically indicate at least one corrupted object in the Map, Topology, or Object database. The procedure immediately below typically resolves the issue. If not, it may be necessary to contact HP support. It may also be necessary to delete and rebuild the databases then rediscover the network (see page 12).

Finding the offending object may not be that easy, however. Usually, the output of repeated invocations of `ovtopofix` and `ovw -mapcount` (using the options suggested below) can help identify the object that is causing issues.

Remove a stubborn object from all maps and databases

Typically this is required when an object is corrupted because its configuration has drastically changed and NNM holds stale information about the object. Before an object can be deleted from the topology and object DBs, it must be deleted from all maps. Objects are not deleted from maps until they are opened. If an object is deleted from one map, it is marked for removal in the object DB and should be removed from maps that subsequently opened during the map synchronization process. Follow these steps to make sure that objects are removed (in highly-scaled environments, remove the –v options to increase performance):

1. Delete object using "delete from all submaps" option in *ovw*
2. Open all maps and let them synchronize; close *all* maps
3. Run: `ovstop netmon`; then run `ovw -mapcount -cruDRv`
4. Repeat #3 until no errors are reported
5. Run: `ovtopofix -chs0v`
6. Run: `xnmsnmpconf -clearCache`, then start *netmon*, *ovw*
7. Confirm object is removed from DBs using find from *ovw* or by running: `ovtopodump -RISC <object>`
8. If object is still in DB, run: `ovtopofix -r <object>`
9. Rediscover device using: `loadhosts` (see page 47)

Remove "REMOVED" objects from databases

Typically, opening all maps and running the above procedure takes care of most situations. Still, objects marked for removal may still persist. In this case:

1. Select "Locate->Objects->By Selection Name" and enter REMOVED in the "Regular Expression" field then hit "Apply" or "Enter"
2. This finds all REMOVED objects and "Highlights" them on the map
3. Click "View->Highlights->Select Highlighted"
4. Next click: "Edit->Delete->From All Submaps"

If the REMOVED objects still persist in the database, stop *netmon* and run the following commands:

```
ovw -mapcount -RuD
ovtopofix -a
xnmsnmpconf -clearCache
```

Manually add objects

The command `loadhosts` (see page 47) exists to automatically force the discovery of objects that *netmon* cannot discover by itself. `loadhosts` is typically attempted when *netmon* fails to discover desired objects. Use this procedure when `loadhosts` itself fails.

A typical example is a device (perhaps in a DMZ) that is on the other side of a firewall from the NNM server. Commonly, the firewall permits SNMP traffic, but blocks incoming or outgoing ICMP traffic or both. A similar scenario is often seen when using MPLS or IPVPN tunnels/clouds where access to an ISP's devices is restricted. It is easy to add an object for which the appropriate segment-level submap already exists. Simply choose Edit-Add Object. It is trickier when the segment or the network symbol above it don't exist.

Before attempting such operations, search the topology using "find" for the IP subnet to make sure it not hidden from view or placed in a hard to find container in the topology. When adding a network object into the internet map, be sure to choose the "IP Network" network symbol from the Add Object palette; IPMAP won't recognize any other symbol type at this topology layer. Give it a label and note that the "Add Object" dialog has the "IP Map" Object Attributes available, and not grayed out. If it is grayed out, something is amiss.

It's important to select and set the "IP Map" attributes. Minimally, set the network Name, Address, and Subnet mask. All subsequent entries into this object's submap must map to these attributes in order to be recognized by IPMAP. A "verify" should return: "OK." Once the network object is added, it should not show up in the user plane.

In addition, it is a good practice to use /etc/networks or your DNS to enter information about the network, and the use the -m option to loadhosts to set the correct netmask.

Now, open the network object and create a segment object, which also must be configured with the proper "IP Map" attributes such as subnet mask. Open the segment object, then add a generic node device, with the "IP Map" attribute minimally containing the IP address, and then demand poll it.

Externally manage or unmanage objects

Version 6.31 introduced the -g and -G options to the ovotopofix command. Earlier version on NNM past version 6.0 provide support for the -g and -G options via patches.

Version 6.41 introduced the following Dynamic Views URL's which allow objects to be managed or unmanaged remotely:

> http:// <NNM-Server>::7510/topology/manage
> http:// <NNM-Server>::7510/topology/unmanage

For all NNM versions, the DIM command: xnmtopoconf – manage/unmanage can be used to externally manage or unmange devices, but this only works with AE version of NNM.

Overriding IPMAP symbol changes

IPMAP has rather narrow logic about mapping constructs. When a symbol is created by IPMAP, it is considered "managed" by IPMAP, and any subsequent symbol edits are subject to IPMAP's review for correctness. When *netmon* issues a configuration poll, any changes to such an object may be reset by IPMAP.

For example, if the symbol is updated with a preferred name, the name may change back to the original name that IPMAP chose for it. Use the following environment variable setting to preserve manual settings of IPMAP objects:

```
IPMAP_NO_SYMBOL_CHANGES=TRUE
```

Or, set the "-u" option to the IPMAP application call in the IPMAP registration file. See page 5 for more on the ARF process. See page 3 for more on setting environment variables.

Map status propagation rules
Default:
This is defined by the number of symbols that are normal, compared to the number of symbols that are not normal. Administrative status values are ignored (Unmanaged, Testing, Restricted, Disabled.) The calculation is:

Unknown:	No Normal or abnormal symbols
Normal:	All symbols normal
Warning:	One symbol abnormal; multiple normal:
Minor:	Multiple symbols abnormal; multiple normal
Major:	One symbol normal; all others abnormal
Critical:	All symbols are abnormal

Propagate Most Critical
This setting simply takes the most critical status and propagates it from the interface to the node, from the node to the segment, from the segment to the network, and from the network to the internet symbol in the root submap.

Customizing map status propagation rules
The user can define the percentage of symbols in a given state that cause that state to be used. If two states are satisfied then the most severe state should be used. Here are the default values for this option:

>5%	Critical
>10%	Major
>20%	Minor
>30%	Warning
>0	Normal
else	Unknown

For example, if 25% of the symbols are Minor and 15% are Major then Major is the status that is used, since it is the more severe status.

Symbol status
ovw supports three different ways in which color (status) can be set on a symbol: "Compound Status", "Symbol Status" and "Object Status". These options allow applications and/or IPMAP control over the color of the symbol. To determine or change a symbol's status, simply right click over the symbol and select "Symbol Properties".

Compound Status

Compound status is used when the parent symbol wants to reflect the combined status of the symbols in the symbol's submap. e.g. Networks, Segments etc.

Symbol Status

Symbol Status is used when an application wishes to have control over the color of symbol that may differ depending on which submap the symbol is on.

Object Status

ovw propagates the status the same way to all the symbols in the map that represent this object. The value of this status is stored in the object in the map.

Symbol status influences

Status is stored in the map database as well as in the topology database. Map synchronization reconciles differences.

IPMAP uses the following rules to assign status source :

- Interface symbols are set to object status source.
- Devices in segments and networks are set to symbol status.
- Segments and networks are set to compound status.
- Routers in internet submap are set to compound status.

Note that this rule suggests that router symbol on a network submap uses symbol status, while the symbol on the internet submap uses compound status. This means the router symbol on the network submap reflects only the interface status of the router in that network, however the status reflects all the router's interfaces on the internet submap. See the "-s compoundNodeOn" switch (discussed below) to change this behavior so all symbols reflect the more global status of the devices.

Fine tuning *ovw* symbol status

IPMAP has options that allow some interesting levels of granular control with respect to status that goes beyond setting simple status propagation rules. The "-s" switch to IPMAP affects a map behavior, but only at the initial creation time of the map, in the following ways:

Connections reflect the status of underlying interface:

```
-s connStatusOn
```

Connections do not reflect the status of underlying interface:

```
-s connStatusOff
```

Status of node symbols reflects the status of all components. This means that symbols on multiple levels and submaps representing the same object reflect more consistent status:

```
-s compoundNodeOn
```

Transient, persistent and on-demand submaps

To improve scalability, HP added the ability to specify the levels of the IPMAP topology which are loaded into memory upon start up of the *ovw* map in version 5.0. This is called the 'on-demand submap feature'.

A transient submap is one that is not loaded into memory and a persistent submap is one that is. Transient submaps take longer to load from the GUI and their contained objects are not available to *ovw* API actions such as the ability to change their status programmatically.

The persistence filter was implemented to allow filter-based rules to determine what submaps are loaded. Persistent filters are mostly needed by a few third party products that require their objects being in memory. In highly-scaled environments, they can also be used to keep submaps containing particular devices in memory for quicker GUI access.

By default, all levels are persistent for UNIX installations. For Windows installations, only the internet level and the containment realms are persistent.

Persistent levels are set through map options in the *ovw* GUI or via the "-d level" switch option to the ipmap callback in the $OV_REGISTRATION/C/ipmap ARF registration file. See the IPMAP man/ref page for switch level values and page 6 for more on updating ARFs.

Care is needed, though, in making higher IPMAP levels transient. For example, router symbols on the internet submap which would normally take "compound status" could potentially not properly update their status since there may not be a node submap in memory from which to calculate its status.

Note that only persistent submaps are included in map snapshots.

setStatus utility

This contributed utility sets the "object status" value of a map symbol. For `setStatus` to work, the symbol representing the object must have its status source set to "object". Also, the *ovw* map must be open in order to change the status of the object. This means that a `setStatus` issued on an object when the map happens to be closed is not subsequently changed when the map is eventually opened. The path to the script is:

```
$OV_CONTRIB/NNM/setStatus/setstatus.ovpl
```

In order to manually set a symbol to allow its status to be changed by the script, right click on the icon and choose Symbol Properties. Change Status Source to "Object."

Occasionally, an error may be generated when the object source doesn't properly map to the selection name of the target of the `setStatus` command:

```
Could Not set status color for XXXX - Object not on map
```

This error can be suppressed by setting the following $APP_DEF xnmevents resource (see page 9 for more info):

```
warnOnUnknownSource:false
```

If `setStatus` is unworkable and insufficient for externally manipulating an object's status, it is very easy to change the status source for an object or a set of objects using the NNM APIs. See page 182 for more on the *ovw* API.

Lining up symbols in a perfect line or row

Perfectly lining up symbols using manual drag operations is very difficult. Another method is to export the map, then edit the export file, modify the X and/or Y coordinates in the file to match the line which the symbols fall on, then import the file back into the map.

Note that editing the export files is not supported and could result in map database corruption if syntax errors are introduced through editing. Back up the mapdb prior to attempting to edit export files. See page 281 for the proper backup procedure.

Forcing icons to scale down in size

Consider that each submap is a default pixel width and height. That default affords the largest icon that is registered. Things tend to get cluttered when there are a lot of icons are on a submap. So, to make the icons scale down in size, the default pixel width and height for the submap needs to be made larger while keeping the window size the same.

To do this, turn auto layout on. If there are any background graphics, they have to be temporarily removed because OV locks the pixel width and height to the background. Now, drag the icons to the extreme left, right, top, and bottom of the window and notice that auto-layout automatically shrinks the icons as the pixel width and height expand.

Keep repeating this process until the icons are small enough to get the number of nodes desired onto the submap. Once this is complete, auto layout can be turned back off, background graphics can be re-applied. At this point, save the geometry for the submap in the View menu.

Forcing icons to scale up in size

In general, turning auto layout off and manually spreading out the icons may cause the map to redraw the icons at a larger pixel size. See also the section above on lining up icons to specific XY coordinates. The following $APP_DEF parameter can be used to set the minimum icon size for maps with many objects:

```
OVw*layoutMinSymbol Radius
```

This setting is useful when it is important to visually display the color changes on very busy maps. Details on updating $APP_DEF parameters can be found on page 9.

Finding and closing open *ovw* maps

To determine how many and which *ovw* maps are open, run:

```
ovstatus -v ovuispmd
```

To determine which users have maps open (UNIX only), run the following command, which may show users of the default map:

```
fuser -u $OV_DB/openview/mapdb/default/current/map.lock
```

To stop all *ovw* sessions:

210

```
ovstop ovuispmd
```

IPMAP tracing

Assign the name of a logfile to the following environment variable and IPMAP tracing is logged to that file when *ovw* is started in that environment:

IPMAP_LOG_FILE

See page 3 for details on setting environment variables.

Network named "10" or "arpanet" on internet submap

NNM names network symbols by using the name found in /etc/networks or ..\system32\drivers\etc\networks. The default version of that file found in an unmodified state on some UNIX systems (particularly HP-UX) has only the "10" network defined with "arpanet" as the historical name. See page 115 for a discussion of this issue.

The solution may be as simple as changing the default entry in /etc/networks, then deleting and rediscovering the devices in the affected network. If a name for the corresponding subnet number isn't found in /etc/networks, then NNM will name the network symbol as the subnet number.

Note that NNM removes trailing zeros from the name. Therefore, 10/8, 10.0/16, 10.0.0/24 and 10.0.0.0/30 might all look like "10" when named. It may be a good idea to assign different names in the networks file to these networks if they exist. See page 28 for more details on how network objects are named. Also, avoid having any /8 - /22 networks in your network.

NU0 interfaces turn red in map

In some instances, null interfaces are used for route advertising aggregation, and they may be important depending on how the network is setup. In most cases, these interfaces can safely be unmanaged. If there are many, globally filtering them out using the following procedure may be an option:

If using the APA poller, set up an ifType filter to unmanage them (see page 89); if using *netmon*, use ovautoifmgr (see page 44). In either case, the

211

affected nodes should be rediscovered, or use netmon.interfaceNoDiscover (7.5+), which is used by both the netmon and APA pollers.

Symbols superimposed on each other in submap

This is a bug in NNM 6.2 and it was fixed with a patch. The problem was seen when doing cut-and-paste operations into submaps with auto-layout turned off. This only affected only read-only maps.

Managing VLANs

A discussion on managing VLAN's for Cisco devices can be found on page 187. In general, VLAN SNMP info is virtualized in the Bridge MIB via the SNMP community string. For example, to list MAC address for a VLAN for vtpVlanState.1.3, where 3 is the VLAN number:

```
snmpwalk -c passwd@3 <switch> .1.3.6.1.2.1.17.4.3.1.2
```

ET's VLAN View provides support for a limited number of switches and protocols. Cisco VLANs are discovered via the bridge MIB, the Cisco Stack and CDP MIBs. Other vendors that provide good support for VLAN View discovery include Enterasys, Extreme, and HP.

Sometimes, interconnected switches which carry VLAN traffic that are not on the management VLAN can cause the NNM topology segment to change, depending on which switch is polled. In this case, the netmon.equivPorts file can be useful in hard coding to port connections from the NNM perspective. See page 202 for more information on using netmon.equivPorts. Also, assure you have the most up-to-date ET device agents for your critical connector devices. See Page 227 for more on device support.

Managing VPN endpoints

How NNM manages VPN's depends on how the VPN behaves. If the VPN is always stable and present, it just looks like an IP tunnel. Even if there is at least one device on the other side of the tunnel that is pingable and SNMP supported, it probably won't be discovered by *netmon*, but in this case, the reachable devices can be loaded into the topology via loadhosts (see page 47).

Other devices on the remote subnet may be discovered naturally after demand polling the first pingable, SNMP-supported object, but they also may not. ARP usage (required for NNM to auto-discover) is not standard across VPNs. Again, use `loadhosts` to force everything to be discovered.

If the VPN is not stable, those links might be managed in an indirect manner, perhaps via VPN-related enterprise MIBs using an SNMP data collection that generated threshold alarms based on a change in a particular MIB table entry. Or, perhaps the upstream device might support VPN-specific traps. Another possibility is that the upstream device can be configured to log important messages with the syslog facility (see page 148).

Managing ISDN interfaces

Polling dormant backup ISDN links may cause them to activate. The best practice is to set up an ACL in the router to block certain types of traffic that could activate them, i.e. ICMP, SNMP, RIP, etc.

Most vendors' SNMP agents, including Cisco, report inactive ISDN interfaces as "dormant" in the ifOperStatus MIB2 table. Setting the "-d" oid_to_type flag (see page 7) also restricts status polling (via *netmon*) to these interfaces. Observe that this flag will not restrict polling of downstream devices on the LAN segment connected to the node with the ISDN interface.

Switching routers and routing switches in *ovw*

Also called multi-layer switches, there is an increasing presence of chassis with support for boards that route and boards that switch. NNM's *ovw* maps have a hard time mapping switches that contain router modules or routers that contain switching modules. This is because those devices often don't consolidate SNMP functions. For IPMAP topology in general, level 3 data comes from RFC 1213 MIB2 tables and level 2 data comes from RFC 1493 bridge MIB tables. Extended Topology works differently in this respect and more details on that can be found on Page 237.

Some of these devices support separate SNMP agents for the router module and the switch module and may not be able to be addressed properly via SNMP unless separate IP addresses are assigned to the discrete management agents.

In some cases, the device may be represented as two separate objects in the *ovw* maps, particularly if separate names have been assigned to the management addresses in DNS. This may be desirable depending on the network administrator's preferences.

If this is not desirable, use DNS A records for the unique addresses, but also assign CNAME records that are the same - then *netmon* can resolve multiple addresses as being aliased to the same name. The objects might have to be deleted and rediscovered after such a change. ET is better at representing these devices. In NNM 7.5, there is support in ET for board-level discovery and mapping, and this greatly helps with this sort of device. While *ovw* maps may still have difficulty properly representing these devices, the ET representations should be just fine with this newer capability.

One issue, though, is that APA polling may be reading data from one discreet agent or the other and the agent being polled is not the desired agent. *netmon* discovery picks a preferred SNMP address and the APA uses this address. See page 46 for the procedure which explains how to change the preferred SNMP address.

Wireless

NNM started supporting wireless network discovery in V6.4 (ET 2.0). Wireless access points are discovered by *netmon* via SNMP and NNM assigns the devices the "isWireless" *ovwdb* attribute.

Tuning *ovwdb* for large numbers of objects

If `ovobjprint -S` shows more than 5000 objects, use the `-n` LRF flag to adjust the database to the proper size for the number of objects being managed. The number should be set to 5-10% above the number of objects reported. See page 5 for the LRF procedure.

Limiting *ovw* menu bar access for some users

The basic process to limit menu bar access is to copy the registration tree to another location, pare down the registration files in the copied location by searching for the registration file entries that are to be removed, then set the OVwRegDir environment variable to point to the modified registration tree directory in the user login shells for the users who are invoking the modified trees. To set environment variables, see the procedure on page 3.

On Windows, be careful to set %OVwRegDir% in all users' profiles or logon scripts, especially the default profile for new users.

Limiting usage of read-write maps

Normally, the first instance of map is opened in read-write mode; subsequent maps are opened in read-only mode. Only one read-write instance (*ovw* session) of a map can be open at any one time. The $OV_CONF/ovw.auth file was introduced in NNM 6.0 and is the preferred method for control user access to maps. This does not provide some of the granularity of control offered by the below methods, however. Add the following OVw app-defaults setting to change the default map open state to read-only:

```
OVw*readOnly:   true
```

For instructions on how to modify application defaults, see page 9. With this setting, read-write maps can be opened only by explicitly using the -rw option to the *ovw* command. Another method for forcing users to be able to only open read-only maps is to alias or hard code the *ovw* command in the users shell account (UNIX), to the ovw -ro command. Similar tricks can be played in Windows environments. Note that users who invoke *ovw* with the -rw option get read-only maps if the map permissions don't permit access via ovwchown or ovwchmod commands (UNIX only).

Limiting access to certain NNM applications

NNM V7.51 Intermediate Patch 18 introduced the ovprocess.allow configuration file in $OV_CONF to allow some processes to have limited user-based access by user id. The applications this applies to in V7.53 inlcude:

> *xnmsnmpconf*
> *ovalarmadm*
> *xnmevents*
> *xnmtrap*

Manipulating map ownership and permissions

ovwperms is a front end to the following three utilities:

ovwchown	allows maps to associated with UNIX users
ovwchgrp	allows maps to associated with UNIX groups
ovwchmod	sets maps with UNIX-like permissions

These commands are not supported under Windows. Any attempts to try to duplicate ovwperms-like activities on Windows systems, for example trying to change ACL's on the NNM DB files or directories, could result in database corruption. Note the command `ovwls`, which may be familiar to users of older NNM versions, is deprecated in later versions of NNM.

ovw.auth, ovwdb.auth, ovspmd.auth, and ovserver files

The ovw.auth, ovwdb.auth, and ovspmd.auth files were introduced in NNM 6.0. They control, respectively, user access to the *ovw* GUI, client access to *ovwdb* for remote consoles, and user access to the ovstop, ovstart and ovstatus commands.

With NNM 6.0, the $OV_DB/openview/ovwdb/ovserver file was introduced as well. This file is simply a text file with the NNM hostname and needs to be checked when restoring databases from backups from hot standbys, when hostnames change, and when migrating NNM to new hosts.

Windows-specific monitoring tools in NNM Menus

Windows NT Menu options are not actually defined in any registration files. These menu entries seem to be generated by a program called `ovwNTtools.exe`. The execution of this file, however, is itself defined in a registration file, namely $OV_REGISTRATION/NTtools. Move this file out of the registration tree to disable these Windows-specific menu bar options. See page 5 for details on the LRF Procedure

Add right-click pop-up menu items to *ovw* GUI

The following ARF adds a right-click pop-up menu item that issues a `ping` to the target node. Also, see notes on `natping` on page 177.

```
Application "Popup_Ping"
{    Description { "HP OpenView", }
DisplayString "Ping";
/* Use -Shared to make sure only one instance of the process is
executed at any one time.
*/
Command -Shared "xnmappmon";

PopupItem <100> "Ping"        Context (AllContexts || isIP ||
isRouter || WantPopupMenus)
TargetSymbolType ANY f.action "natping";

Action "natping" {
        MinSelected 0 ;
        SelectionRule (isNode || isInterface) && isIP;
    #ifdef NT
        CallbackArgs "-helpBrowser nnm:netPingTsk\
                    -commandTitle \"Ping\" \
                    -appendSelectList -
                            appendSelectListToTitle \
```

216

```
                    -cmd Perl/bin/perl -S natping ";
#else
    CallbackArgs "-helpBrowser nnm:netPingTsk\
                    -commandTitle \"Ping\" \
                    -appendSelectList -
                          appendSelectListToTitle \
                    -cmd natping "; 
#endif }
```

Add the above into a file with any name under the $OV_REGISTRATION/C directory and check the syntax with the command: `regverify -arf <filename>`. A restart of *ovw* sessions is then required.

Add menu item to launch SSH on selection (UNIX)

See above for full procedure and use this ARF snippet in the action block of the registration file:

```
Action "ssh" {
MinSelected 1;
MaxSelected 1;
Command "/usr/dt/bin/dtterm -title "${OVwSelection1}" -e
ssh ${OVwSelection1}&"; }
```

Another approach is to call a script and pass it a specific username that differs from the default, which in the above ARF will be the user who opened the *ovw* session. Also, such a script could not require a selection name so a host can be provided if a node is not selected. In this case, simply remove the "MinSelected" requirement from the ARF. Such a script might look like this:

```
#!/bin/sh
stty erase '^H'
target=$1
if [ "$target" = "" ] then /usr/bin/echo "Enter host to
connect to: \c"
    read target
    echo ""
fi
/usr/bin/echo "Enter Username: \c"
read logon
/usr/bin/ssh $logon@$target
/usr/bin/echo ""
```

19. Web Interface

The Web GUI is based on legacy *ovw* GUI topology and only provides visibility to legacy IPMAP topology. This interface is to be distinguished from the Dynamic Views JAVA interface discussed in Section 21. The legacy web interface requires an open *ovw* session to be running and the user sessions are always read-only views. In the past, the Web GUI was a CGI-based application. With NNM 6.4, Jakarta Tomcat becomes the operative servlet.

URLs

Note that the UNIX Web GUI access port changes from 8880 to 3443 in NNM Version 6.4

Web GUI:

      http://nodename/OvCgi/ovlaunch.exe (Windows)
      http://nodename:3443/OvCgi/ovlaunch.exe (UNIX)

Launch a specific map name :

      http://nodename:port/OvCgi/jovw.exe?MapName=MyMap

Launch a specific map submap name :

      http://nodename:port/OvCgi/jovw.exe?MapName=MyMap&ObjectName
      =MySubmap

Alarm Browser:

      http://nodename:port/OvCgi/ovalarm.exe

Reporter:

      http://nodename:port/OvCgi/nnmReportPresenter.exe

NNM V7.51 Intermediate Patch 18 added the following additional URL options which are documented in the NetworkPresenterURLoption.pdf white paper in the $OV_DOC/WhitePapers directory: `ServerName`, `objectName` and `PreferredSubmapType`, for example:

http://hostname[:port]/OvCgi/jovw.exe?[MapName=<*mapname*>&Object
Name=<*selectionname*>&ServerName=<*servername*>(PreferredSubmapType
=<*submaptype*> | SubmapName=<*submapname*>)]

Maintaining open *ovw* map sessions for web clients

Web clients require open *ovw* sessions. (note that Dynamic Views do
not require open *ovw* sessions). There are creative ways to make sure
ovw sessions are available to serve web clients without having to
dedicate a workstation to maintaining *ovw* sessions for this purpose.

xvfb:

The UNIX X Virtual Frame Buffer can be used to support *ovw*
sessions. xvfb is free and supported by the X consortium and can be
downloaded from www.x.org. Once installed, set up an rc file to
automatically launch a session on system startup. Don't forget to set
up a kill script as well. Make sure to give the numbered startup link
file a higher number than the one used by the OpenView daemon
startup rc file. In the script, enter:

```
/usr/bin/X11/Xvfb :10 &
DISPLAY=:10 ovw &
```

Or, a slightly more verbose version:

```
/usr/X11R6/bin/Xvfb :10 -screen 0 1152x900x8 2>>
/var/adm/Xvfb.log&
```

VNC:

VNC (also known as REALvnc) is only one of many virtual
windowing products. VNC is free, multi-platform, and widely used
in the user community. It can be found at: www.vnc.com

Also consider a more actively-developed and stable VNC derivative,
tightVNC: www.tightvnc.com. To configure an *ovw* session to start
when the system starts up or whenever ovstart is issued, add an LRF
file for *ovw* (details on LRF procedure on page 5):

1. Create a LRF file, named ovw.lrf with the following lines:
   ```
   ovw:ovw:    OVs_YES_START:ovuispmd:-
   ro:OVs_NON_WELL_BEHAVED:15:
   ```
2. Register the new LRF via: ovaddobj ovw.lrf
3. Note the –ro option makes the session read-only. Map options can also
   be added to open a particular map name.
4. The session can be controlled from other windows via `ovstop ovw`
   and `ovstart ovw` commands

219

There is a very handy newer option to the *ovw* command that checks the health of XServer periodically:

```
ovw -pollXServer
```

This option is also available as an OVw $APP_DEFS resource so it can be invoked automatically (see page 9).

On any virtual windows server, make sure that the color depth is set for 24. If it is set lower, *ovw* may generate the following error: "Cannot allocate 128 colors, Using monochrome images." More about this error can be found on page 21. There are several tools that can be used to make sure the virtual console stays locked. The following site, for example, has a tool for Windows that locks out the keyboard and mouse:

www.e-motional.com/tscreenlock.htm

An open source UNIX client to open Windows Terminal Server sessions can be found at: www.rdesktop.org

Web GUI login password

The default username/password for web GUI login is ovuser/ovuser. The password can be changed by running:

```
ovhtpasswd <user>
```

Web GUI access using jovw registration files

Jovw registration files can be used to control WEB GUI user access using standard htgroup file definitions. In the htgroup file, add groups with the users needed. In the jovw registration file add sections like this:

```
<110> "map1 IP Network"
Access group1
Icon "launcher/network.16.gif"
ActiveHelp { "><Access to the Network Presenter which
displays the objects based on map1's Network."}
f.action "map1";
```

Adding Web GUI menu and toolbar items

To add a toolbar button, modify the jovw files in both:

```
$OV_WWW_REG/Launcher/C/Jovw
$OV_WWW_REG/Jovw/C/Jovw
```

Example of a toolbar item to `ping` the selected device:

```
ToolbarButton <100> @"C/toolbar/newwin.24.gif"
        Context "AllContexts" f.action "ping";
    Action "ping"
        {
        MinSelected 1;
    URL
    "/OvCgi/webappmon.exe?app=IP+Tables&act=ping&help=on&sel=OV
    wSelections;
        WebWindow "ping"
            {
            Type limited;
            Width 600;
            Height 300;
            }
    }
```

Note the use of `webappmon`, which is the Web GUI equivalent of `xnmappmon` (see page 175). The code example above adds the button, but uses the same GIF as another button on the toolbar. Change the GIF by adding the path to a 24x24 bit picture.

Menu bar items for the Web GUI are spread amongst several files. For example, the "ping" menu item in jovw is located in:

$OV_WWW_REG/jovw/C/snmpviewer

Jovw menu registration files use the same syntax as standard NNM ARFs (see page 6).

Icons OK in *ovw* but not OK in web GUI

Some third party products developed for NNM create custom bitmaps for *ovw* (which supports several graphic formats), but not in gif format for the Web GUI. The gif format files cause question marks to appear in the web GUI. The following utility can be used to convert the bitmaps to gif format:

$OV_CONTRIB/NNM/ImageMagik/convertBitmaps.ovpl

Note that on UNIX, $OV_CONTRIB/NNM/ImageMagik should be added to the LD_LIBRARY_PATH environment variable and convertBitmaps.ovpl needs to be run as the root user.

The new symbols should be deceted right away for *jovw* views. To force Dynamic Views to recomputed its symbol mappings after converting bitmaps, run the `ovdvstylereset` command found in $OV_BIN and then refresh any open dynamic views to apply the new symbols.

javaGrapher contributed data collection tool

javaGrapher is a contributed application and is a tool for live queries of the *snmpCollect* data. It does not, however, pick up user-configured collections and is designed for more ad-hoc-type queries of SNMP objects. It also doesn't seem to work with the base installation of NNM 7.5. It is located in:

```
$OV_CONTRIB/NNM/javaGrapher
```

Running JAVA apps in event action callbacks

Use caution when calling JAVA applications as automatic actions associated with NNM events because a separate JVM is started for each instance for each event launched and this can consume a lot of system overhead. That said, the typical problem one encounters is that the classpath is not set in the calling script, for example, the following error is seen in ovactiond.log:

```
Exception in thread "main"
java.lang.NoClassDefFoundError:
```

To resolve this problem, set the classpath in the calling script using:

```
java -classpath <path_to_script>
```

Secure JAVA-based telnet or ssh

In some environments, GUI users don't have the ability to locally access the devices managed by NNM (jovw relies on this to launch local utilities for telnet, etc). There are a few free JAVA-based telnet clients that fit nicely in this situation; here are links to two of them:

```
http://javassh.org/
http://www.mud.de/se/jta/
```

Setting the preferred web browser

To configure the browser used to launch URLs from within NNM menus and additional actions, see the ovweb.conf man page and use the $OV_CONF/ovweb.conf configuration file. An example entry (UNIX):

```
Browser: /opt/ns-communicator/netscape -install %s
Port: 3443
```

To reuse an open Netscape instance rather than open a new one:

```
Browser: /opt/netscape/netscape -remote "openUrl
(%s,_blank)" || /opt/netscape/netscape %s
```

Web GUI access control

User control for Web GUI access This can be achieved by creating groups in the $OV_WWW/etc/htgroup file with particular users assigned to a group. Then, by assigning an access clause for that group in the action block of a specific action in the application's launcher registration file, the action can be restricted to the users of the group. The application's registration file for ovlauncher is found in the directory:

$OV_WWW/registration/launcher/C/

Here is an example $OV_WWW/etc/htgroup file:

```
NetworkAdmin: Mary
NetworkOper: Rachel
NTOper: +
UNIXAdmin: Charlie
UNIXOper: Jake
OVAdmin: Charlie Jake
Su: Molly Max Goldie
NOC: Molly
```

Here is an example jovw registration file snippet to restrict the display of map options within ovlauncher to certain groups.

```
/*
 * jovw.exe takes MapName and ObjectName parameters.
 * MapName specifies the map for the Network Presenter
 * to open, and ObjectName specifies the selection name
 * of an OVW object to display.
 */
Action "NNMNetworkPresenter" {
URL "/OvCgi/jovw.exe?MapName=default";
WebWindow "OvWwwNetworkPresenter" {
Type limited;
} }
Action "NNMNetworkPresenterIP" {
URL
"/OvCgi/jovw.exe?MapName=default&ObjectName=IP+Internet";
WebWindow "OvWwwNetworkPresenter" {
Type limited;
}
Access NetworkAdmin;
}
/* The following two entries to the Action block are provided as
examples of how to add personalized maps. You must also update
the List blocks within this file.
*/
Action "NetAdmn" {
URL
"/OvCgi/jovw.exe?MapName=NetAdmin&ObjectName=IP+Internet";
WebWindow "OvWwwNetworkPresenter" {
Type limited;
```

```
        }
    Access NetworkAdmin;
        }
    Action "NNMNOC" {
    URL
    "/OvCgi/jovw.exe?MapName=NOC&ObjectName=IP+Internet";
    WebWindow "OvWwwNetworkPresenter" {
    Type limited;
        }
    Access NOC;
        }
    Action "NNMSu" {
    URL
    "/OvCgi/jovw.exe?MapName=Su&ObjectName=IP+Internet";

    WebWindow "OvWwwNetworkPresenter" {
    Type limited;
        }
    Access Su;
        }
    Action "NNMNetworkPresenterHelp" {
    URL
    "/OvCgi/OvWebHelp.exe?Content=cntref&Context=cxtref&Scope=sc
    pref&Topic=Network_Presenter";
    WebWindow "OvHelp" {
    Type intermediate;
        }
        }
        }
```

Web GUI and ovw auth files

Which remote systems that have access to the Web GUI can be controlled through the $OV_CONF/ovw.auth and $OV_CONF/ovwdb.auth files. By default, all systems have access to the Web GUI. Both files must be updated if using these files to set granularity to specific nodes. Always make sure there is an entry for the NNM server itself in these files.

20. Extended Topology

Extended Topology (ET) is literally an entire product within the NNM product. In 2000, the ET source code was licensed by HP from Riversoft Technologies (Riversoft was acquired by Micromuse in 2002 and Micromuse was acquired by IBM in 2005). HP has been integrating ET into NNM in stages ever since and ET has increasingly become the dominant architectural component of NNM in terms of user interface development and representation of new topologies. This has manifested itself as Dynamic Views in NNM (See section 22). In essence, Extended Topology provides visibility to Layer 2 connectivity, HSRP, VRRP, VLANS, IPv6, and overlapping address spaces that are otherwise impossible with legacy NNM.

When NNM is first installed, Extended Topology is not enabled. The reason for this is that in highly-scaled environments, zones must be configured or ET may become a performance burden. Also, a successful ET discovery is dependent on a well-discovered *netmon*-based topology, and it is a good idea to take a hard look at the results of *netmon* discovery before enabling ET. Several rediscoveries of *netmon*-based topology should be expected during the implementation phase of most NNM deployments.

Enabling Extended Topology

Read the guide to Using Extended Topology thoroughly before enabling ET. When running for the first time, use:

```
$OV_BIN/setupExtTopo.ovpl
```

If this command is being run for the first time, it prompts for zone configuration. In environments where there are fewer than 200 connector devices, selecting automatic zoning should be OK. Zone configuration can always be updated through the Extended Topology Configuration window available from the Discovery Status tab in Homebase.

In general, zoning in smaller NNM deployments will adversely affect performance. The best practice is to avoid using more than one zone. Depending on the environment (and the version of NMM), discovery may take some time. It can be monitored in Homebase under the Discovery Status tab.

ET autozoning

Autozoning is prompted for by setupExtTopo.ovpl. The zones created by this feature are strictly based on Layer 3 information from the classic NNM topology. All subsequent topology discovery runs will not use the autozone feature and will then place any newly-discovered devices into the default zone.

A best practice, then, is to manually run the autozone script before running a new ET discovery. By default, a new discovery is run when a threshold of newly discovered nodes is reached, but the discovery can be adjusted in the HomeBase extended topology configuration window. The autozoning feature can be launched using the "Configure zones automatically" option in the extended topology configuration window or by launching the following command:

> $OV_BIN/autozone.ovpl

Monitor progress in the $OV_PRIV_LOG/autozone.log file. Restart *ovas* after running autozoning using `ovstop/ovstart`. Test the zones using the test zones option in the extended topology configuration window.

If running NNM on more powerful hardware, the number of nodes that are placed in a single zone can be increased by modifying the `numManagedObjects` parameter in the following file, but HP recommends not using a value of more than 10,000:

> $OV_CONF/nnmet/recVals.conf

Manual zoning tips

If experiencing troubles with the autozone feature, consider creating the zones manually. Use these guidelines for the zones:

Create one zone for core network devices

Create one or more zones for the central site's L2 connecting devices and key components

Create one or more zones for external sites L2 connecting devices and key components

Use device naming standards as wildcards in the zone definitions. Supported wildcards in zone definitions are:

*	Any number of characters up to the next period (.)
?	A single character
[..]	A single character or a range of characters [acd] or [a-f]
[!..]	Strings NOT containing a character or range [!acd] or [!a-f]
n-n	From-to for ranges of IP addresses

Remember to test all zones using the test zones option in the extended topology configuration window. The output files created by this operation is $OV_TMP/etzonetest.out and this file contains a list of all the discovered nodes and what zones they are placed in.

Restart or force ET discovery

See procedure on page 10

ET device agents

Extended Topology makes device-specific queries to supported devices to build connectivity, topology, and intelligence for the polling engine. The following URL'

NNM device and protocol support:
   www.openview.hp.com/products/nnmet/support/device_support.html
NNM device support:
   openview.hp.com/products/nnmet/support/device_requirements.html

ET discovery and SNMP configuration

SNMP community strings are transferred to NNM/ET from the legacy SNMP configuration subsystem, but inV7.53 and prior, SNMP polling timeout and retry values are not transferred. In V7.53, two options are available for customizing timeouts and retries in ET: the first is to import the settings from legacy SNMP configuration; the second it to configure ET Discovery polling timeouts and retries independently.

To enable importing of classic SNMP configuration timeouts and retries, run: `ovstop ovet_dhsnmp` then add the `-useNNMSNMPConf` switch to the ovet_dhsnmp.lrf file per the LRF procedure on page 5, then restart the `ovet_dhsnmp` process.

For ET-based Discovery timeouts and retries, they are configured in the m_TimeOut and m_NumRetries paramters near the end of the following configuration file:

$OV_CONF/nnmet/DiscoSnmpHelperSchema.cfg.

For changes to take effect, restart the ET processes using etrestart.ovpl. The below logfile will indicate if timeouts are occurring during ET discovery:

$OV_PRIV_LOG/ovet_dhsnmp.log

ET discovery considerations and limitations

ET makes use of data in the forwarding (FDB) tables of LAN Switches when computing topological relationships. Many switches do not generate layer-2 packets that contain their own layer-2 addresses. This results in the forwarding tables of neighboring switches not having entries for each other. This results in too many switch-to-switch connections to be created by ET when switches are not directly connected to each other.

ET can take advantage of protocols like CDP to eliminate non-neighbor connections in the topology. Such protocols "advertise" the physical addresses via layer-2 packets. This results in useful connectivity information being available in SNMP forwarding tables. Also, when VLANs are in use in an environment (and discoverable via supported vendor-specific SNMP agents), "non-neighbor connections" can often be recognized as such. Below are additional considerations regarding switches:

- Expect HP to develop improvements to the "topology stitching" algorithms in future releases to NNM, keep up-to-date on NNM patches and on ET device agents.
- With Cisco devices, CDC should be understood and customized for the environment. See page 188 for more information on CDC.
- ATM switches that support the ILMI MIB produce more accurate and complete ATM switch connectivity. The ILMI discovery agent only discovers remote neighbors for interfaces with ifType of atm(37). Devices supporting the ATM MIB that

report ILMI neighbors for other interface types, for example sonet(39) will not be discovered.

- Extreme Networks devices running OS version 6.1.7b7 or later, enable SNMP access to the forwarding database:

```
enable snmp dot1dTpFdbTable
```

ET discovery may treat certain routers as "end-nodes" under circumstances where there is not enough data to create router-to-router connections. ET in NNM V7.53 and prior does not have support for the Repeater MIB (rfc2018) or for enterprise-specific repeater and/or hub MIBs. NNM, however, continues to interrogate devices supporting rfc2018, as well as the HP Interconnect Functionality (ICF) MIBs, which supply connectivity information for Neighbor and Node Views.

Improving ET discovery accuracy

The following steps may improve the accuracy of the topology discovered by ET:

1. Enable discovery protocol (CDP, FDP, EDP) to improve accuracy
2. If the above protocols aren't available, run discovery during an active time on the network to better grab Forwarding Database tables in switches
3. Consider the need to manage end-nodes. Managing end-nodes improves L2 connectivity accuracy but may cause more events
4. Check DNS performance. ET uses DNS lookups extensively

The CDC introduced in V7.51 (See Page 188) may affect the accuracy of discovered data. The CDC is not enabled by default however.

Improving ET discovery performance

The performance of ET discovery and the APA poller has been dramatically improved through several versions of NNM and particularly through incremental patches to V7.5. When encountering issues with performance always make sure the latest version and the latest patches are installed. As with *netmon*, ET discovery performance is also directly affected by DNS performance. See Section 4 on DNS for more on this.

NNM V7.51 introduced CDC to provide administrators a way to control how much data is pulled from Cisco devices during ET discovery. This feature can greatly improve the performance of ET discovery, but does so at the potential expense of accurate topology representations. See Page 188 for details on the CDC.

Interface filtering, which was introduced in a patch to V7.5 can greatly speed ET discovery in highly-switched environments. More information on this feature can be found in the InterfaceFiltering white paper and on the section on the netmon.interfaceNoDiscover file on Page 55.

Dynamic Views by default uses a combination of filters from ET filter files (paConfig.xml and TopoFilters.xml) and the legacy NNM "filters" file ($OV_CONF/C/filters). Disabling the legacy filters file simplifies filters definitions and boosts performance. If running NNM versions previous to NNM 7.53, change the "enableETFilters" parameter from 0 to 1 in:

> $OV_AS/webapps/topology/WEB-INF/web.xml

If running NNM 7.53, change the "enableETFilters" parameter from 0 to 1 in:

> $OV_AS/webapps/topology/WEB-INF/servletRegistration/1NodeServlet.xml

Reducing ovet_poll startup time

If startup time for ovet_poll is taking more than a minute or two, there may be a large number of unconnected interfaces in the environment. The following setting may reduce startup time:

Edit $OV_CONF/nnmet/topology/filter/TopoFilters.xml
Find the section below and comment it out:

```
<!--
<filter name="NotConnectedIF" objectType="Interface"
title="NotConnectedInterfaces" description="Interfaces
without Layer 2 Connection">
  <operator oper="NOT">
  <filterName>ConnectedIF</filterName>
  </operator>
</filter>
-->
```

It is commented by adding <!-- as comment start, and --> at the end.

Then, locate the following line:

```
<interfaceAssertion name="ConnectedIF"
title="ConnectedInterfaces" description="Interface with L2
Connection">
```

And add this section above it:

```
<interfaceAssertion name="ConnectedIF"
title="NotConnectedInterfaces" description="Interface
without L2 Connection">
  <operator oper="NOT">
  <attribute>
    <capability>isL2Connected</capability>
  </attribute>
  </operator>
</interfaceAssertion>
```

Check filter validity with `ovet_topodump.ovpl -lfilt`, the restart *ovet_poll*.

ET and *ovw* database synchronization issues

Trouble can result when objects are discovered by *netmon*, but have not yet been discovered by ET. Prior to V7.51, there is no single command to force a single object or set of objects to be discovered by ET. To force a complete ET discovery, or a single zone discovery, see the procedure on page 10. To synchronize a node that has not been discovered by ET but has been discovered by *netmon* in V7.51, see the procedure immediately below.

ET single/incremental node discovery

After V7.51, single nodes that are subsequently added by netmon can be made a part of Extended Topology, but there are some limits in the initial support for this feature. For example, connectivity for newly added nodes is not yet supported. It is important to read the IncrementalNodeDiscovery.pdf white paper for more information on using this feature. In V7.53, this documentation is rolled up into the Guide to Using Extended Topology user manual.

This feature is disabled by default. To enable this feature, add the following LRF flag to the ovet_bridge.lrf file and using the LRF procedure on Page 5:

231

-single_node_discovery

Restart the *ovet_bridge* process after updating the LRF using `ovstop/ovstart`. Prior to V7.53 Intermediate Patch 20, Single Node Discovery discovers interfaces on non SNMP nodes and marks them as disabled.

Since the interfaces are unconnected, polling is controlled by a paConfig.xml filter that uses the new isNewNode and isNewInterface attributes on the newly added nodes. These attributes are cleared after a full or incremental zone discovery occurs.

To initiate a node discovery after enabling this feature, simply issue a standard demand poll to the node using ovw map function or from the command line using `nmdemandpoll`. Incremental node discovery activities are logged to:

$OV_PRIV_LOG/ovet_bridge.log

Detect interface configuration changes

The below configuration settings should be considered if the APA is enabled. Added in NNM V7.53, the following LRF flag added to the ovet_bridge.lrf file (using the LRF procedure on Page 5) will enable automatic discovery of interface configuration changes:

-interface_config_change

Similarly, the following LRF flag will automatically detect SNMP interface index table renumbering:

-handle_interface_renumber

Note that automatic discovery of interface changes and interface renumbering settings are disabled by default. Restart the *ovet_bridge* process after updating the LRF using `ovstop/ovstart`.

Detection of the above changes occurs through the APA's monitoring of the `sysUpTime` and `entLastChangeTime` MIB variables. By default, the former is enabled by default, but the later isn't. To enable entLastChangeTime monitoring, edit the paConfig.xml file and set the `entityMibEnable` parameter in the `ConfigPollSettings` to "true."

HP recommends that if the above parameter is set to true, a new filter is created to identify devices that supports the `entLastChangeTime` MIB variable and then setting up the `ConfigPollSettings` so that the `entLastChangeTime` parameter is set to "true" only for supported devices. Also, limitations apply to the classes of interfaces that the above settings apply to. The documentation for this may be found in the Guide to Using Extended Topology user manual.

Detect interface table additions

NNM V7.53 introduced the `ifNumberQueryEnable` paConfig.xml file parameter setting in the config group which when set to true (false by default), will cause the APA to poll the ifNumber variable with every APA status poll. If ifNumber increments, the APA will generate the new event OV_APA_IF_ADDED.

Zone discovery tips and performance tricks

Zones are an ET scalability feature and an absolute necessity for environments that manage more than a few hundred connector devices.

As a general rule, zones should correspond to geographic locations or other logical groupings where the number of links between the groups is minimized. Do not separate directly-connected switches, switches connected to routers, or switches in the same global VLAN. Zones should be connected by having at least one router from each zone in another zone.

`setupExtTopo.ovpl` automatically partitions devices into discovery zones. It suggests zones that maintain switch and router connection, minimize overlap and duplicate SNMP queries, and improve performance. Zone configuration occurs after ET discovery, and is based on the assumption that the discovery was complete and accurate. Manual manipulation of the the zone of a particular device can be accomplished by editing the following file then restarting ET:

$OV_DB/nnmet/hosts.nnm

Note that "0" is the default zone and the file is overwritten whenever ET discovery takes place (editing this file is not supported by HP).

The sizing of the zones is configured when enabling ET with setupExtTopo.ovpl. The values used are stored in:

> $OV_CONF/nnmet/recVals.conf.

The values used are based on the available RAM, swapspace, and the number and speed of CPU's in the system. The values can be changed after running setupExtTopo.ovpl, but before running Autozone. Note changed values will be overwritten when re-running setupExtTopo.ovpl. The values which give most performance improvements are: numManagedNodes and numManagedObject. Be careful increasing them too much, however, since lack of accuracy in the topology can result.

Password to access ET Configuration page

`setupExtTopo.ovpl` prompts for a username and password when run. This info is stored in administrator block in the following xml file under the main NNM installation directory:

> `$OV_AS\webapps\topology\WEB-INF\dynamicViewsUsers.xml`

Connection editor

Introduced in V7.01, the connection editior allows direct manipulation of the ET topology data. HP added some documentation on the Connection Editor feature in V7.51 which can be found in:

> $OV_DOC/WhitePapers/ConnectionEditor.pdf

In V7.53, this documentation is rolled up in Chapter 2 of the Guide to Using Extended Topology user manual.

The documentation discusses a more generalized approach to connection edits that can be used to span nodes in separate zones and uses the following file:

> $OV_DB/nnmet/generalConnsEdits

Prior to v7.51, HP provided more a bit more limited connection edit functionality through the follwing file:

> $OV_DB/nnmet/connectionEdits

Only endpoints that already exist in topology database can be connected through both files. The files contain OQL queries that perform the desired operations, for example:

To add a connection between nodes Bobby and Jerry, both using
`ifIndex 91`:

```
insert into disco.connectionEdits (m_Name, m_NbrName,
m_Command) values ('bobby.dead.net [ 0 [ 91 ] ]',
'jerry.dead.net[ 0 [ 91 ] ]', 1);
```

To remove an invalid connection between nodes Bobby and Jerry, both
using ifIndex 91:

```
insert into disco.connectionEdits (m_Name, m_NbrName,
m_Command) values ('bobby.dead.net[ 0 [ 91 ] ]',
'jerry.dead.net[ 0 [ 91 ] ]', 2);
```

The last digit in the target statement is the command and is one of
the following:

```
1    Add connection
2    Delete connection
0    Do nothing
```

To use the connection editor, Create, then edit:

```
$OV_DB/nnmet/connectionEdits
```

Once the above file is created, run:

```
ovet_topoconnedit.ovpl
```

Discovery should not have to be re-initiated, but if the expected
updates do not occur, force an ET discovery per procedure on page
10. To determine the proper ifIndex to specify, use:

```
$OV_SUPPORT/NM/ovet_topoquery getNodeByName <target>
```

To dump all the level 2 connection in the NNM/ET topology:

```
ovet_topoconndump.ovpl
```

End nodes not in same zone as connector

To discover connections for nodes that end up in different zones from
their corresponding connector devices, modify the DiscoSchema.cfg
file per the instructions in the section on Connectivity in Chapter 2 of
the Guide to Using Extended Topology user manual.

Add connections for unsupported devices

ET topology may not be complete, or, in some cases, incorrect when a device that is not supported by the device agents is in play. In general, the connection editor can be used to delete inaccurate connections that may be assumed by ET from the device and add new connections to properly show the correct connections. An excellent example is provided in Chapter 2 the Guide to Using Extended Topology user manual.

Layer 3 edge connectivity

Edge connectity is assumed by ET when a subnet is shared by only two addressed interfaces. This assumption may lead to erroneous layer 3 connections in the ET topology. To stop ET from creating connections based on this assumption, uncomment the line that reads: `#enableConnectivity:1` and change "1" to "0" so the line reads: `enableConnectivity:0` in the following file:

$OV_CONF/nnmet/EdgeL3Conn.cfg

Run a new ET discovery cycle per the procedure on page 225.

Exclude nodes from ET discovery

The bridge.noDiscover file can be used to exclude *netmon*-discovered devices from being placed in the ET topology. Also, with the release of NNM 6.31, HP introduced the ability of filters to be used to prevent discovery of whole classes of nodes based on standard NNM filters. For more information on Discovery Filters, see Page 41.

Showing device details for non-SNMP devices

Information for nodes that ET can't otherwise discover can be imported into the ET database for some limited fields including SysName, SysContact, and user definable fields. The ETNonSnmpNodeDataImport.pdf white paper (or, if running V7.53, the Guide to Using Extended Topology user manual.) describes this feature, which requires 10 explicit fields and is configured via the following configuration file:

$OV_CONF/nnmet/nonsnmpnodes.nnm

Use the following command to check the syntax of the configuration file after making changes to it:

```
$OV_SUPPORT/NM/testnonSnmpFile.ovpl nonsnmpnodes.nnm
```

Custom Icons/Symbols can be assigned to non-SNMP devices by using the following special sysObjectID:

```
1.3.6.1.4.1.11.2.3.16.n
```

"n" is the OID instance assigned in the nonsnmpnodes.nnm that corresponds to a specific entry in that file.

Switching routers and routing switches in ET

ET issues custom SNMP polls to devices that are then used to convey topology, connectivity and status information. Since many devices in this class provide multiple management cards, it is important that they are configured to best reflect the actual use of the device and its relationship to other devices in the network.

In essence, if the device is set up to function more like a switch than a router, the management card for switch functions should be enabled, and vice versa if the device acts more in a layer 3 rhelm. If the device truly provides both functions, it may be possible, using DNS, to address both management cards as separate entities which will show up in the topology as separate devices. See Page 90 for more on ET interaction with devices of this type from an APA polling perspective and Page 213 for more on *netmon* discovery considerations and legacy *ovw* implications.

ET command summary, support tools, log files

The following commands are used to create and manipulate the Extended Topology:

```
setupExtTopo.ovpl                  Enable Extended Topology
autozone.ovpl                      Run autozoning
etrestart.ovpl -verbose -disco     Force ET discovery
ovet_topoconnedit.ovpl             ET connection editor
```

The following log files can be used to troubleshoot issues with ET:

```
$OV_PRIV_LOG/ovet_bridge.log       Bridge logfile
$OV_LOG/ovas.log                   Tomcat server logfile
$OV_PRIV_LOG/ovet_disco.log        ET Discovery logfile
```

The support commands listed below can all be found in the following directory: $OV_SUPPORT/NM

`$OV_BIN/ovet_topodump.ovpl`

> There is good documentation in the man/ref pages for this command which dumps ET topology data.

`ovet_demandpoll.ovpl`

> Poll nodes, update status bridge,, enable/disable polling, and tracing. Note the -d (dump) parameter changed in patch 15 to NNM V7.51 and gives detailed info on which filters are in use for interfaces and nodes. More on page 74.

`checkPollCfg`

> This tool displays the APA polling settings for a node, its interfaces, addresses and boards that are configured in paConfig.xml. Note that the displayed values only reflect settings in the paConfig.xml file, not the runtime ovet_poll process.

`ovet_topoquery`

> Use this versatile tool to dump detailed data from the ET database. Also, this tool can be used to change the status of ET topology objects with the setNodeStatus and setIfState flags. Run this tool with the undocumented -internal flag to dump an extensive list of flags for this command.

`ovet_fixTopology.ovpl`

> This tool helps fix anomalies that are attributable to SNMP timeouts during discovery. The script can be run with the -checkDanglingConn option to see if the fix option is needed.

`ovet_generateTopoDeltaReport.ovpl`

> This tool compares the current discovery pass with the last one.

`ovet_ toponame2id.ovpl`

> This tool converts a *ovw* selection name to the ET object ID

`ovet_ toposet.ovpl`

> This tool sets or unsets polling for a object, see page 77

`ovet_reloadTopoDBTbls.ovpl`

> This tool drops and recreates all NNM Extended Topology tables without dropping the NNM data warehouse tables.

`ovet_topoobjcount.ovpl`

> This tool outputs totals for different kinds of objects in the ET database if called with the -all option.

`ovtopodbsnapshot.ovpl`

> This tool makes a snapshot of the ET topology data.

`dumpDiscoStatus.ovpl`

> Displays ET discovery status. All configured agents must get to state 4. Valid state values are:

0: Undefined

> 1: Not Running
> 2: StartUp
> 3: Running
> 4: Finished
> 5: Died

`dumpAgentProgress.ovpl`
> Displays ET discovery status for an ET agent.

`ETsNoSnmpNodes.ovpl`
> This tool outputs the IP addresses of nodes that did not respond to Extended Topology setup SNMP query and can help identify unresponsive SNMP nodes.

`ovet_truncatetopotbls_all.ovpl`
> This script is used to truncate all Solid tables used by the topology service. It can be used to determine if there are interfaces that are misconfigured in ET.

`misconfigIfaces.ovpl`
> This script finds interfaces with speed and/or duplex mismatch.

`zoneTime.ovpl`
> This tool gives info about the time used for discovery during the last ET discovery..

ET and DNS issues

Errors similar to the following may appear in $OV_LOG/ovet_auth.log:

```
2002-05-15 17:07:48 rvd: unrecoverable IP configuration error:
    gethostname() returns '<hostname>',
    gethostbyname() for that returns IP address '15.2.113.5',
    but that address does not match any listed interface.
2002-05-15 17:08:07 rvd: startup aborted: Initialization failed.
Fatal warning : A critical bus error occurred. in ../CRivRvNet.cc at
line 367
```

These errors incicate DNS configuration issues and ovet_auth may dump core and exit. Check the forward and reverse DNS configuration for the affected node.

21. Dynamic Views

Dynamic views are available through the Homebase GUI, which provides Extended Topology representations. Dynamic views are not available unless Extended Topology is enabled, which it is not when NNM is initially installed.

It is important to have a well-discovered network topology before enabling ET. Dynamic Views are controlled by the *ovas* daemon, which is registered through the LRF process. See page 5 for tips on controlling LRF daemons.

Homebase is able to properly display the familiar level 3 representations typical of the legacy *ovw* or Web GUI, neither of which is architecturally able to support ET views. Homebase is completely independent of *ovw* and the legacy databases that support it.

ET still relies on *netmon* for network discovery (except for OAD discovery). From *netmon* discovery data, only basic object data is conveyed to the extended topology database, which ET uses to again poll the devices for ET configuration once ET is enabled. ET probes devices specific agents for in-depth topology data and HP maintains a separate support matrix for extended topology device agents.

Dynamic Views has both server (*ovas*) and client (web page with Java Plug-in) components. Dynamic Views features include:

- Add and Delete nodes
- Expand all or connecting neighbors, path
- Poster printing: large views can be printed in chunks
- Toggle port labels
- Tomcat-based authentication

Dynamic views available

Dynamic views available with NNM 7.5x. Note that some of these views require additional licenses. HSRP, VRRP, OSPF, and IPv6 views require purchase of the Advanced Routing SPI. They are enabled by default when NNM Evaluation code is installed, but expire along with the eval key.

Home Base	Node View
Container View	Access Path View
ET Discovery Status	Path View
Alarm View(APA only)(T)	Node/If Status(APA only)(T)
Neighbor View	Station View
Internet View	Network View
Segment View	VLAN View
Problem Diagnosis View	OSPF View
CDP View	HSRP View (T)
IPV6 Network View	IPV6 Node Detail (T)
IPV6 Interface Detail (T)	IPV6 Prefix Groups (T)
Overlapping Address Domain View	Container View
Interface View (T)	VRRP View (T)

(T) indicates table view

V7.51 added container views (Page 243) and access path view (Page 176). Several other views can be added if using one or more of the add-on SPI's for NNM. V7.53 added the Alarm View, Node Status View and Interface Status View. All three of these new views are only available in the APA is enabled.

Dynamic Views URLs

Dynamic Views URLS changed between NNM V6.31 and NNM V6.41. This is when the Tomcat server replaced the ovpl/ov-cgi-based dynamic views. The former and newer locations are respectively:

    http://<NNM-Server>:3443/OvCgi/ovlaunch.exe
    http://<NNM-Server>:7510/topology/

Specific views can be accessed by URL directly, for example:

    http://<NNM-Server>:3443/OvCgi/nodeView.ovpl
    http://<NNM-Server>:7510/topology/nodeView
    http://<NNM-Server>:7510/topology/segmentView
    http://<NNM-Server>:7510/topology/ospfView
    http://<NNM-Server>:7510/topology/vlanView

Dynamic Views configuration

The following two files are the master configuration entry points for Dynamic Views:

```
$OV_AS/webapps/topology/WEB-INF/web.xml
$OV_CONF/dynamicViews.conf
```

With the release of NNM 7.53, many configuration paramters were split off from web.xml and placed in context-specific xml files in:

```
$OV_AS/webapps/topology/WEB-INF/servletRegistration/
```

To merge xml files in the servletRegistration directory with web.xml, run the following command:

```
$OV_WWW_REG/dynamicViews/oneXmlFileCreator/oneXmlFileCreator.ovpl
```

Dynamic Views concurrent views/users

The number of concurrent users that can access Dynamic Views is not limited to the actual number of users, rather to the number of dynamic views open at any given time. `acceptCount` is the parameter which defines this maximum. Change the default by modifying the `acceptCount` value for the connector classname for port 7510 in the $OV_AS/server.xml file and then `ovstop/ovstart` the *ovas* daemon:

```
<Connector className="org.apache.catalina.connector.http.HttpConnector"
           port="7510" minProcessors="5" maxProcessors="125"
           enableLookups="true" redirectPort="8443"
           acceptCount="10" debug="1" connectionTimeout="-1"/>
```

Dynamic Views access via Webstart

On Windows clients, JAVA Webstart can be used to access the Dynamic View GUI without using a standard web-browser. This is documented in the following user manual: Network Node Manager v7.5 Dynamic Views application integration with Java Web Start Application Manager. Webstart can be installed from:

```
http://nnm-server:7510/topology/webstart
```

Problems may arise in accessing webstart due to the fact that HP populates the .jnlp file with the short name for the server. If an "Unable to load resource" error message is displayed, find the three lines with the NNM server name in the following file and change them to use the FQDN:

$OV_AS/webapps/topology/webstart/dvclient.jnlp

Dynamic views access control

The following script provides the front-end for managing users who have access to dynamic views:

$OV_BIN/dvUsersManager.ovpl

By default, dynamic views are open to all, except for:

- Configuring Extended Topology
- Managing/unmanaging nodes
- Adding/deleting nodes

To add a user role for an operator or an administrator via Tomcat realms if running versions of NNM previous to 7.53, uncomment the block similar to below in $OV_AS/webapps/topology/WEB-INF/web.xml:

```
<security-constraint>
<web-resource-collection>
<web-resource-name>DV Access Secure</web-resource-name>
<url-pattern>/*</url-pattern>
</web-resource-collection>
<auth-constraint>
<role-name>operator</role-name>
<role-name>administrator</role-name>
</auth-constraint>
</security-constraint>
```

If running NNM 7.53, update the similar block in the following file:

$OV_AS/webapps/topology/WEB-INF/servletRegistration/userAuthentication.xml

Then run the following script to add your changes in the userAuthentication.xml file to the web.xml file:

$OV_WWW_REG/dynamicViews/oneXmlFileCreator/oneXmlFileCreator.ovpl

Then add the users and assign roles in:

$OV_AS/webapps/topology/WEB-INF/dynamicViewsUsers.xml

```
<tomcat-users>
<user name="ovuser1" password="mypw"
```

243

```
        roles="operator"/>
    <user name="ovadmin" password="adminpw"
        roles="administrator"/>
</tomcat-users>
```

After any of the above changes restart *ovas* via:

```
ovstop ovas; ovstart ovas
```

The above autheticalion method is BASIC (cleartext passwords are sent over the network). To use MD5 passwords instead, enter the results of the following command as the password above, where <passwd> below is the password to be encrypted:

```
"$OV_JRE"/bin/java -classpath \
"$OV_AS"/server/lib/catalina.jar:"$OV_AS"/bin/bootstrap.jar \
org.apache.catalina.realm.RealmBase -a MD5 <paawd>
```

Note on IPF, the path for the command is: `$OV_JRE"/bin/IA64N/java`

Make sure LD_LIBRARY_PATH is set to:

```
$OV_JRE/lib/IA64N:$OV_JRE/lib/IA64N/server
```

Next, edit the $OV_AS/conf/server.xml file and add the digest parameter of the <Realm> element of the topology Context to digest="MD5", e.g:

```
<Context path="/topology" docBase="topology" debug="0">
    <Realm className="org.apache.catalina.realm.MemoryRealm"
        pathname="webapps/topology/WEB-INF/dynamicViewsUsers.xml"
        digest="MD5"
    />
</Context>
```

Dynamic views via SSL

The following Manual was shipped with NNM V7.53 to explain how to enable SSL for launching Dynamic Views through Java WebStart:

```
$OV_WWW/htdocs/C/manuals/Configuring_SSL_for_DynamicViews.pdf
```

Container views

V7.5.1 introduced this powerful view set to replace the traditional role of *ovw* views in representing customized views of the network with background graphics, etc. A white paper describing this feature can be found in:

```
$OV_DOC/WhitePapers/ContainerAdministration.pdf
```

In V7.53, this documentation is rolled up into the Guide to Using Extended Topology user manual. Unlike *ovw*-based containers, ET containers are not limited to the strict hierarchical constraints of IPMAP. In fact, containers can even be contructed using circular references. Containers can be defined dynamically using filters, which are evaluated each time the container is opened. APA status is propagated through containers. The only real restriction on containers is that they must be hierarchical and each container name must be unique.

The Container Views menus provide a set of container creation and customization options, which are written to an xml file:

$OV_DB/nnmet/containers.xml

This file should not be manipulated directly to create containers. Use the following procedure to manually update the containers.xmll file:

- Backup the existing containers.xml file
- Create a working copy of containers.xml and edit as desired
- overwrite the runtime copy in $OV_DB/nnmet with the working copy
- Run `ovstop ovas ; ovstart ovas`
- Reload the views using the following url option:

http://<hostname>:7510/topology/home?reloadContainers=true

The white paper mentioned above contains an example .xml file and describes the various tags allowed in this file. There are also tips on troubleshooting issues with container views.

Container View customization best practices

Adding nodes directly to the cointainers.xml is always preferable to expanding a particular container's view using GUI operation and then using the "Save Layout" option in the Container Setup drop down menu. The reason for this is that any objects which are added to the containers via the "Expand" options are only saved by object ID in the containers.xml file. This makes ongoing management using the xml file difficult.

Avoid use of the "Include Node . . ." menu item when using filters. The two don't mix well. It's best to create filters and then strictly use filters for containment. The "Include Node. . ." menu is really best used to test out a container view. For deployment, try to stick with filter-based containers.

Jpeg (.jpg) files for background images resize better than other image files types. It is best not to show connectivity between containers by setting showContainerConnectivity="false" on all containers. There is an example in the whitepaper.

Don't put too many nodes in a container. They are recalculated every time they are opened. Try to cap the size around 200 nodes or so. If connectivity is not important to show in a container, set the below flag:

> showNodeConnectivity="false"

This makes the view's performance improve greatly, so consider setting this for all containers. A neighbor view for connectivity from a node can always be launched to show connectivity. Connectivity within a container can be problematic because key nodes may not pass the filter and may not be in the container, thus possibly degrading the accuracy of the connectivity.

Make a second backup of the containers.xml file and call it containers.raw.xml. Edit this file and remove all references to object IDs. This will be useful if the ET database has to be wiped and re-created from scratch.

Container View operations

If running versions prior to V7.53, the below operations are *not* covered in:

> $OV_DOC/WhitePapers/ContainerAdministration.pdf.

In V7.53, this documentation is rolled up into the Guide to Using Extended Topology user manual.

Delete a container:

> Edit the file: $OV_DB/nnmet/containers.xml.

> `ovstop ovas` when editing this file since it could be changed by *ovas*. Remove any containerReference tags and the entire container tag for the container to be deleted.

Rename a container:

> `ovstop ovas` and edit $OV_DB/nnmet/containers.xml and simple replace the name in the container name tag and in the containerReference name tag.

Remove selected objects from a container:

> Objects that had been saved from the GUI do not have node names associated with them in the container.xml file. To remove objects of this type, move the objects to be deleted into a corner of the screen, then "Save Layout." Edit the containers.xml file and the desired objects can be identified by their X and Y coordinates.

Scaling container icons:

> To change the size of the container relative to the background graphic, the size of the background graphic graphic must be increased. This can be done in any graphics editing tool such as Microsoft Picture Manager. Replace the image files in:

> > $OV_WWW/htdocs/images/backgrounds.

> Restart *ovas* or call the following URL to reload the new image:

> > http://<hostname>:7510/topology/home?reloadContainers=true

Container Views access control

Container Views access control is only available in NNM V7.53 and later. By default, every container is accessible to every user. An access list can include a list of users and/or a list of roles. User-based access lists provide a way to grant access to individual users. Users with the role of administrator automatically have access to all containers, even if the container has an access list. An empty access control list allows only administrators to access the container.

Users and roles are defined as a part of the user authentication process. Before enabling container access control, enabling user authentication is required. See page 243 for more information on Dynamic Views access control. To enable access control for a container, set the `enableAccessControl` to "true" or "false" in the container definition in the containers.xml file. Then, add an access list similar to the following example:

```
<accessList>
    <user name="myuser"/>
    <role name="myrole"/>
</accessList>
```

If user access is configured for containers, the access assignments apply to the Node Status View, Interface Status View, and Alarm View. In these views, the nodes, interfaces, or alarms a user can see are determined by the total set of nodes in all the containers to which the user has access.

Container View example

The example below (Figure 21.1) shows a container view that is partially containerized. That is, some of the objects on the maps represent containers, and some represent parts of the standard L3 view. Screenshot is from an active installation at MøllerGruppen in Norway, with permission to use by Bjørn Asprem.

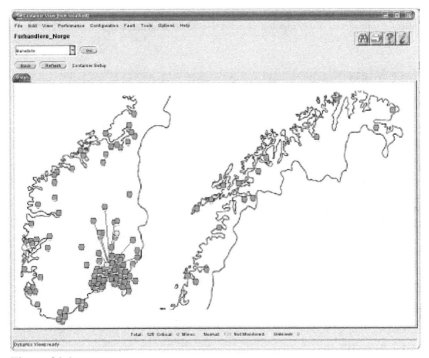

Figure 21.1

Node View

Support for filtering of node views was added in V7.5. This was based, however, on legacy NNM filter definitions. V7.51 added support for ET topology filters to be used instead. This is more efficient, consistent and scalable. If running V7.51 or above, the procedure to switch to ET-based filters is found in:

$OV_DOC/WhitePapers/nodeView_ETfilters.pdf

249

In V7.53, this documentation is rolled up into the Guide to Using Extended Topology user manual.

A node view that employs a filter can be called by url:

http://"nnmserver":7510/topology/nodeView?filter=filtername

V7.51 Intermediate Patch 18 fixed a problem with the URL ipRange specification, so these can now be used to qualify node views, e.g.:

http://"nnmserver":7510/topology/nodeView?filter=filtername&ipRange=10.2.*.*

Interface View

To set Interface View to not show disabled interfaces, change the includeDisabled parameter from 1 to 0 in the following file and restart *ovas* using `ovstart/ovstop`, but only if running versions of NNM previous to 7.53:

$OV_AS/webapps/topology/WEB-INF/web.xml

If running NNM 7.53, change the includeDisabled parameter from 1 to 0 in the following file:

$OV_AS/webapps/topology/WEB-INF/servletRegistration/1IfaceServlet.xml

Then run the following script to add your changes to the web.xml file:

$OV_WWW_REG/dynamicViews/oneXmlFileCreator/oneXmlFileCreator.ovpl

Restart *ovas* using `ovstart/ovstop`.

Node Status and Interface Status Views

These views were added in V7.53 to display service oriented management information about nodes and interfaces such as who is assigned to oversee the node, the current lifecycle state of the node, and notes that can be added by an operator.

These views are note enabled by default and require that ET and the APA are enabled. Use the following commands to enable or disable these two views:

$OV_BIN/enableNSVandISV.ovpl

$OV_BIN/disableNSVandISV.ovpl

Alarm View

Introduced in NNM V7.53, this tabular view is designed to replace the Java Alarm Browser and has all the same functionality. The Alarm view requires that ET and the APA are enabled. Note that Container View Access Control (Page 247) applies to Alarm View as well.

Neighbor View

In NNM V7.51 and higher, the default Neighbor View hop count can be changed. In complex networks, the default of "2" may create views that are too complex. To change the default, edit the following file and change the `defaultNumHops` value and restart *ovas* using `ovstart/ovstop`, but only if running versions of NNM previous to 7.53:

$OV_AS/webapps/topology/WEB-INF/web.xml

If running NNM 7.53, change the `defaultNumHops` value in the following file:

$OV_AS/webapps/topology/WEB-INF/servletRegistration/1NeighborServlet.xml

Then run the following script to add your changes to the web.xml file:

$OV_WWW_REG/dynamicViews/oneXmlFileCreator/oneXmlFileCreator.ovpl

Restart *ovas* using `ovstart/ovstop`:

VRRP View

Support for this view appeared in a patch to V7.5 and a white paper was supplied with V7.51 in $OV_DOC/WhitePapers/VRRP.pdf. This documentation was rolled into the Guide to Using Extended Topology in V7.53. VRRP View requires purchase of the Advanced Routing SPI. VRRP support by NNM has the following capabilities:

- Discover virtual router groups on devices that support RFC 2787
- RC-VRRP MIB allows Nortel devices to discover VRRP groups
- FOUNDRY-SN-IP-VRRP-MIB discovers virtual router groups

Special VRRP OpenView enterprise events are generated with VRRP protocol support and special VRRP correlators are also used. Check the following LRF flag to netmon to see if it is set to true:

251

migrateHsrpVirtualIP=true

If not, set this flag per the LRF procedure on page 5 and then verify that any VRRP virtual interfaces have not been added to the NNM topology using `ovtopodump`. Remove them using: `ovtopofix -r <router_name>`.

Interpreting VRRP Group Status:

Unknown (blue)	State undetermined
Normal (green)	The VRRP Group is operational
Warning (cyan)	The VRRP group has an interface in the Active State and an interface in the Standby state, but it also has at least one interface that is not in the Listen state.
Minor (yellow)	The VRRP Group has an interface in the Active state, but there is no interface in the VRRP group which is in the Standby state.
Major (orange)	Multiple interfaces in the VRRP group are in the Active state, or multiple interfaces in the VRRP group are in the Standby state.
Critical (red)	The group has no interface in the Active state.

OSPF View

ET's OSPF View provides a representation of an OSPF Area. By default, it shows Area 0 (0.0.0.0). Tables show routers filtered by the area, with basic data including neighbors. OSPF View requires purchase of the Advanced Routing SPI.

OSPF discovery uses RFC 1253 or RFC 1850 MIBS. The RFC 1850 MIB (OSPF V2) is backwards-compatible with RFC 1253.

A seed IP address of an OSPF router running the MIB is required to start the discovery. Enter this seed router in the configuration file below. The seed file can be configured to discover via an inclusive rule or an exclusive rule, but *not* both. Once the seed file is populated, run the startup script and check the log file for errors.

OSPF Disco configuration file:	$OV_CONF/nnmet/Ospf.cfg
OSPF Disco startup script:	$OV_BIN/ospfdis.ovpl
Error log:	$OV_PRIV_LOG/ospfdis.err
Database:	$OV_DB/ospf/ospfdis.data

Path View

Path View computes paths using SNMP queries in real time. Contrast this with Problem Diagnosis, which uses probes and maintains usage data over time (page 175) and Access Path View, a contributed application also known as Smart Path (page 176.) NNM 7.53 introduced the ability to use ET data to provide more intelligent paths. To enable this feature, set the value for `restrictToET` to `true` in the following file:

$OV_AS/webapps/topology/WEB-INF/servletRegistration/1IPathServlet.xml

Then run the following script to add your changes to the web.xml file:

$OV_WWW_REG/dynamicViews/oneXmlFileCreator/oneXmlFileCreator.ovpl

Restart *ovas* using `ovstart/ovstop`.

The following configuration file can be used to change the Extended Topology algorithms for computing paths:

$OV_CONF/nnmet/topology/NMActiveRoute.Conf

The V7.53 Guide to Using Extended Topology lists the conf file parameters and how they can be changed in Chapter 6.

HSRP View

HSRP management requires purchase of the Advanced Routing SPI. Note that some upgrade packages for NNM included the Advanced Routing SPI. HSRP management is supported only for Cisco HSRP and HSRP EXT MIBs.

Cisco IOS's 12.1(14) and 12.2(13) require manual configuration for the tracked interface information (standby IPs) to appear in the MIB. Older versions automatically populate this info.

To configure NNM to manage HSRP routers see the Guide to Using Extended Topology. To force an ET Discovery, see the procedure on page 10. To check to see if ET discovered any HSRP groups:

```
UNIX:   $OV_SUPPORT/NM/ovet_topoquery \getAllHSRPs |
        grep EntityName | cut -d: -f2
```

Windows: Run: `ovet_topoquery > out.txt` and search out.txt for EntityName, and look for the IP address on that line

Interpreting HSRP Status:

Unknown (blue)	State undetermined
Normal (green)	All standby routers are available.
Warning (cyan)	One IF in the Active state, and one IF in the Standby state, but also at least one that is not in the Listen state. One or more standbys are unavailable.
Minor (yellow)	One IF in the Active state, no IFs in the Standby state. No standby available.
Major (orange)	Multiple IFs are in Active state, or multiple IFs in the Standby state. Routing functionality likely affected.
Critical (red)	No interface in the Active state.

Troubleshooting HSRP:

The log file is $OV_PRIV_LOG/ovet_daHSRPSnmp.log

Managing overlapping address spaces (OAD)

Also known as DupIP and OAD, this capability is only supported in NNM versions 7.0 or higher and requires the AE version. In addition, extended topology discovery must be enabled. OADs are discovered and monitored by the *ovet_poll* daemon and OAD objects are maintained in the ET databases, but the APA need not be enabled to manage OADs. Discovered OAD nodes are not visible to any of the NNM legacy databases or GUIs, and thus are not displayed in *ovw* maps. OAD configuration and troubleshooting is covered in Chapter 3 of the Guide to Using Extended Topology and in Chapter of that guide in V7.53.

The devices in the address space must be reachable from the NNM server via a device that provides Static NAT and those devices must have valid route to the NNM server. Status can be managed on the overlapping devices, only if ICMP and/or SNMP are not firewalled along the way. In order for NNM's OAD to properly work, the NAT implementation needs to be compliant with the RFC's, not dynamic, and not nested.

An example of dupip.conf can be found in the directory: $OV_CONF/nnmet/dupip. A customized copy of this dupip.conf needs to be created for each overlapping address space. A unique address space name defines a subdirectory under

$OV_CONF/nnmet/dupip so the configuration file name for the address space named "phil" would have to be:

```
$OV_CONF/nnmet/dupip/phil/dupip.conf
```

The ovdupip command can be used to test and to query the OAD configuration. There is no man/ref page for dupip.conf in NNM 7.01 or 7.5, but the file itself has very good help. There is a man/ref for ovdupip.

Seed files, as explained in the dupip.conf file, are necessary for proper discovery of the OADs by ET. Once the configuration has been validated using ovdupip, "refresh configuration" must be selected in the OAD section of the ET configuration GUI, then discovery for the new OAD can be initiated in the discovery section.

Use the below command to specify an overlapping address domain ID (OADID) for an entity to be polled. If this option is used then the nodename or virtualIP is assumed to be a private IP address. The OADID must be the ID and not the overlapping domain name. To map the name to an OADID, perform the command ovdupip -i a:

```
ovet_demandpoll.ovpl -r <OADID>
```

Any nodes listed in the OAD Configuration file should also be entered into the *netmon*.nodiscover file and existing NNM-discovered nodes must be purged from the IPMAP topology for the OAD to be properly discovered by ET.

When the OAD is discovered, the OAD table display shows the node name, the management IP address, the private IP address, the route distinguisher, and the node's status. In the event browser, the address space name is postfixed to the management IP address.

On Windows, when migrating from NNM version 7.0 to 7.5x, run the following command to update OAD zone ID's to the new 7.5x format:

```
%OV_BIN%\migrate70to701ZoneNumber.ovpl
```

In NNM 7.0, deleting an OAD (Overlapping Address Domain) required running a full discovery. In NNM 7.01, a full discovery is no longer necessary.

Delete an overlapping address spaces (OAD)

Follow this procedure to delete an OAD called "haze" without initiating full discovery:

1. Go to the $OV_CONF/nnmet/dupip/haze directory
2. Edit "dupip.seed" file and comment out all entries using a "#"
3. Go to the ET Config GUI
4. Select the "Overlapping Address Domains" tab
5. Press the "Refresh Configuration and Activate Changes"
6. After a message indicating success, press the "Continue"
7. Select "haze" OAD from the table and press "Discover Zone"
8. Wait until "Please wait" message disappears, then press "Continue"
9. Wait to see a "Discovery Complete" pop-up message from Home Base
10. Go to OAD View from Home Base, and confirm "haze" is not in the Table
11. Delete directory "$OV_CONF/nnmet/dupip/haze" and its contents
12. Go to the ET Config GUI
13. Select the "Overlapping Address Domains" tab
14. Press the "Refresh Configuration and Activate Changes"
15. After a message indicating success, press the "Continue"

NNM 7.0, deleting an OAD (Overlapping Address Domain) required running a full discovery. In NNM 7.01, a full discovery is no longer

IPV6

NNM's IPV6 support is an ET feature - IPV6-discovered devices are not visible under legacy NNM databases or GUIs. IPV6 devices are discovered and polled via ICMPv6 ping, and IPV6 discovery is not enabled by default. IPV6 discovery can be enabled by running:

```
setupExtTopo.ovpl
```

The IPV6 dynamic views in NNM 7.5 and higher shows layer 3 connectivity. Licenses are required for both IPV4 (NNM) & IPV6 (ET), and only dual-stacked (IPV4 & IPV6) routers are supported (i.e. the supporting router must be discovered via *netmon* first). Hitachi, NEC, Juniper and Cisco equipment is supported, and IPV6 discovery is only supported on HP-UX 11.11 and Solaris 8 & 9 NNM installations.

Only RFC 2465-supported devices can be fully managed (i.e. properly mapped in topology), but v6 end-nodes are discovered and polled for status via ICMPv6 ping. An additional license for the IPV6 nodes is required. For HP-UX, version 11i is required along with the appropriate OS bundles. More info can be found under the IPV6 SPI for NNM at HP's web site.

Configure IPv6 discovery using the procedure outlines in the Guide to Using Extended Topology. There, the following five control files in the $OV_CONF/nnmet directory are documented:

>
> IPv6.conf
> IPv6Polling.conf
> IPv6Prefix.conf
> IPv6Scope.conf
> IPv6Seed.conf

The following IPV6 Status events are supported in NNM 7.x:

>
> - Address DOWN
> - Address UP (log only)
> - Interface Status Change (log only)
> - Node Status Change (log only)
> - Prefix Group Status Change (log only)

There is a Pair-wise correlation for Address UP and Address DOWN. If Address UP occurs less than 10 minutes after a corresponding Address DOWN, both events are suppressed. See page 130 for more about this correlation.

If an IPv6 node is down or unreachable during NNM Extended Topology discovery, NNM may not include that node in the ET database (depending on the presence of that node's addresses in the ARP caches of IPv6-responsive nodes). This differs from the behavior of IPv4 nodes, which will be treated as "unresponsive" nodes due to their presence in NNM's databases.

On Solaris platforms, if IPv6 nodes are not configured with hostnames, *pmd* performance will suffer as the monitorIPv6Agent sends (many) status events about these nodes. To address this issue, configure the ipNoLookup cache to prevent these lookups by:

1. Discover IPv6 devices
2. Add the addresses discovered to a file called <filename>
3. Run `snmpnolookupconf -file <filename>`

Port Admin tool

This tool introduced in V7.53 provides a GUI for disabling/enabling APA status polling to ports of interfaces that formerly required using the `ovet_toposet.ovpl` command. To launch the tool, select a target node in any Dynamic View and choose menu selection Edit -> ET Monitoring Manager -> Port Admin Tool.

Aggregated port support

Support for aggregated ports in ET started with V7.5, where multiple physical ports on devices that support Cisco PAgP would be represented via trunk virtual ports. V7.51 added support for Nortel's MLT and SMLT via the ovet_daBaySSw(BaystackSwitchAgent) and ovet_daPassSw (PassportSwitch) device agents. For more information on support for Nortel aggregated ports, see the following white paper:

> $OV_DOC/Whitepapers/MLT.pdf

In V7.53, this documentation is rolled up into the Guide to Using Extended Topology user manual. For details on how aggregated ports are handled by the APA, see Page 79.

Suport for discovery of aggregated ports on Alcatel Timetra and Riverston switches was added via new device agents in June, 2007. See Page 227 for how to check for latest device agents.

Increase JAVA heap size

In large environments, increasing JAVA heap size will help reduce running out of memory issues that may crop up. Add the following LRF flag "-Xmx384m" to ovas.lrf per the procedure on Page 5. This specifies a heap size of 384 Meg. The max is 512m but this is not recommended and the default is 128 MB.

Add, delete, manage or unmanage objects via URLs

This handy feature was added in NNM 6.41 to provide a remote facility to replace `loadhosts`, `ovtopofix` and other assorted local facilities for manipulating objects. The URLs are:

> http:// <NNM-Server>::7510/topology/add
> http:// <NNM-Server>::7510/topology/delete
> http:// <NNM-Server>::7510/topology/manage
> http:// <NNM-Server>::7510/topology/unmanage

These URLs are configured via the following xml files:

> All: $OV_AS/webapps/topology/WEB-INF/dynamicViewsUsers.xml
> Prior to NNM 7.53: $OV_AS/webapps/topology/WEB-INF/web.xml
> 7.53: ...webapps/topology/WEB-INF/servletRegistration/1ManageServlets.xml

Troubleshooting dynamic views

The first place to look when troubleshooting Dynamic Views issues is the JAVA console.

On UNIX use: /opt/java1.4/jre/binControlPanel
On Windows: Control panel -> Java Plug-in

Always confirm the Web server is running.

On UNIX: ps –ef | grep ovhttpd
On Windows: Control panel ->Admin Tools ->
                     Internet Information Manager ->
                     Web server

Confirm there is a match between topology views and topology databases. For more information on ovet_topoquery, see page 94. For more information on ovtopodump see page 69.

Several problems with dynamic views may arise due to JAVA caching. Caching can be safely disable from the JAVA control panel mentioned above.

Dynamic views update issues due to caching

There are several layers of caching possible that could lead to stale topology information (due to lack of update) in dynamic views.

Browser cache: For IE, clear via Tools -> Internet Options
                ->General tab -> Temporary Internet files -> Delete Files.

Proxy servers: These also often do caching. The best practice is to disable. For IE
                do the following: Tools -> Internet Options -> Connections tab ->
                LAN Settings -> Uncheck "Use a proxy server for your LAN".

Java Plug-in Cache:
                On Windows, navigate: Start -> Control Panel -> Java Plug-in ->
                Cache tab -> Clear.

                On UNIX, browse to ${JPIDIR}/jre/ControlPanel.html, where ${JPIDIR}
                is the location where the Java Plug-in is installed. The cache can be cleared
                at this point.

Web content optimizers or internet accelerators:

259

These network devices can hijack URL requests and serve content that is stale. In most cases, these servers can be configured to pass either requests from certain clients or content from certain servers.

Dynamic views registration files

Extensions to dynamic views are added using XML files under:

$OV_WWW_REG/dynamicViews/C/

HP menus are in dynamicViews.xml (do not modify this file). All files get merged automatically into menusettings.xml located in:

$OV_WWW/htdocs/$LANG/dynamicViews

Many traditional ovw menu settings are only visible to dynamic views that are launched locally. Most SNMP graphing tools under the performance menu bar fall into this category. To enable these menu items to be visible to those who launch dynamic views from remote browsers, change the localOnly flag from true to false for each menu item in the dynamicViews.xml file.

Dynamic views and edge connectivity

Dynamic Views has special support for displaying layer 3 edge router connectivity across WANs in V7.5 and later. In that version, point-to-point connectivity is addressed, but not point-to-multi-point.

Examples of supported protocols include ATM, Frame Relay, t1/t3 and Sonet. Typically, such connections will be two-node subnets with 30-bit subnet masks, and this is configurable in the following file:

$OV_CONF/nnmet/Edge3Conn.cfg

Transfer MIB application builder apps to Dynamic views

Follow the steps below to transfer *ovw* Menu bar applications that were built using the MIB Application Builder into Dynamic Views:

1. To invoke MIB Application Builder app through a "traditional" web interface; use:

    http://nnmserver:3443/OvCgi/snmpviewer.exe

    Select MIB Application Builder application, select "Display in New Window." In new window, right click and look at Properties, e.g.:

```
http://nnmserver.xx.com:3443/OvCgi/webappmon.exe?ins=res
new&sel=somenode.xx.com&app=IP+Tables&act=Disk+Space&arg
=helpBrowser+ovw%3aHPdiskSpace+%09%09++++++appendSelectL
ist+appendSelectListToTitle+%09%09++++++headingLine+1+co
mmandTitle+%22Disk+Space%22+%09%09++++++iconName+%22Disk
+Space%22+%09%09++++++cmd+rbdf&cache=2795
```

2. In menu items XML file, copy the URL from properties window and modify slightly, as below:

```
<!-- A C T I O N S  -->
<Actions>
<action actionId="Disk Space"
url="http://${localhost}${localport}/OvCgi/webappmon.exe?i
ns=resnew&amp;sel=${names}&amp;app=IP+Tables&amp;act=Disk+
Space&amp;arg=helpBrowser+ovw%3aHPdiskSpace+%09%09++++++ap
pendSelectList+appendSelectListToTitle+%09%09++++++heading
Line+1+commandTitle+%22Disk+Space%22+%09%09++++++iconName+
%22Disk+Space%22+%09%09++++++cmd+rbdf&amp;cache=2795"/>
</Actions>
```

3. Define <menu> entry to use new action.

Customize dynamic views-based alarm browser

The following file can be used to configure the JAVA-based alarm browser:

$OV_WWW/conf/NNM.spec

Examples of configuration entry points include color definitions, filter group and action definitions.

A useful customization to this file is to disable access to the event correlation configuration screens . Do this but commenting out the following line:

CATGETS(14, 11, "Event Correlation Configuration") f.action "a_id11";

After making changes to the NNM.spec file, stop and retart the *ovalarmsrv* daemon and refresh any open browser views.

22. Databases and Reporting

There are several distinct databases used within recent versions of NNM. Some are relational and some are flat file databases. The NDBM flat file operational databases include: map, object, topology, snmpCollect, Binary Event Store.

The SNMP configuration database: ovsnmp.conf, is not considered an operational database. It is composed of 5 NDBM database files, three of which hold polling and SNMP configuration data, and the other two are caching databases. *cachedb* holds a list of hostname to IP address mappings and IP address to hostname mappings; *nolookupdb* holds hostnames that will not be resolved to an IP Address. Problem Diagnosis (PD), which has been bundled with NNM AE since version 6.4, stores probe data in a text file database.

Relational databases used by NNM include the data warehouse and the Extended Topology DB. The data warehouse (DW) holds exported trend, topology, and event data for relational use by the reporting subsystem. This is also referred to as the "embedded" database, and it uses the Solid DBMS OEM'd from Solidtech. Extended Topology uses the same Solid DB instance as the DW, but is a separate database that is not exposed (the schema is not available). The DW part of the Solid DB can be changed to use Oracle (or on Windows, MSSQL) instead, but the ET part cannot.

Data warehouse

Solid DB gets data via automatic export of Events, *snmpCollect* and topology data. The export happens through the *ovrequestd* daemon's internal scheduler. The command `request_list schedule` shows the exact timing for each export in UNIX `cron` format). Events get exported every 30 minutes, topology twice daily, and trend data every 40 minutes. The exports can be changed by editing the `request.properties` files in the subdirectories under:

```
$OV_ANALYSIS\ovrequestd\requests\C\export
```

Events are exported to the nnm_event_detail table, *snmpCollect* data is exported to the snmp_raw_trend table. The following directory contains the Solid DB backups, which can be entirely removed if there is a need to recover disk space:

```
$OV_DB/analysis/default/backup
```

You can stop Solid from doing backups by editing solid.ini in $OV_DB/analysis/default and commenting the following line with a semicolon:

```
At=23:00 backup
```

After making changes to solid.ini, run `ovstop ovdbcheck` and then `ovstart ovdbcheck`.

Solid database

Details for the data warehouse's use of Solid are given above. The extended topology database is on the same instance of Solid but it cannot be queried with `ovdwquery`. The ET database schemas are not publicly available. ET data can be queried, however, using:

```
$OV_SUPPORT/NM/ovet_topoquery
```

Solid DB documentation:

```
http://www.solidtech.com/devresources/documentation.html
```

Solid ODBC Drivers:

```
$OV_NEW_CONF/OVDB-RUN/conf/analysis (UNIX), or
$OV_WWW/htdocs/classes/solid (Windows), or
$OV_CONF/analysis/reportTemplates/Solid/driver, or
http://www.solidtech.com/library/software.html
```

Data warehouse queries

Queries can be made to the data warehouse data via the `ovdwquery` command. SQL commands can be directly entered, or placed in a file, and then called in with the `-file` option. The default user and password are shown in the below example query:

```
ovdwquery -u ovdb -password ovdb -file router.query
```

The `-x pwdfile <password file>` was added and the `-securefile`
option was updated in NNM V7.51 to make this command NIAP
compliant. Thus –u and –password options shown above were
deprecated. See the man/ref pages for usage details.

The Solid DB schema can be unraveled by looking at the table creation
scripts in:

```
$OV_CONF/analysis/sqlScripts/tables_*
```

The following predefined built-in parameters may be used in the
SQL WHERE clauses:

```
$NOW, $BEGIN_TODAY, $BEGIN_YESTERDAY, $BEGIN_WEEK,
$BEGIN_LAST_WEEK, $BEGIN_MONTH, $BEGIN_LAST_MONTH,
$BEGIN_YEAR, and $BEGIN_LAST_YEAR
```

Some examples of SQL queries follow:

Return all nodes by hostname:
```
SELECT ip_hostname FROM nnm_nodes;
```

Return all nodes by SNMP sysname:
```
SELECT sysname FROM nnm_nodes;
```

Return all managed interfaces from certain hosts:
```
SELECT a.snmp_ifphysaddr,  b.ip_hostname,
       c.ip_address
FROM  nnm_objects a, nnm_nodes b, nnm_interfaces c,
      nnm_objects d
WHERE c.topo_id = a.topo_id
       and c.node_id = d.ovw_id
       and d.topo_id = b.topo_id
       and b.ip_hostname like 'S%lab'
       and a.ip_status != 5;
```

Return all managed interfaces matching SNMP ifDescr:
```
SELECT  a.snmp_ifphysaddr, c.ip_address
FROM nnm_objects a,nnm_interfaces c
WHERE c.snmp_ifdescr = 'Compaq
       Ethernet/FastEthernet or Gigabit NIC'
       and c.topo_id = a.topo_id;
```

Return today's exported events:
```
SELECT * from nnm_event_detail
WHERE event_timestamp > $BEGIN_TODAY;
```

Return only IP addressed nodes and interfaces:
```
SELECT n."ip_hostname", n."sysname", i."snmp_ifname",
       i."ip_address"
FROM "ovdb"."nnm_nodes" n,"ovdb"."nnm_objects" o,
```

264

```
    "ovdb"."nnm_interfaces" i
WHERE n."topo_id" = o."topo_id"
      and o."ovw_id" = i."node_id"
      and i."ip_address" <> '0.0.0.0';
```

Solid database performance

In highly-scaled environments, there is no performance advantage to switching from Solid to Oracle. Oracle handles simultaneous access better than Solid, but overall, Solid is faster than Oracle per HP's documentation. In highly-scaled environments, be sure that the Solid DB is not on the same drive as the OS. Using Raid 0 or some other RAID in combination with moving Solid off the OS drive can facilitate an increase in performance of 10% or more.

With the release of V7.51, a white paper appeared on how to improve Solid database performance in the $OV_DOC/WhitePapers directory. It is not clear from the white paper whether the recommendations provided can apply to earlier versions of NNM/Solid. Some of them are known to do so. All of the below paramers are set in the following file:

$OV_DB/analysis/default/solid.ini

For CacheSize, the white paper recommend increasing this from the default of 10MB to 512MB. The minimum is 512KB and there is no maximum, but HP recommends the maximum not exceed the amount of physical memory.

The Threads default is 5, which HP says is adequate for systems with one or two processors. Increase Threads if the NNM server has more than two processors. A common recommendation is to set threads to (2x (num CPU's) + 1). Setting ForceThreadsToSystemScope to "yes" on NNM Servers running Solaris can dramatically improve performance on that platform only. After making changes to solid.ini, stop and restart all openview processes.

Determining the version of Solid

On UNIX:

```
what /opt/OV/bin/ovdbrun |grep Embedded
```

On Windows:

```
find /i "embedded" "%OV_DB%\analysis\default\solmsg.*"
```

265

Database command utilities

Data warehouse configuration tools:

ovdbcheck	Start, stop or monitor DW
ovdbdebug	Validates DB connections
ovdwconfig.ovpl	Configure ODBC source, security
ovdbsetup	Integrate DB into existing Oracle
ovdwloader	Reload data into DW
ovdwunloader	Copies DW to special file or to CSV

Raw database maintenance tools:

ovcoltosql	Convert *snmpCollect* data to trend
ovcoldelsql	Reduce or delete raw trend data
ovcolqsql	Retrieve and summarize trend data
ovdwtopo	Retrieve topology data to DW
ovdwtrend	Export, sum and trims trend data
(combines ovcoltosql & ovcoldelsql)	
ovdwevent	Export, trim event to/from DW
ovdweventflt	Restrict events exported to DW

Reporter URLs

Use the following URLs to access the NNM reporting interface:

http://nnmserver[:port]/OvCgi/nnmRptPresenter.exe
http://nnmserver[:port]/OvCgi/nnmRptConfig.exe

nnmRptConfig.exe is the program used to configure reports and nnmRptPresenter.exe is the program to view web reports.

Connecting Crystal Reports to NNM (Windows)

Connecting NNM report data to Crystal Reports requires Crystal Report 9 Professional version or greater. To do this, follow these steps:

1. Copy stcw3230fe.dll to C:\winnt\system32 on NNM system.
2. Go to ODBC in System DSN
   Datasource name : ovdbrun
   Description   :
   Network Name   : tcpip <NNM server IP> 2690
3. Within Crystal Reports:
   Select create a new connection -> ODBC (RDO)
   username : ovdb
   password : ovdb

Using Oracle for the data warehouse

The most commonly asked question posed by those who are trying to decide whether to use Oracle for NNM's data warehouse in place of Solid is: "Can NNM share the same DB instance with an OVO installation?" The NNM DW can indeed share an OVO Oracle instance, which is named "openview" by default. A common problem with Oracle as DW for NNM in large-scale environments is that the `ovdb.nnm_event_varbinds` table tends to fill up. To extend this table, issue the following SQL command:

```
ALTER TABLE ovdb.nnm_event_varbinds storage maxextents
unlimited;
```

See the "Managing" guide for instructions on changing from Solid to Oracle for a given platform. In summary, the following commands are used to manage the switch:

```
ovdbsetup
ovdbcheck
ovdbdebug
```

On UNIX platforms, if the Oracle SID is set to anything other than the default "openview," subsequent invocations of `ovdbsetup` may generate errors. To correct this, make sure the correct value of $ORACLE_SID is placed in the listener.ora file, located as listed below:

HPUX:	/etc/listener.ora
SOLARIS:	/var/opt/oracle/listener.ora
LINUX:	$ORACLE_HOME/network/admin/listener.ora

NNM does support 64-bit Oracle databases. A comment in the Support Matrix references that Oracle is only supported in 32-bit versions on HP-UX and Solaris. This statement was removed in the NNM 7.5 Release Notes. It is not the case that the Oracle database server is 64-bit. Some versions of 64-bit Oracle did not deliver 32-bit Oracle database drivers. Given that NNM is 32-bit, NNM would not have a valid database driver to operate, but NNM now relies upon a database driver provided by the ODBC vendor called OVoraWire. With this driver, NNM is assured that a 32-bit driver exists.

ODBC Driver Manager Version errors

When using a external DB under Windows, the following ODBC Driver Manager pop-up window for a version mismatch for various ODBC utilities may occur, for example:

```
The ODBC resource DLL
(C:\WINNT40\System32\odbcint.dll)
 is a different version than the ODBC driver manager
(C:\WINNT40\System32\ODBC32.dll).
```

If these occur, reinstall the ODBC components to ensure proper operation by applying the latest Service Pack. This mismatched DLL problem is a known issue with Windows and is not unique to NNM. See Microsoft Knowledge Base article: Q170769 for more information.

Accessing DW data directly from Microsoft Excel

Install the solid ODBC drivers (see above) on a Windows client running Excel. In the control panel create a data source with the driver and the machines details. From Excel, select: Data -> Get External Data -> New Database Query. Select the data source created above and follow the prompts.

Data warehouse compatibility: NNM 6.0 to NNM 6.1

The ODBC interface between NNM and Solid changed from NNM 6.01 to NNM 6.1. In 6.01, shared memory was used, in 6.1 TCP/IP is used. NNM 6.01 (Windows) was the last version to provide Excel templates and NNM 6.1 introduced the web-based reporting infrastructure. Excel templates no longer work after NNM 6.1.

Disable the data warehouse

Disabling the data warehouse is not a catastrophic operation. In fact, it can greatly improve the performance of the Solid DB in highly-scaled environments. The only consequence to disabling the DW is that reports will have missing data. To disable the data warehouse, run:

```
ovstop ovrequestd
ovdelobj $OV_LRF/ovrequestd.lrf
```

More information about LRF files can be found on page 5. The scripts that populate and aggregate this data are:

```
ovdwquery, ovdwevent and ovcoltosql
```

These scripts are called by *ovrequestd* daemon to populate the data warehouse. The population of data into the data warehouse can also be stopped by commenting out the at job in the following file:

```
%OV_DV/analysis/default/solid.ini
```

Rebuild the data warehouse

Run the below command on any version of NNM above v6.1 to rebuild the data warehouse from scratch. All data will be cleared in this process, and the default tables will be populated. This is an easy way to recover disk space. Note that running this command will stop all OpenView processes, so make sure user sessions are closed.

```
$OV_BIN/ovdwconfig.ovpl -type embedded -reload
```

Rebuild the ET Database

Run the below command on any version of NNM above v6.1 to rebuild the Extended Topology database, which is a separate SOLID database. Stopping the OpenView daemons will cause this script to fail, so leave them running:

```
$OV_SUPPORT/NM/ovet_reloadTopoDBTbls.ovpl
```

Re-run `setupExtTopo.ovpl` after the above command successfully completes.

Disabling NNM 6.2 default data collections

After version 6.2 of NNM, default reporting configurations were a lot less consumptive of system and disk resources. But v6.2 in particular had lots of default data collections and reporting enabled. To disable these collections and reports, invoke the Report Config GUI either through the *ovw* GUI or via the url:

```
http://<nnm_server>:8880/OvCgi/nnmRptConfig.exe
```
or
```
http://<nnm_server>/OvCgi/nnmRptConfig.exe
```

Double-click 'View Selected Reports', select a report and press 'stop'; repeat for all of the reports listed. Exit this GUI and invoke the data collections and thresholds GUI, either from the *ovw* GUI or from the command line via `xnmcollect`. Select the collections that are "collecting" by default and "suspend" them. See the procedure below for recovering *snmpCollect* database disk space if desired.

Follow the procedure below to completely remove all the SNMP collected data. Note the command `snmpColDump` can be used to selectively pare the *snmpCollect* database as well, and examples of those command are found in the man/ref pages:

```
Run: ovstop snmpCollect
Delete all files under:
   $OV_DB/snmpCollect/
   $OV_DB/snmpCollect/stringData/
Run: ovstart snmpCollect
```

Extend and customize router performance reports

Cisco Router General Performance Reports (CPU and Free memory), are limited in the scope of devices which this report applies to. Note that in the report configuration, the "SysObjectID" field is .1.3.6.1.4.1.9.1.* which supports only some Cisco devices. To include other devices, modify the following line in the availability.ovpl script:

```
$report_qualifier  =  "AND  node.snmp_sysobjid  LIKE
'.1.3.6.1.4.1.9.1%'\n"
```

Extending the number of instances in the TopN report

To accomplish this, change the `topn_count` value in:

```
$OV_CONF/analysis/global.conf
```

Support and contributed reporting tools

Some useful reports can be derived from data produced by the scripts in the support and contrib directories. The support directory scripts in particular contain some interesting topology data dump tools.

Support Directory:

getConnectedPort.sh (UNIX)	Dump connected port info
mineETDB.ovpl	Gather device discovery data
ovet_topoconndump.ovpl	Dump address and entity totals

Contrib Directory:

TopoInventory.ovpl	Various topology reports
Trend directory	Various SQL for trend reports
writeSelList	Dumps OVwSelections to file
Event Directory	Various event reports

Database maintenance

Use the following commands to maintain the databases that feed the data warehouse:

```
ovdwevent, ovdwtrend, and ovdwtopo
```

Note that `ovdwtrend` combines `ovcoltosql` and `ovcoldelsql` functions.

`ovdwtrend -trim`	remove *all* from SNMP tables
`ovdwevent -trim`	remove oldest from events
`ovdwevent -trimdetail 0`	removes *all* event table data

Delete old reports

This can be done from the report configuration GUI, or by manually deleting files located in:

$OV_SHARE_HTDOCS/C/nnm/reportPresenter/

The following commands are useful for selectively deleting older reports on Windows:

cd %OV_WWW%, then replace yyyymm with year and month below and run the 2 following commands :

```
for /f "delims=#" %a in ('dir daily.yyyymm*.* /s /b') do del "%a\*.*" /q
for /f "delims=#" %a in ('dir daily.yyyymm*.* /s /b') do rmdir "%a" /q
```

If using some regional setting other than EN-US, you might end up with several copies of each report, and this eats diskspace, not to mention time needed to run `ovbackup`.

Rebuild DW after trim to recover space (UNIX)

This procedure is available in Versions 6.1 and higher:

$OV_CONTRIB/NNM/dataWarehouse/repackDb.sh

This script resizes the Solid data warehouse by trimming unused space taken by the database. Since the Solid database never gives back any disk allocated when reaching new high-water marks, this script allows recovery of unused disk space after trimming old data. This script: 1) backs up the database (just in case), 2) unloads the database into a flat file, 3) removes and recreate an empty database, 4) reloads the database and 5) cleans-up. To limit size of Solid DB in NNM V6.1 or V6.2, see HP's SSO document number KBRC00004254 at:

openview.hp.com/sso/ecare/getsupportdoc?docid=KBRC00004254

Remove Default Reports:

```
ovstop ovrequestdovdumpevents
Delete $OV_CONF/analysis/requests/C/*
Delete $OV_ANALYSIS/ovrequestd/requests/*
Delete $OV_WWW/htdocs/C/nnm/reportPresenter/Reports/*
```

```
ovstart -v ovrequestd
```

Disable Default Reports: Backup `snmpRep.conf`, edit and comment all lines

Delete/recreate Solid data warehouse and ET DB:
```
$OV_SUPPORT/redoSolid.ovpl
```

Unload DW data to flat files:
```
ovdwunloader -file trend_output_file -trend -v
ovdwunloader -file event_output_file -event -v
```

Disable Solid:
   Prior to NNM 6.41, Solid was only used for DW operations and could be completely disabled without much impact to NNM operations. More recent versions use Solid for the Extended Topology database and disabling Solid would render all ET functions useless. Procedures for completely disabling Solid vary with NNM version and platform.

Maintain/preen web reports:
   The web reports are stored in :
```
$OV_SHARE_HTDOCS /C/nnm/reportPresenter/Reports
```

Subdirectories hold reports by type, then by time period. If the subdirectory is deleted for any particular day, for example, that day simply is no longer be available in the Web report. Once deleted, the reports cannot be recreated.

Configure DW, connect to ODBC: `ovdwconfig.ovpl`

Resolving errors with database maintenance programs
If the following error is seeen:

   Error: `"Data warehouse maintenance program (ovcoldelsql) exited with a non-zero return code of 1 and the following message: Data specified to trim has not been aggregated"`

This is a non-critical error that indicates an unsuccessful data-deletion from the embedded database or an unsuccessful attempt to delete data that's not present in database. In most cases, it can be ignored.

Extreme filtering in event data exports
Only the following events are exported by default: node up, node down, interface up, interface down, node added, node deleted,

threshold violation and threshold rearm. To export *all* alarms, create an empty file in the $OV_CONF\analysis sub-directory called:

```
NO_EXTREME_EVENT_FILTERING
```

Make sure that no extension is appended to this file name, then run the following command to enable it:

```
ovdweventflt -n '*' -o '*' -i N
```

Database size limitations

Raw databases:
  - The binary event store DB (BES) default size is 16 MB and it can grow up to 32 MB.
  - The *SnmpCollect* database can grow without bounds, and can be trimmed with the `ovdwtrend` or `snmpColDump` commands
  - Topology, Map, and Object databases are boundless, but in practice rarely grow beyond a few dozens of MBs.

Solid DB

Solid DB can be extended up to about 16 GB (2x8 files of 2GB). 16GB is the default maximum database size in V7.5.

Increase size of the binary event store (BES)

The BES is also called the event database or *eventdb*. More information can be found in the ov_event man/ref pages. Do not attempt to decrease the size of *eventdb*, as this may cause the data warehouse to fail. To increase the BES beyond the default maximum of 32 MB, set the following LRF switch (page 5) on *pmd* to increase the size (in this example to 128MB):

```
-SOV_EVENT;b128
```

If the option to log events to trapd.log is also selected (see page 103), use the "-l" (ell) option to increase the maximum size of that file, for example:

```
-SOV_EVENT;t;l128;b128
```

If reducing the size of the BES, clear the eventdb (see below) before restarting OpenView processes.

Clear the event database (BES)

To clear the contents of the event database, issue and `ovstop` command, then delete the OV_DB/eventdb directory. Restart NNM using `ovstart`. The eventdb directory will be re-created automatically.

Dump list of managed nodes into CSV file (UNIX only)

This is a typical example use of `ovtopodump`:

```
ovtopodump | awk '/NODES/, length < 2' | grep -v
Unmanaged | grep IP | awk '{print $3}' | sort -u
```

Dump a clean list of all managed nodes (UNIX only)

In the command below, do not substitute a hostname where it says HOSTNAME, use that exact text:

```
ovtopodump -lr | grep '^HOSTNAME' |
sed -e 's/^HOSTNAME:[      ]*//g' | sort
```

Dump interface list for all nodes (UNIX only)

```
for a in `ovobjprint -a "Selection Name" isNode=1 | awk
'{print $2}'|sed -e 's/"//g'|sort`
  do
    print $a;
    ovobjprint -a "TopM Interface List" "Selection
    Name"=$a |grep -v "TopM Interface" |grep -v
    "OBJECT ID" | grep -v "for all objects"
  done
```

23. Distributed NNM

Multiple copies of NNM can be set up to share data and distribute polling loads in a DIM configuration. DIM is Distributed Internet Discovery and it is described in the NNM Guide to Scalability and Distribution.

A CS is an NNM Collection Station. An MS is an NNM Management Station. Any copy of NNM can be a CS, but not all versions of NNM can be an MS. Setting up DIM requires multiple licenses for the NNM product.

Note that several important newer NNM features, like APA, may not be fully supported in DIM environments. The APA in some cases can eliminate the need for DIM. Note also that if DIM is in use on an MS and the APA is enabled, failover polling will no longer work. If failover polling is required for a particular architecture on an MS, the APA cannot be enabled.

DIM limitations

DIM requires the use of *netmon*-based discovery and polling for the MS. APA polling is supported on CSs only.

The Starter Edition and NNM 250-Node Edition of NNM do not support MS features.

Extended Topology views only discover the managed, local and primary topology objects on a CS or MS; as of NNM 7.5 there is no integration of ET under DIM.

Generally, mixed versions of NNM cannot participate in DIM, but there are exceptions. Typically, same versions on varying platforms are supported.

DIM can operate across firewalls. The ports that need to be open are listed on page 291 and there is more information on this below.

DIM overlap modes

These modes define the behavior of the relationship between CSs and MSs:

allowOverlap:
> MS manages 2 collection stations with overlapping domains. With thi mode, there will be two entries in the topodb and one entry in the objdb on the MS.

unmanageSecondary (unmanage local):
> MS has own collection domain; secondary objects unmanaged until failover.

deleteSecondary (delete local):
> MS deletes CS copies of locally managed objects in topodb. *netmon* discovery is on.

Ports used by MS and CS:

This chart may not be accurate for every version of NNM.

Source	Dest.	Protocol	SRC Ports	DST Ports
MS	Mgd nodes	UDP	1024-65535	161 SNMP
Mgd nodes	MS	UDP	1024-65535	162 SNMP
CS	MS	TCP	1024-65535	162 *pmd*
MS	Mgd nodes	ICMP	N/A	N/A
Any	CS or MS	TCP	8880	*ovw* web
Any	CS or MS	TCP	8888	*ovw* web
Any	CS or MS	TCP	9999	*ovw* web
Any	CS or MS	TCP	3700	*ovw* web

Polling through firewalls using DIM

To configure the port that *nmdemandpoll* opens when listening for incoming demand poll output from a local or remote collection station, edit the $OV_CONF\nmdemandpoll.ports file. Each line in the file may contain a single port number, a comma-delimited list of port numbers, or an integer range. A valid integer range is of the form m-n, where m and n are valid integers, and m is less than or equal to n. Comments are denoted by a number sign (#), and cause the remainder of the line to be ignored. Blank lines are allowed.

Filtering

NNM filters are used in several places for differing NNM functions, and with NNM 7.0+, a second separate filtering facility is provided for ET functions such as the APA Poller. ET topology filtering is discussed separately on page 85.

- *Discovery filters* limit which objects the local topology database contains.

- *Topology filters* limit which objects on a CS are passed to a MS.

- *Map filters* limit which objects are shown on user maps.

- *Failover filters* specify the most critical nodes for which the MS takes over polling control should a CS become unreachable from the MS.

- *Important Node filters* determine which nodes should never be flagged as secondary failures by *netmon* polling, and are discussed on page 60. APA Important node filtering uses a different methodology as described on page 85.

- *Object filters* define *netmon*-based devices to which object-based polling applies.

- *Persistence filters* define objects that are placed in memory for backward compatibility with certain third party API applications by disabling on-demand submaps for those submaps containing objects that pass the filter.

- *DHCP filters* identify shared or floating IP addresses.

ovfiltercheck, ovfiltertest and ovtopodump

These commands can be used to troubleshoot and verify filters:

`ovfiltercheck -v`	Check filter syntax
`ovfiltertest`	Produce the results of the filter and test against the topology database
`ovtopodump -f <filt>`	Test topology database against filter

V7.51 Intermediate Patch 18 introduced the "-x" option to the command `ovtopodump`. This option is similar to `ovtopodump -l`, which prints a summary of data for the local node, only it prints a summary of data consolidated from all collection stations.

Examples of filter expressions

Here are some commonly used expressions:

```
CiscoDevices   "Match  all  Cisco  Routers"  {  "SNMP
    sysObjectID" ~ 1.3.6.1.4.1.9.* }
DevicesWith3orMoreInterfaces "" { numInterfaces > 2 }
```

These examples show map filters that both exclude or include:

```
Sets {
    EXCLUDEDNODELIST "Excluded Nodes"
{ "DAVE.acompany.int", "BILL.acompany.int" }
    INCLUDEDNODELIST "Included Nodes"
{"JOHN.acompany.int", "FRED.acompany.int" }
}

Filters {
    NetsNSegs "All networks & segments" {isNetwork ||
isSegment}
    NTServer "sysObjectID for NT servers"
{ "SNMP sysObjectID" == ".1.3.6.1.4.1.311.1.1.3.1.2" }
    INCLUDEDNODES "Included Nodes"
        { "IP Hostname" IN INCLUDEDNODELIST }
    EXCLUDEDNODES "Excluded nodes"
        { "IP Hostname" IN EXCLUDEDNODELIST }
}

FilterExpressions {
    NtServerMap "NT Managed Systems"
        { !EXCLUDEDNODES && (NetsNSegs || NTServer ||
INCLUDEDNODES)
}
}
```

Exclusion filter for VLAN Interfaces. Note use of "||" vs. "&&":

```
NotVlan "Not Vlan" isInterface && (("Selection Name" !~
"Vl") || ("Selection Name" !~ "VLAN")) }
```

Using external files within filters

To help separate lists of sources from making the filters file grow too large, external files can be referred to within the filters file. Note that while wildcards are supported in filter definitions directly within the filters file, they are not supported in the external files. The example below shows filters based on external files populated with valid NNM node names or IP Addresses, one on each line:

```
LRouters "Set of Routers from list"
    { c\:/cfg_files/routers }

LTerminalServers "Set of Terminal Servers from list"
    { c\:/cfg_files/terminalservers }

ListNodes "All nodes from list"
    { ( "IP Hostname" in LRouters ) ||
      ( "IP Hostname" in LTerminalServers ) }
```

Filtering idiosyncracies

Filters using SNMP entities return results for the node entity and cannot be used to produce results for interface entities.

Any defined map filters show up in the Homebase selection criteria. This can be a powerful tool for better customizing dynamic views.

Examples of xnmtopoconf commands

These are the DIM control commands:

To add :	`xnmtopoconf -add collection_station`
To delete :	`xnmtopoconf -delete collection_station`
To check status:	`xnmtopoconf -print`
To test:	`xnmtopoconf -test collection_station`

Remove secondary objects from the database

When disabling DIM, secondary objects can be removed from the database using the following command in running NNM V7.51 with Intermediate Patch 18 or greater:

```
ovtopofix -C -X
```

DIM set-up in a nutshell

On the collection station:

Edit /etc/snmpd.conf to establish set community string
Edit filters file to set up topology filter
Edit ovtopmd.lrf to add filter using LRF process (page 5), for example:

```
OVs_YES_START:pmd,ovwdb:O -f Routers:
OVs_WELL_BEHAVED:15:
```

On the management station:

Run: `xnmtopoconf -print` to see if CS is known.
If not, add using: `xnmtopoconf -add -unmanage <CS>`
Options - Configure SNMP to set the SNMP set string for CS
Test collection station : `xnmtopoconf -test <CS>`
Configure failover: `xnmtopoconf -failover <CS>`
Set status check interval : `xnmtopoconf -interval [n] <CS>`
Manage CS: `xnmtopoconf -manage <CS>`
Run: `ovtopodump -RISC` on the MS to monitor progress

279

Migrating to non-DIM with APA

Because of substantial improvements to scalability between version 6 and 7.5 on NNM, it may be desirable to migrate from multiple NNM collection stations back to a single server architecture. The advantages for doing this are: fewer NNM licenses, a single topology to maintain, better analysis across polling boundaries by the APA, and better dynamic maps. Disadvantages are: a loss of failover ability if using DIM for failover, more complex and sensitive performance tuning tasks and non-distributed polling. Note that if *netmon*-based polling is not managing Level 2, there may be a large increase in the number of managed interfaces when switching to APA.

Using WEB interface with an MS as Management Console

The following white paper in the $OV_DOC/WhitePaper directory provides some tips about configuring web consoles to act as a "third tier" to the management hierachry and thus increase the number of operators who can access a distributed NNM installation:

> WebUIFromRemoteConsoles.doc

CS views from MS Alarm Browser

NNM V7.51 Intermediate Patch 18 introduced an enhancement to the *ovalarmsrv* process that allows some Collection Station views to be accessed via the Management Station's Web Alarm browser by configuring the following file:

> $OV_CONF/C/xnmeventsExt.conf

See the following White Paper for details on how to configure this:

> $OV_DOC/WhitePapers/CrossLaunch.pdf

24. High Availability and Backup

NNM provides the `ovbackup.ovpl` script to perform backups of the NNM databases and important data. This script calls the `ovpause` and `ovresume` commands that respectively quiet and awaken the daemons and force in-memory data to be written out to the appropriate files. Any open *ovw* sessions will receive a popup informing them that OV daemons have been paused.

The object, topology, snmpCollect, and map databases use NDBM flat file databases. These are "sparse" files, and thus there can be issues when restoring if the backup facility used isn't sparse file-aware.

`ovbackup.ovpl` backs up operational and/or analytical files only. Base installation files like binaries and configuration files are not backed up by `ovbackup.ovpl`. Also, if `ovbackup.ovpl` is customized, be sure to save copies of the customized file since NNM upgrades may over-write the file.

To piggyback onto the `ovbackup.ovpl` process, write a script that copies additional data to be backed up (as well as restored with `ovrestore.ovpl`) and place it in the following directory:

$OV_TMP/ovbackup

Automated database backups

Data warehouse backups occur automatically by default. Daily transaction log consolidation also occurs by default. If `ovbackup.ovpl` is being used regularly, then the DW is being backed up twice. Often, errors arise if the automated DW backup and the `ovbackup.ovpl`-based backups step on each other.

To disable automated DW backups, modify the following file and add ";" before the line that starts with "at":

$OV_ANALYSIS/default/solid.ini

Then, remove old backups in:

$OV_DB/analysis/default/backup

To prevent `ovbackup.ovpl` from backing up the DW, run it with the `-operational` command line option.

DW backup files:

Config file:	$OV_DB/analysis/default/solid.ini
Transaction logs:	$OV_DB/analysis/default/log
Backups:	$OV_DB/analysis/default/backup
Error log:	$OV_DB/analysis/default/solerror.out

Force backup: `ovbackup.ovpl -analytical -d dest_dir`

ovbackup and OpenView data protector (OmniBack)

A best practice is to run: `ovbackup.ovpl` before running Data Protector via `cron` or scheduler. If `ovbackup.ovpl` is run as a pre-exec using Data Protector, a wrapper script is required to establish the appropriate environment variables.

ovresume times out

In higher scale deployments, the default timeout of 5 minutes can easily be reached, particularly when there are a lot of data collections, causing `ovbackup.ovpl` to fail. To increase the timeout, find the system call to ovresume within the script and add the "-t" option to increase the timeout, for example:

```
system "$OV_BIN/ovresume -v -t900 > \
$OV_TMP/ovresume.output 2>&1";
```

Running ovbackup.ovpl as non-root user (UNIX)

`ovbackup.ovpl` runs the `ovpause` and `ovresume` commands, which can only be run by root (by default). See the procedure on page 12 for instructions on how to allow non-root users to execute these commands.

ovbackup.ovpl and Data Warehouse interaction

When the `ovbackup.ovpl` command is executed, it will instruct the Embedded Database server to initiate an online backup. In order to allow a roll-forward recovery, the default backup schedule must be deactivated. The process for doing this is:

1. Copy $OV_DB/analysis/default/solid.ini file to $OV_DB/analysis/default/solid.ini.old file.
2. Edit $OV_DB/analysis/default/solid.ini file.
3. Comment out "At=<time> backup" entry, by inserting a ";" at the beginning of the line. For example: ;At=01:00 backup
4. Save $OV_DB/analysis/default/solid.ini file.
5.

The embedded database will now be backed up only when the ovbackup.ovpl command is run. If use of ovbackup.ovpl is stopped in the future, the default backup should be restored by copying the solid.ini.old file back to solid.ini.

ovdbcheck daemon not starting (MS SQL)

On Windows system after a reboot, if *ovdbcheck* fails to start it may be because the SQL server is still recovering from the reboot and is not available to NNM yet. Simply waiting for the DB to recover should suffice. To avoid this issue, always try to stop NNM with the `ovstop` command prior to rebooting the server.

Backing up SNMP configuration data

The command to save SNMP configuration database, which contains polling and SNMP community name settings is:

```
xnmsnmpconf -export <outputfile>
```

Integrating NNM with OVO database backup

Use this when running NNM on a server along with OVO (OpenView Operations). The database backup integration scripts are in $OV_CONF/ovbackup/checkpoint/operational directory, and contain both `nnm_checkpoint.ovpl` and `ito_checkpoint.sh` and `$OV_CONF/ovbackup/pre-pause` (which contains `ito_oracle.sh`).

Backing up the Solid database

Solid DB grows very large in highly-scaled environments using ET. A Solid DB greater than 2 gigabytes in size is not unusual. The Solid database resides in:

```
$OV_DB/analysis/default
```

By default, the Solid backup program is automatically launched daily at 11pm. So if `ovbackup.ovpl` is in use, then the Solid database is uneccessarily backed up twice. The automatic backup is made to:

$OV_DB/analysis/default/backup

To disable the automatic Solid backup, put a semicolon before the following line in the $OV_DB/analysis/default/solidini.file then restart the OpenView daemons: `At=23:00 backup`

To disable Solid backup when running `ovbackup.ovpl`, run instead:

```
ovbackup.ovpl -operational
```

To change the location of the Solid database backup, specify a new path in the solid.ini file that is relative to $OV_DB/analysis/default, for example:

[General]
BackupDirectory=../../../../../tmp/solidbak

Map exports and imports

The *ovw* GUI Map Export/Import facility preserves IPMAP customizations made for a specific topology. Legacy databases require occasional rebuilding, particularly in dynamic environments. Most NNM administrators create customizations to their maps using "containerized" realms and cut-and-paste operations.

These customizations can be preserved using the Map Export feature. When restoring a map using an exported map file, the assumption is that the underlying topology data in the databases is essentially the same. If it is not, many objects may be placed in the "New Object Holding Area." Before importing a map, first make sure that the discovery is complete and that any objects that were manually populated into the databases via `loadhosts` are in place before performing the map import.

Map snapshots

A map snapshot, which is also performed from the *ovw* GUI, captures a copy of the entire map database, and allows for the "freezing" of IPMAP topology status at a particular point in time. Use snapshots only for that purpose: to capture the status of the topology at that particular moment in time. Map snapshots can also be issued externally using the ovmapsnap command.

ovtopodbsnapshot.ovpl

This support tool was introduced in NNM V7.5 and it is useful for creating backups and restoration points for both NNM's *ovw* and ET topology databases and associated configuration files. Note that it issues a complete NNM daemon shutdown (ovstop) when it is executed:

```
$OV_SUPOPORT/NM/ovtopodbsnapshot -c <outputfile>
```

This tool can also be used effectively to to maintain a hot-standby server.

Native backup and restore commands (UNIX)

Use these when choosing not to use the ovbackup.ovpl script. Note NNM legacy databases are "sparse" files, so must be backed up with sparse file-aware tools. For HP-UX, use fbackup/frestore and for Solaris, use ufsdump/ufsrestore. cpio is also sparse file-aware.

Backup sparse file databases using cpio:

```
cd $OV_DB/openview ; find . | cpio -pdmux \
/dir/backupfile >> /dir/logfile 2 >> /dir/logfile
```

Backup and restore sparse file DB's using fbackup or frecover to or from tape:

```
fbackup -oi $OV_DB/openview -f /dir/backupfile

frecover -x -v -o -f -s /dev/rmt/om \
-i $OV_DB/openview
```

DIM Configuration for a hot standby system

The following implementation of DIM as a hot standby uses the cooperative-independent DIM model described in the guide to Distribution and Scalability for NNM. An additional license is required, but in most cases, a discount can be negotiated through the sales process. The two NNM servers should have the same visibility to the network. Generally, the hot standby should be running the same OS versions and have a similar hardware configuration as the primary system.

First, make sure both stations have discovered the same topology. Copy the configuration files of interest from the primary to the standby server when configuring the standby for the first time. Of particular interest will be any *netmon* seed files that may have been configured and the netmon.noDiscover file. Also, copy the trapd.conf file for the primary.

Create the topology filters as follows:

For Primary NNM server named "Primary," create filters:

```
Primary "" { "IP Address"  ~ "1.2.3.4" }
UnManaged "" { "IP Status" ~ "Unmanaged" }
```

For the same primary server, create FilterExpression:

```
Topofilter ""{ !Primary && !UnManaged }
```

Create the same filters on the standby server, substituting the name of the standby server where it says "Primary" above.

Update *ovtopmd* LRF files to call the new topology filters on each server, per the detailed procedure in the Scalability and Distribution guide.

On the primary server, run:

```
xnmtopoconf -add -over AllowOverlap ServerB
xnmtopoconf -failover ServerB
```

Set the status check interval on the primary server using:

```
xnmtopoconf -interval <n> <node>
```

<n> is number of minutes between status checks between the manager and the collection station, and <node> is the name of the standby server. It may take a few hours for *ovrepld* to stabilize the two topologies.

Non-DIM configuration for a "hot standby"

A hot standby can be configured using the following outline. An additional license is required, but in most cases, a discount can be negotiated through the sales process. Generally, the hot standby should be running the same OS versions and a similar hardware configuration. The two servers must be running the same version of

NNM at the same patch level. The two NNM servers should have the same visibility to the network. There are actually several ways this can be accomplished, and this method is neither the best nor the most efficient.

Copy configuration files of interest from the primary to the standby server when configuring the standby for the first time. Of particular interest will be any *netmon* seed files that may have been configured and the netmon.noDiscover file. Also, copy the trapd.conf file from the primary. On the primary server, export the SNMP configuration database and copy to the standby. Import it on the standby using:

```
$OV_BIN/xnmsnmpconf -import <file>
```

Allow the standby server to discover the entire network. In doing so, the standby server will set itself as a trap recipient on the managed nodes. Compare the results of this server's discovery to that of the primary. Differences may be attributable to network visibility if the primary and standby are on different segments.

Run: `ovbackup.ovpl` on primary NNM server
Copy `ovbackup.ovpl` results to standby server.
Run: `ovstop` the run `ovrestore.ovpl` on standby server.
Populate the standby server's FQDN in:

$OV_DB/openview/ovwdb/ovserver

In essence, the idea is to let discovery polling run on the standby server, but not status polling. To do this, run:

```
xnmpolling -statPollOff
```

When using APA polling instead of *netmon* polling:

```
ovdelobj $OV_LRF/ovet_poll.lrf; ovstart ovet_poll
```

To enable the standby:

```
xnmpolling -statPollOn
```
or:
```
ovaddobj $OV_LRF/ovet_poll
ovstart ovet_poll
```

The above steps provide an outline for getting started, and they can be included in a nightly or weekly set of scripts to keep the server's synchronized. Remember, that when switching from standby back to primary, the procedure should be reversed so that any changes that occurred while the primary was down are not lost when the primary is brought back online.

NNM as a highly available service

NNM as a highly available application in UNIX clusters has enjoyed increasing support from HP, but with problematic support in earlier versions. After NNM V7.01, clustering is supported for HP's MC ServiceGuard 10.06 or greater, Sun Cluster 2.2 or greater, and Veritas Cluster 2.0 or greater. NNM's added support in V7.01 for migratable IP addresses has enhanced NNM's clusterability.

V7.51 Intermediate Patch 18 added support for Windows Clusters, and a white paper describing its configuration in the V7.53 $OV_DOC/WhitePapers directory.

NNM 6.2 (patched) and higher supports MC ServiceGuard and Veritas Cluster, but floating IP addresses must be undiscovered by placing them in the netmon.noDiscover file. NNM can read the ServiceGuard MIBs in the *cmsnmpd* agent, which allows NNM to separate floating IPs, but if this agent stops running, instability could result. Note that clustered solutions have very specific hardware requirements. MC ServiceGuard, for example, won't run on most of HP's workstation-class hardware. Similarly for SUN hardware, there are minimum requirements for high-speed channel connects.

The $OV_CONF/ov.conf file contains configuration settings that pertain to using NNM in a cluster. It has its own man/ref page. Additional NNM licenses are required to run NNM on cluster member nodes, but these licenses should be available at substantial discounts.

The choice as to whether to achieve high availability via clustering technology or via implementing a DIM solution is a hard one, and almost always comes down maintainability issues rather than cost or complexity issues. A general rule of thumb is that if the staff is familiar and comfortable with clustered environments, clustering is the preferred method. Likewise, DIM should be the choice for a DIM-competent staff. See page 285 for an example DIM configuration that provides a highly-available NNM configuration.

Increasing favor towards disaster recovery architectures suggest DIM-based solutions, which lend themselves more easily to disaster recovery architectures because clustering solutions can be problematic over great distances.

Syslog in an HA environment

If the syslog facility is to be used in an HA environment, then syslogTrap requires being installed on all nodes in a HA cluster. This is due to updating files that are not under the shared disks. Additionally, it is necessary to stop syslogTrap when bringing down the NNM package. To do this, it is recommended that the following commands be added to the cluster run commands and halt commands:

> Run commands:
> /opt/OV/bin/OpC/opcagt –start
>
> Halt commands:
> /opt/OV/bin/OpC/opcagt -stop
> /opt/OV/bin/OpC/opcagt –kill

The order between opcagt and ovstart/ovstop calls does not matter.

NNM and multiple NIC cards

Highly-scaled NNM installations can benefit from using multiple NICS on the management server, but this option has strict limits, mostly due to OS processing requirements within the network stack. NNM's default poller *netmon* is single-threaded, so outbound polls are likely to be bound to the same interface anyway. NNM 7.01 introduced the APA poller, which is multi-threaded; this poller can take advantage of multiple interfaces for issuing polls and receiving replies.

For redundancy, extra NICs may be set up to act as standbys. In this case, set up the backup NIC(s) with the same default routes as the primary NIC. Set the route metric for the backup NICs higher than the primary, and the router should simply use the backup if the primary fails or becomes too congested. Also, the USE_LOOPBACK setting in the $OV_CONF/ov.conf file will stop NNM from binding to a specific NIC.

Managing migratable IP addresses

Cluster virtual IP addresses that do not fall under NNM's ability to handle HSRP (see page 253) can be handled using the

289

netmon.migratable configuration file. For more information, see the man/ref page for netmon.migratable, which was introduced in V6.31.

When *netmon* finds that an interface flagged as migratable appears on a new device, it does not attempt to merge the nodes. Instead, it allows movement of the interface to the new device.

The IP address belonging to a migratable interface is given a lower priority for use within the node naming algorithm. More information on the order that is used to determine node names can be found on page 25.

The configuration file accepts single IP addresses, IP address ranges, or IP address wildcards. The file is read upon *netmon* daemon startup, but a re-read of the configuration file is forced by running:

```
xnmpolling -event
```

Troubleshoot issues stemming from netmon.migratable by using the *netmon* -a 115 tracemask. See page 69 for details on *netmon* tracing.

25. Firewalls and Security

Many issues arise when attempting to manage nodes through firewalls. There is a whitepaper that ships with NNM on firewall details, but it is possible this is out of date with the most recent versions of NNM.

NNM Ports used

Many of these ports are only accessed via the local loopback of the NNM server.

Used by NNM daemons:

> SNMP requests (*netmon*, APA):
> > source port udp 1024-65535
> > dest port udp 161
>
> SNMP replies (*netmon*, APA):
> > source port udp 161
> > dest port udp 162
>
> SNMP traps (*ovtrapd*):
> > dest port udp 1024-6553
> > source port udp 162
>
> ICMP requests and responses (*netmon*, APA)

Used by NNM Web interface:

ovalarmsrv :	source port tcp 2345 (V6.1-) 2953 (V6.2+)
	source port tcp 2346 (V6.1 2954 (V6.2+)
ovhttpd :	source port tcp 8880 (V6.2- UNIX)
	source port tcp 3443 (V6.31+ UNIX)
	source port tcp 80 (Windows)
ovas :	source port tcp 7510 (V6.31+) ; 8005 (V7.01+)
ovwdb :	source port tcp 9999 (V6.1-) 2447 (V6.2+)
	source port tcp 37XX, one for each *jovw* session, sequentially from port 3700

Reconfiguring ports used by NNM

The ports used by most daemons can be configured via LRF switches. See page 5 for how to modify LRF files. Some ports which certain daemons listen on, however, cannot be reconfigured. NNM's *ovtrapd* must listen on UDP port 162 and this cannot be changed. The port it send traps from (UDP 161), however, can be changed. Note that even if the trap receiver port could be changed, every SNMP agent in the enterprise would also have to be reconfigured to send traps on a different port, and it is an unlikely feat to accomplish for all agents.

pmd uses TCP (not UDP) port 162 for talking to other copies of NNM, and this port apparently cannot be changed. This is an issue, though, only if *ovrepld* is running, which it does only when using DIM (see page 275) or NNM-to-NNM event forwarding.

Highly-secure network management scenario

Most network managers would consider the following recommendations extreme, but some unusual or out-of-control environments call for extreme measures to successfully and securely manage them.

The following scenario provides such an example:

> Create a separate VLAN or management network for the LAN infrastructure.
>
> Protect this management network from the rest of the network via a firewall or at a minimum using access-lists.
>
> Use device-based access lists or similar technology to limit SNMP access to the WAN infrastructure from the management network.
>
> Similarly limit access to the network management servers. Consider the use of SNMPv3 on particularly critical and vulnerable devices. Finally, always make sure the appropriate version of code and or patches is running in the managed environment.

NNM ICMP polls versus ping sweep attacks

Some firewalls report ping sweep attacks from the NNM server. NNM-issued ICMP polls contain a string of all zeros in the payload, and the packet is always 64 bytes. This is an unusual packet configuration and cannot be re-configured. If the "-b" option is set in the netmon.lrf file, this may be the source of unusually heavy ICMP traffic. See the *netmon* man/ref for details.

Security issue with ICMP ping (UNIX only)

Some IT security departments express concern about NNM's status polls. NNM uses root to execute ping. This is a requirement as only root user can open raw sockets on UNIX. The raw socket is only open for a short time and only to send and receive 64 bytes of data. It only accepts the ICMP echo response packet coming back.

Discovering into subnets using NAT

NNM reads a target's SNMP ip.ipAddrTable and may report addresses that produce confusing topology views and report down status since they are only reachable within the discovered subnet, and not from the NNM server. One way to avoid this is to block the visibility of the offending IP address tables using SNMP cut views.

If seeing the non-NAT addresses is desirable, sometimes these addresses are treated as secondary and not reported in the IP Address table, then NNM ignores them by default. In this case, the "S" flag in the oid_to_type or HPoid2type files can be set to force reading of secondary addresses. See page 7 for more on modifying these files.

Here is an example set of Cisco IOS commands to allow NNM to view NAT and to exclude ip.ipAddrTable:

```
snmp-server view NAT-view mgmt included
snmp-server view NAT-view enterprises included
snmp-server view NAT-view ip.20 excluded snmp-server
community whatever view NAT-view rw 1
```

Monitoring DMZ devices

Sometimes, it is not desirable to loosen DMZ-intranet firewall rules to allow network monitoring inside a DMZ. One alternative is to set up a single host within the DMZ to act as an SNMP proxy. ICMP-based polling would be precluded, but if all the DMZ hosts support SNMP, either *netmon's* netmon.snmpStatus file can be used (see page 60), or ET topology filters in conjunction with APA polling can be used to control what devices get polled (see page 85).

In environments where there is a large number of hosts in the DMZ, setting up another copy of NNM in the DMZ and using

DIM (see page 276) is also a workable solution. Some third party products, such as Tavve's eprobe (www.tavve.com), are specifically designed to gather network management data and securely communicate to an internal network management server.

Extended Topology configuration GUI password

The Extended Topology configuration GUI password is in cleartext in:

$OV_AS\webapps\topology\WEB-INF\dynamicViewsUsers.xml

26. Product Details

This section summarizes new NNM version release notes, differences between NNM product bundles, OS-based functionality differences and a summary of major IT management products in the OpenView suite.

NNM 8i

NNM 8i (V8.00) was released in November, 2007 and is a completely different product that any previous version of NNM. Up until this version, virtually every feature ever introduced to NNM since version 3 has remained with the product for backward compatibility. That changes dramatically with NNM 8i. The author estimates that 85% of the code in NNM 8i is brand new.

There is no upgrade path from previous versions of NNM; it must be installed on a fresh system. HP plans to support and release new versions of NNM 7.x in parallel with NNM 8.x for at least the whole of 2008. Migration tools for some legacy NNM customizations and some database data will be available with NNM 8.10, due in the fall of 2008. Most familiar NNM features and product elements are totally absent from 8i, including the *ovw* GUI, all *xnm* applications and all the databases.

NNM 8i is a 64-bit application that requires 64-bit hardware running 64-bit OS versions and is built on a J2EE application server. It consists of functional subsystems in an n-tier architecture. The modules are organized around a central notification bus that provides for communications between modules and, in the future, communications between distributed copies of NNM 8.x.

The only major subsystem that was ported over from older code is the Extended Topology code, but with a different database, a different GUI, and different configuration entry points. The *pmd* event subsystem remains in place, but only to act as a forwarder or receivers of NNM events to/from legacy copies of NNM. The new GUI can also connect to legacy installations of NNM and display those product elements that were web-based. One curious artifact from legacy NNM is the *ovspmd* process and the familiar ARF process (see page 6).

The author prepared a presentation on NNM 8i for the 2008 HP Software Universe conference in Las Vegas, but the presentation was rejected by HP and not presented there. It was presented for some Vivit local chapter user group meetings, however. It can be downloaded from:

www.fognet.com/hpsu08.pdf

NNM 8i architecture

Use the diagram below to compare and contrast 8i's architecture with previous versions. Note that it's completely different from the architecture depicted on page 71.

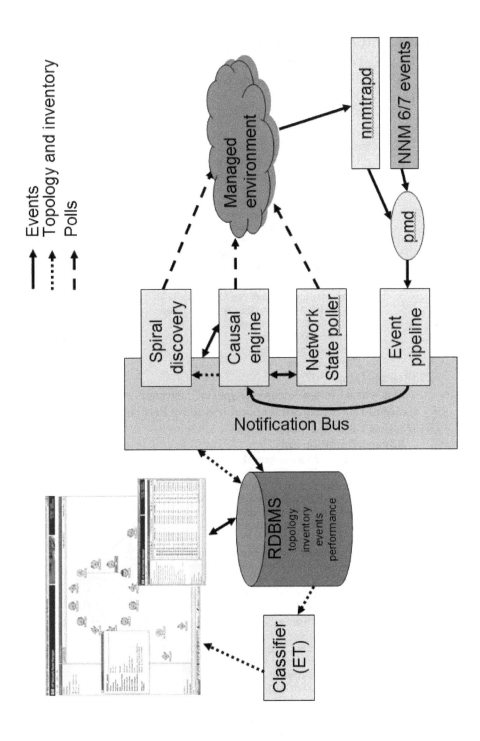

Product feature deltas by NNM version

8.01 (Release Date: 1/17/08):
    AKA NNM 8i. See section on NNM 8i above.

8.00 (Release Date: 11/26/07):
    AKA NNM 8i. See section on NNM 8i above.

7.53 (Release Date: 4/03/08):
    Advanced Edition only:
        Container View Access Control
        Node Status and Interface Status Views
        Alarm View
        Use ET data in Path View
        Connect end nodes from another ET zone
        Interface configuration change detection in APA
        Import xnmsnmpconf timeouts & retries into ET
        ET community string discovery
        Port admin tool in Dynamic Views
    Standard Edition & Advanced Edition:
        Linux platform support (See OS section below)
        HP-UX 11iv3 support (See OS section below)
        Solaris Containers/virtualization support
        VMware ESX3.0 support
        Windows Cluster support
        JRE 1.5 support

7.52 (Release Date: ?/07):
    This was a limited release for special customers asking for extend Linux platform support including Redhat Linux 2.6

7.51 (Release Date: 8/24/06):
    Advanced Edition only:
        Container Views – *ovw*-like views for ET
        Interface Views
        Interface Discovery Filtering
        Incremental Node Discovery for ET
        Cisco Discovery Configuration
        Connection Editor Enhancements
        APA Improvements
        Improved ET Disvovery performance
        Topology API stability improvements
        Contrib App: SmartPath
    Standard Edition & Advanced Edition:
        NNM & OVPI integration pack
        Automatic merging of user-configurable files during patch updates
        Default number of hops in Neighbor view is now configurable
        Support for Std & Ent Editions of Windows 2003 R2
        Support for Tomcat v5
        Support for Apache v2
        Support for Solid DB v4.5

7.5 assorted patch release features:

Advanced Edition only:
> APA parameters added to load only polled objects into memory
> APA parameters added for backoff polling for particularl devices
> APA preferred IP management address paramters added
> Improved SNMP NoSuchObject handling in APA
> ET-based filters for Node View added
> VRRP View
> Expanded ET device support

Standard Edition & Advanced Edition:
> Java Web Start for windows-based Dynamic Views clients
> IPMAP Filter of network symbols connected to a gateway
> *ovtrapd* can block traps based on combo of IP addr's and event OID's
> *ovtrapd* automatically unblocks blocked devices after trap storm
> ovtrapd.conf switch for rate of event flow
> *netmon* switch to disable default Anycast functionaility
> *netmon* switch to disable BGP routing tables queries

7.5 (Release Date: 8/12/04):

Advanced Edition only:
> Cisco Card support shows "board" entity details
> Trunk Support improvements with new icons
> OAD Improvements: VLAN, HSRP, Pathview, Telnet
> Removal of ovet_auth and ovet_dffile
> Improved Topology Filtering
> Improved Layer Three connectivity in dynamic views
> New APA Status for Dynamic Views: "Not Monitored"
> New Topology Report for ET: Not SNMP Supported
> Neighbor View context-sensitive VLAN View launch
> Improvements to syslog template
> Support for MS SQL (NT Version)

Standard Edition & Advanced Edition:
> View alarms for selected nodes in dynamic views
> Support for Windows 2003 (NT Version)
> Updated Java Browsers, Plug-Ins, and Virtual Machines
> Display layer 3 edge connectivity across WANs
> ovtrapd.conf suppresses trap storms and traps from addr's

7.01 (Release Date: 1/14/04):

AE Only:
> APA Poller can take over all *netmon* status polling
> Fixes 7.0 issues with OID_to_sym
> Fixes 7.0 issues with deleting an OAD

SE Only:
> Support for HP-UX on Itanium with HP-UX 11.23
> Support for Red Hat Linux Advanced Server 2.1

7.0 (Release Date: 10/8/03):

> SE/AE Product Structure introduced

AE Only:

> Introduction of syslog parser (AE UNIX versions only)
> Extended Topology features supported on NT version
> OAD Support introduced
> APA introduced only for HSRP and OAD polling (Active Problem Analyzer)
> Support for filters in bridge.noDiscover file
> ET discovery status moved to Home Base
> ovet_topodump.ovpl introduced
> ET Discovery improvements (VLAN, autozone, etc)

SE & AE:

> Improved dynamic views:
> Introduction of Home Base, multi-framed views, "active tables," Authorization, authentication manage nodes via DynamicViewsUsers.xml, better scalability, many new icons, extensible menus, poster printing, toggle port labels, node, interface details pages.
> New event correlations introduced and updated
> Mapping of SNMP sysObjectID to symbol moved from $OV_CONF/oid_to_sym to $OV_CONF/oid_to_sym_reg/
> Support for 31 bit subnet masks
> netmon.migratable introduced
> netmon.MACnoDiscover introduced

SE Only:

> Support for Red Hat Linux Advanced Server 2.1

6.41 (ET 2.01) (Release Date: 3/12/03):

> Correlation Composer Introduced
> New correlations, including DeDup and dedup.conf
> Cisco HSRP discovery, monitoring, and 3 new HSRP Views
> IPV6 discovery & monitoring, including 4 new IPV6 views
> Improved Dynamic Views:
>> Dynamic Views menu bar, Neighbor View, Summary View, Print, Icon Label Control, Improved zooming, signed applets, Discovery/device support for MPLS (isMPLS), IPV6 (isIPV6), BGP4 (isBGP4), HSRP (isHSRP), OSPF (isOSPF), STP (isSTP), VRRP (isVRRP), Wireless (isWireless), ET introduces Zoning and conversion to Solid Database
> Data warehouse support for Oracle 9
> AutoPass Licensing introduced
> Jakarta Tomcat ($OV_AS) replaces $OV_HPAS (App Server)
> JRE 1.4.1 support in $OV_JRE
> Data Collector improvements and new (suspended) collections
> NNM and OVPI integration (Performance Insight)

6.31 (ET 1.51) (Release Date: 6/19/02):

> Web server port moved from 8880 to 3443 (UNIX versions)
> Major Event Correlation changes (NodeIf) affecting status
> *netmon* status event change: node-centric to interface-centric
> Web Based alarm browser support for xnmeventsExt.conf
> Dynamic Views introduced with Stations, Internet,

Network, Segment, Path, Neighbor and Node Views
JRE 1.3.1 support in $OV_JRE, 1.4 on NT
Connected Nodes renamed Port-Address Mapping

6.2 (Release Date: 4/25/01):

Node View introduced using Java Plug-in V 1.2
Cisco CDP View introduced
Port Labeling Introduced via Show Connection Labels
Show Path and ovtopodump.ovpl
SNMP and object-based status polling by *netmon*
connectorL2Ports, nonConnectorL2Ports *netmon* switches
Discover/device support for isFrameRelay, isRMON,
    isRMON2, isCDP, isATM, isDS1, isDS3, isSONET.
Display Bridge MIB table configuration menu bar item
View Connected Nodes menu item sorted by port, VLAN
netmon.equivPorts introduced for improved port aggregation
Attribute-based Data Collection Using Filters
Baseline Threshold Setting using Standard Deviation based
    on the data collected and stored in the data warehouse. See
    statTimeRanges.conf(4)
Collection of Ping Response Time and Ping Retries
Data collection throughput rate has improved more than 10x
Out-of-the-box data collections configured
Improved support for devices that change their SNMP
    instance to interface mappings after a reconfiguration.
SNMPCollect performance via ovstatus -v snmpCollect.
ovdwquery -secureFile and -force options
New Reports - Top ICMP Ping Response Time, Top ICMP
    Ping Retries, Top RMON Segments By Octets, Top Frame Relay
    Congestion
Automatic Report Generation - Availability, and Inventory
Trend data exports and trim are now enabled by default
New, faster ECS 3.1 engine - Circuits improved, faster
Zoom to Highlight - Highlight node using xnmevents or Find Edit:Find is
available in the Java-based Network Presenter.
Menu Graying in Network Presenter
New telnet, traceroute, and RMON menu and pop-up items
Link Management Menu Items in *ovw* :ATM, Frame Relay,
    DS1/E1 Serial Line, DS3/E3 Serial Line, SONET/SDH, along with
    various Performance, and Fault menu items.
Tools:Unused IP Addresses.
OV_EventStorm event if an event storm is detected.
Name Service Response Time events:
    OV_DNS_PerformErr, OV_DNS_PerformWarn
Data Collector (snmpCollect) response time event:
    OV_DataColl_Busy
netmon performance via ovstatus -v netmon
ovactiond Trusted Commands in trustedCmds.conf
$OV_CONF/trustedCmds.conf/ALLOW_ALL file
SNMP Community String Discovery via netmon.cmstr
New ovwdb field: Preferred SNMP Address
Firewall Support of Traps Received Through a NAT
    device via -u option in ov_event

ovdumpevents -t and -l options for tail and for time window

M Flag in HPoid2type File for multi-homed nodes

Manuals Available as .pdf Files

ovwdb TCP port number change from 9999 to 2447

ovalarmsrv ,ovalarmsrv_cmd: 2345 to 2953, 2346 to 2954

Obsolescence of Excel report templates

Windows-only Features:

Installation into directories with spaces now supported. Default dir C:\Program Files\HP OpenView\NNM\.

Drag-and-Drop from *ovw* map.

Microsoft Terminal Server on Windows 2000.

Tip-of-the-day.

Use of Winsock-2 instead of Winsock-1 libraries.

OVSHELL and OVHIDESHELL trapd.conf Keywords

NNM 6.1 (Release Date: 10/29/99):

Web Based Reporting Service via JDK 1.1

"SegRedux" - Improved Layout for Switched Environments

NT Support for Windows® 2000

Support of secure web servers (https://)

Microsoft Management Console (MMC) Snap-in

Improved integration with HP OpenView ManageX

Software Update Menu via Help:NNM->Patches

NNM 6.01 (Release Date: 4/5/99):

New capability in xnmgraph to automatically configure data collections for the data currently being shown on the graph via File->Configure Data Collector... menu item.

xnmgraph and rnetstat support invocation for a specific interface (not just a node).

New rnetstat options for node or interface

ovexprguru introduced to graph statistics based on the configuration of the particular device being graphed

Some new expressions are shipped as part of mibExpr.conf

NNM 6.0 (Release Date: 10/27/98):

Event Correlation Services (ECS) Support introduced

Data warehouse introduced

Lightweight embedded database for NNM (Solid) Support for relational databases via ODBC

ovtopmd -Ro/-Ri options (Oracle/Ingres) obsoleted

Support for export of topology (inventory) data

Support for export of *snmpCollect* (trend) data

Support for export of alarm (events) data

Excel templates to retrieve data into Excel spreadsheets

Improved Alarm Browser

Support for relational event display of correlated alarms Support for multiple operators - when one operator an All operators see acknowledges/deletes/reclassifies

New indicator for correlated events

event browser (xnmevents) renamed 'alarm browser'
Menu items have changed from 'event' to 'alarm'.
The Binary Event Store (BES) replaces the trapd.log file
HP OpenView Java-based Web Interface introduced:
  HP OpenView Launcher, Network Presenter, Web alarm browser,
  SNMP Data Presenter
`ovbackup.ovpl` introduced with `ovpause`, `ovresume`
Simpler SPU-keyed licensing replaces Node locks (netls)
Remote Console support across platforms
Collection Station support via ovrepld across platforms
Automatic management station/Collection Station failover
DHCP support
DynaText Browser
Data Collector Enhancements
  performance improvements via -I *snmpCollect* option
  Multiple sysObjectIds per collection
  Multiple node/instance combinations per collection
  Alarm generated when node up but SNMP request fails
  Back-off deferrals of collections within the first hour
Menu Items re-organized for platform compatibility
  Repeater MIB (RFC 2108) support
SNMPv2C support in all NNM applications
Improved status polling performance (connector down ECS)
New "Map->Export..." and "Map->Import..." menu items
Registration files support platform-specific defs (#ifdef)
Integration and auto-detection of HPOV ManageX product
Installation improvements
Perl 5.003 automatically installed
Apache Web server automatically installed (UNIX only)
Java Runtime Environment for NNM automatically installed
ovwdb.auth and ovw.auth files (+ +) by default for web
Discovery via ping sweep capability through loadhosts -c
Support for GIF89a images on the maps
ovspmd generates pop-up when NNM service terminates
New Contributed Applications:
  Java-based grapher, Web-based Report Presenter,
  High Availability Support/Service Guard (HP-UX only)

Windows only:
  Support for WMI via Remote Power On
  DMI 2.0 Support via Intel's DMI 2.0 Service Provider version 1.10 and
  DMI Explorer version 1.11
  Support for pixmap format icons
  Several other formerly UNIX-only features available

NNM Pre-6.0 release history:

Version	Date	Version	Date
5.02:	1/16/98	3.31:	11/93
5.01:	6/23/97	3.1:	7/92
5.0:	3/1/97	3.0:	5/92
4.1:	3/96	2.0:	2/91
4.0:	8/95	1.0:	6/90

303

Product feature deltas by OS

NNM shares a common code base among the four supported operating systems, so OS differences are few, but here are some:

OS-specific menu bar items, e.g., Registry Editor in Windows and Emanate agent metrics in UNIX, access to SAM in HP-UX, etc.

DMI Browser (*ovcapsd*) and RDMI discovery (IPX) is only available in Windows version

UNIX versions use Apache Web Server, Windows uses IIS

UNIX versions support Oracle, Windows, SQL Server 2000

UNIX supports ovwperms command, Windows doesn't

Syslog feature in NNM 7.01+ not available on Windows

Linux platform only supports NNM Standard Edition until V7.53

Linux: integration with Customer Views not supported

Linux & Windows: High availability integrations not supported

Linux supports only the OV_NodeIf event correlation

Linux does not support ovperms.ovpl

NNM relies heavily on individual OS host name lookup algorithms, which differ and can directly impact performance.

UNIX submaps all persistent, Windows: some are transient

IPV6 is only supported on UNIX NNM AE installations

OS and software support matrix

NNM 8.01

2003 Ent x64 SP2
2003 Ent x64 R2 SP2
HP-UX 11iv3
Solaris 10 SPARC
RedHat AS 4.0
RedHat ES 4.0
Optional External DB's: Oracle 10.2.0.x

NNM 8.00

2003 Ent x64 SP2
2003 Ent x64 R2 SP2
HP-UX 11iv3
RedHat AS 4.0
RedHat ES 4.0
Optional External DB's: Oracle 10.2.0.x

NNM 7.53

2000 Pro, Srv, Adv Srv, Term Serv, (SP4), XP Pro SP2,
2003 Std, Ent, SP1 or SP2
2003 R2 Std, Ent
HP-UX 11.0, 11.11 (11iv2), 11.23 (11iv2 PA or IT), 11.31 (11iv3 PA or IT)
Note: HP-UX 11iv3 requires OVSNMP Emanate Agent
Solaris 2.8 2.9 2.10
Redhat Linux AS 2.1, Update 1 (2.4.9-e.3), Update 2 (2.4.9-e.24)
Red Hat Enterprise Linux 4, Update 2, Update 5 (64 bit)
Note: Linux variants support NNM Starter Edition only

Java Plug-in: 11.4.2(Solaris 8), 1.4.2_02(HP-UX 11.0), 1.4.2_04(Red Hat AS2.1), 1.4.2_05(HP-UX 11iv2-PA), HP-UX 11.23-IT), 1.4.2_06(Solaris 10)1.4.2_10(HP-UX 11iv3-PA&IT), 1.5(All except Wndows XP)

Web Srvs: Apache, Apache Stronghold, Raven, MS Peer Web Services, MS IIS 4.0, 5.0

Optional External DB's: Oracle 8.1.7(HP-UX 11.11, Red Hat AS2.1, Solaris 9, Windows 2003), 9.2.0.2(HP-UX 11.23-IT), 9.2.0.3(HP-UX 11.11, Red Hat AS 2.1 & EL4, Solaris 9, Windows 2003), 9.2.0.6 (Solaris 10), 10gR1(HP-UX 11.0, & 11iv2-PA, Red Hat EL4, Solaris 8 & 10, Windows XP), 10gR2(HP-UX 11.11 & 11.23-IT, red Hat EL4, Solaris 9 & 10, Windows 2000), MS SQL 2000-SP3(Windows 2003), MS SQL 2005 (Windows 2003)

NNM 7.51 (*** = with Intermediate Patch 15; **** = with IP 18)

2000 Pro, Srv, Adv Srv, Term Serv, (SP4), XP Pro,
2003 Std, Ent
HP-UX 11.0, 11.11 (11iv2)
Solaris 2.8 2.9 2.10
Redhat Linux Advanced Server 2.1 (SE only)
Java Plug-in: UNIX: 1.4.2(Sun/mozilla), 1.4.2_02(HP-UX), 1.4.2_04(Linux), 1.4.2_05(HP 11.23), 1.4.2_06(Solaris 10), 1.5***, 1.5****
    Windows: 1.4.2, 1.5***
Web Srvs: Apache, Apache Stronghold, Raven, MS
    Peer Web Services, MS IIS 4.0, 5.0
Optional DB's: Oracle 8.1.7(not 11.23), 9.2.0.2(Not
    Windows), 9.2.0.3(not 11.23), 10gR1, 10gR2, MS
    SQL 2000 (SP3)

NNM 7.5

2000 Pro, Srv, Adv Srv, Term Serv, (SP4), XP Pro,
2003 Std, Ent
HP-UX 11.0, 11.11 (11i), (11.23 Itanium w/ SE Only)
Solaris 2.8 2.9
Redhat Linux Advanced Server 2.1 (SE only)
Java Plug-in: Sun: 1.4.1(netscape), 1.4.2(mozilla),
    Windows: 1.4.2, HP: 1.4.2_02, Linux: 1.4.2_04
Web Srvs: Apache, Apache Stronghold, Raven, MS
    Peer Web Services, MS IIS 4.0, 5.0
Optional DB's: Oracle 8.1.7(not 11.23), 9.2.0.2(Not
    Windows), 9.2.0.3(not 11.23), MS SQL 2000 (SP3)

NNM 7.01

2000 Pro, Srv, Adv Srv, Term Serv, (SP1-4),XP Pro
HP-UX 11.0, 11.11 (11i), (11.23 Itanium w/ SE Only)
Solaris 2.8 2.9
Redhat Linux Advanced Server 2.1
Java Plug-in: HP-UX: 1.4.1.05, others: 1.4.2_01
Web Srvs: Apache, Apache Stronghold, Raven, MS
    Peer Web Services, MS IIS 4.0, 5.0
Optional DB's: Oracle 8.1.7(not 11.23), 9.2.0.2(Not
    Windows), 9.2.0.3(not 11.23), MS SQL 2000 (SP3)

NNM 6.41

2000 Pro, Srv, Adv Srv, Term Serv, (SP1-4*), XP Pro
HP-UX 11.0, 11.11 (11i)

Solaris 2.8 2.9
Java Plug-in: 1.4
Web Srvs: Apache, Apache Stronghold, Raven, MS
    Peer Web Services, MS IIS 4.0, 5.0
Optional DB's: Oracle 8.1.7, 9.2.0.1, MS SQL 2000 (SP2)

NNM 6.31

2000 Pro, Srv, Adv Srv, Term Serv, (SP1-3), NT 4.0 (SP6a)
HP-UX 11.0, 11.11 (11i)
Solaris 2.6, 2.7, 2.8
Java Plug-in: 1.3.1 or 1.4
Web Srvs: Apache, Apache Stronghold, Raven, MS
    Peer Web Services, MS IIS 4.0, 5.0
Optional DB's: Oracle 8.0.6, 8.1.7, 9.0.1 , MS SQL 7.0
    (SP3), 2000 (SP2)

NNM 6.2

2000 Pro, Srv, Adv Srv, Term Serv, (SP1-4*), NT 4.0 (SP6a)
HP-UX 10.2, 11.0, 11.11 (11i)
Solaris 2.6, 2.7, 2.8
Java Plug-in: Varies by platform for CDP, Node Views only
Web Srvs: Apache, Apache Stronghold, Raven, MS
    Peer Web Services, MS IIS 4.0, 5.0
Optional DB's: Oracle 7.3.4(10.20 only), 8.0.6, 8.1.7, MS
    SQL 7.0 (SP3), 2000 (SP2)

NNM 6.1

2000 Srv, Adv Srv, Term Serv, (SP1), NT 4.0 (SP4,5,6a)
HP-UX 10.2, 11.0
Solaris 2.51, 2.6, 2.7, 2.8 (Requires installation utilities from
    ftp://ovweb.external.hp.com/pub/download/installs)
Web Srvs: Apache, Apache Stronghold, Raven, MS
    Peer Web Services, MS IIS 2.0, 3.0, 4.0, 5.0
Optional DB's: Oracle 7.2.3.0, 7.3.4, 8.0.4, 8.0.5, 8.0.6,
    8.1.5, 8.1.6, MS SQL 6.5, 7.0

NNM 6.01

NT 4.0 (SP3,4,5,6a)
HP-UX 10.2, 11.0
Solaris 2.51, 2.6, 2.7 (Requires installation utilities from
    ftp://ovweb.external.hp.com/pub/download/installs)
Web Srvs: Apache, MS Peer Web Svcs, MS IIS 2.0, 3.0, 4.0
Optional DB's: Oracle 7.2.3.0, 7.3.4, 8.0.4, 8.0.5,
    MS SQL 6.5, 7.0

NNM 6.0

NT 4.0 (SP3,4,5,6a)
HP-UX 10.2, 11.0
Solaris 2.51, 2.6 (Requires installation utilities from
    ftp://ovweb.external.hp.com/pub/download/installs)
Web Srvs: Apache, MS Peer Web Svcs, MS IIS 2.0, 3.0, 4.0
Optional DB's: Oracle 7.2.3.0, 7.3.4, 8.0.4, MS SQL 6.5, 7.0

*   With Patch
** Not on Windows

Standard edition vs. Advanced edition

AE includes the Problem Diagnostics product
AE Provides Duplicate IP Support for OADs
AE Supports new APA Poller (Active Problem Analyzer)
AE includes Advanced Routing SPI for OSPF, HSRP, IPV6
No Distribution features in SE, i.e., *ovrepld*, *xnmtopoconf*, but an
 SE instance can act as an NNM collection station
AE product support matrix for Level 2 topology at:

openview.hp.com/products/nnmet/support/device_support.html

Node definition

NNM counts nodes towards the license limit by including:

IP addressable nodes with SNMP agents
IP addressable nodes without SNMP agents
Level 2 nodes discovered by *netmon*
IPX nodes on Windows platforms
Nodes in OAD's discovered by ET (AE only)

Any node that is unmanaged (beige) is not counted toward the license node count. To obtain a node counts, run:

```
ovotopodump -l (ell)
```

A chassis with multiple SNMP agents may count as multiple nodes. Non-SNMP entities that share a DNS name are considered a single node. Similarly, if interfaces on a non-SNMP readable device have distinct DNS names, and NNM can't otherwise determine with what node they are associated, they may be treated as separate nodes. This can usually be straightened by adding DNS A and/or CNAME records for the interfaces.

Additional ambiguities may occur on nodes that are assigned multiple addresses for a single interface or where IP addresses float between interfaces. It is recommended to place such addresses in the netmon.noDiscover file and delete them from the topology. Inconsistent responses to SNMP may occur when Round Robin DNS is being used to map requests to multiple application servers.

If managing IPV6, the IPV6 address counts towards the license count for that plug-in, and it consumes an additional node count for the associated IPV4 address, which is required for each IPV6 address to be managed.

The following additional commands may produce node counts that conflict with the results from the `ovotopodump` command above, but these commands are not used by the licensing system in detemining node counts.

```
ovet_topodump.ovpl -info
snmpget <NNM-server> nodeCount.0
ovstatus -v netmon (polled interfaces)
ovobjprint -S (Objects)
```

To prevent nodes from being discovered toward the node count, see the section on limiting discovery on page 41. To discover nodes, then unmanage then, so more nodes will show up on the maps but not count towards the node count, see the section on unmanaing objects on page 43.

NNM smart plug-ins

NNM SPI for Advanced Routing
   HSRP, OSPF, and IPV6 Management. Requires AE and separate license, 60-day demo installed by default with AE
NNM SPI for IP Telephony (One for Avaya and one for Cisco)
NNM SPI for LAN/WAN Edge; formerly Frame Relay SPI
NNM SPI for MPLS VPN
NNM SPI for IP Multicast

HP Software product suite summary

This list is limited to only the most popular IT management applications within the OpenView suite, and it does not include HP's offerings in the storage management, messaging or telecom management spaces.

After acquiring Peregrine and Mercury in 2006 and 2007, HP rebranded all its software to remove the OpenView name. The below listing does not include all the new offerings from those verdors, but the Peregrine Service Center product is now heavily integrated with HP Service Desk offering.

Service Desk (OVSD)
   Help desk application, ITSM/ITIL compliant. HP acquired Prolin in 1997
Network Configuration Manager (NCM)
   Multivendor configuration and compliance manager. Keeps track of configurations and changes for network devices. Checks if configurations are compliant with company standards. OEM-ed from Voyence
Internet Services (OVIS)
   SLA-oriented monitoring via software probes for web services

Transaction Analyzer (OVTA)

Monitoring and diagnostics for both web and non-web J2SE, J2EE, .NET, and COM+

Operations (OVO)

A distributed systems and application management tool, supporting a number of Smart Plug-Ins for application management (SPIs). Operations for UNIX (OVOU) has an embedded copy of NNM. Operations for Windows (OVOW) does not include NNM. Formerly Vantage Point Operations (VPO). Formerly IT/Operations (ITO). Formerly Operations Center (OPC). Formerly ManageX (acquired ManageOne 1999)

Service Navigator

Built into OVOW, and bundled with OVOU to provide service-oriented hierarchical views. No additional license required.

Service Information Portal (SIP)

Web-based portal for serving secure views of data from many OpenView products including OVOU, OVOW, NNM, OVIS, Service Navigator, OVPI, OVPM, Reporter, OVSD and Data Protector.

Performance Insight (OVPI)

Network performance reporting tool. Formerly Trend; HP acquired Trinagy in 2001

Customer Views

Requires NNM; logically organizes network elements
Canned reports for Frame, ATM, SONET, DS-1/E1, DS-3/E3

Performance Suite

GlancePlus: Realtime stats for HP-UX, Solaris, AIX, & Linux
Agent: Gathers and trends system stats, formerly MeasureWare.
Manager: Gather, display data from agents, formerly PerfView.

Reporter

Extensible reporting application generates pre-defined Web reports from Performance agents and OVO.

Problem Diagnostics (PD)

Software probe-based network path analysis
Bundled into NNM 7.0+ AE; no longer a separate product

Event Correlation Services (ECS)

State machine for event correlation runtime bundled with NNM since 6.0; Correlation Composer added in 6.41 allows development of ECS logic; ECS Designer is a separate product for Full ECS circuit development capabilities

Route Analytics Management System (RAMS)

IP Routing analysis and trending probes; Separate Product, works only with NNM 7.5 AE; OEM's from Packet Design in 2004.

SNMP Research's SNMP Security Pack.

Separate, non-HP add-on for SNMPv3 support.
Bundled with NNM 7.5+ (AE only).

Extensible SNMP Agent

Standalone extensible agent for HP-UX or Solaris only.

Radia

HP acquired Novadigm in 2004 to fill out their gap in change, configuration and release management.

Data Protector.
> Enterprise backup application. Formerly OmniBack

Oracle for OpenView
> HP-bundled Oracle database for supported OpenView apps.

PolicyXpert
> Provides packet-level bandwidth metering and QOS management.

Insight manager integration

Systems Insight, formerly Compaq Insight Manager (CIM) Integration:

> http://h18013.www1.hp.com/products/servers/management/openview/index.html

All SIM downloads:

> http://h18000.www1.hp.com/products/servers/management/hpsim/download.html

Core NNM product numbers (U.S), versions 6.4-7.51

Product Number	Version	Description
All operating systems:		
J5323BA	6.4	Manuals, English
J5324BA	6.4	Media
T2489AA/BA	7.0/7.5x	Media
T2490AA/BA	7.0/7.5x	Starter Edition Manuals, English
T2578AA/BA	7.0/7.5x	Advanced Edition Manuals, Eng.
HP-UX:		
J5316BA	6.4	NNM 250 Edition
J5315BA	6.4	Enterprise Edition (Unlimited)
J5330BA	6.4	Upgrade NNM 250 to 6.4 250
J5328BA	6.4	Upgrade NNM 250 to 6.4 Entp
J5329BA	6.4	Upgrade NNM Entp to 6.4 Entp
J1249AB	6.4	NNM 250 Node Increment
J1253UB	6.4	NNM 250 Node Incr. Upgrade
J5310BA	6.4	Developer's Toolkit
T2484AA/BA	7.0/7.5x	Starter Edition 250 Nodes (SE)
T2646BA	7.5	Starter Edition Unlimited
T2688BA	7.5	Upgrade SE 250 to SE Unlimited
T2491AA/BA	7.0/7.5x	Upgrade SE 250 to AE 250
T2692BA	7.5/7.5x	Upgrade SE Unltd to AE 1000
T2700AA/BA	7.0/7.5x	Upgrade AE 250 to AE 1000
T2704AA/BA	7.0/7.5x	Upgrade AE 1000 to AE 5000
T2708AA/BA	7.0/7.5x	Upgrade AE 1000 to Unlimited
T2712AA/BA	7.0/7.5x	Upgrade AE 5000 to Unlimited
T2637AA/BA	7.0/7.5x	Upgrade 6.x 250 to 7.0/5 SE 250
T2640AA/BA	7.0/7.5x	Upgrade 6.x 250 to 7.0/5 AE 250
T2643AA/BA	7.0/7.5x	Upgrd 6.x Enpr to 7.0/5AE 1000
T2651BA	7.5/7.5x	Upgrd 6.x Enpr to 7.0/5SE Unltd
T2495AA/BA	7.0/7.5x	Advanced Edition 250 Nodes
T2500AA/BA	7.0/7.5x	Advanced Edition 1000 Nodes
T2505AA/BA	7.0/7.5x	Advanced Edition 5000 Nodes
T2511AA/BA	7.0/7.5x	Advanced Edition Unlimited
T2579AA/BA	7.0/7.5x	Developers Toolkit
Solaris:		
J5320BA	6.4	NNM 250 Edition
J5317BA	6.4	Enterprise Edition (Unlimited)
J5327BA	6.4	Upgrade NNM 250 to 6.4 250
J5397BA	6.4	Upgrade NNM 250 to 6.4 Entp
J5325BA	6.4	Upgrade NNM Entp to 6.4 Entp
J1256AB	6.4	NNM 250 Node Increment
J1260UB	6.4	NNM 250 Node Incr. Upgrade
J5311BA	6.4	Developer's Toolkit
T2485AA/BA	7.0/7.5	Starter Edition 250 Nodes (SE)
T2647BA	7.5	Starter Edition Unlimited
T2689BA	7.5	Upgrade SE 250 to SE Unlimited

T2492AA/BA	7.0/7.5	Upgrade SE 250 to AE 250
T2693BA	7.5x	Upgrade SE Unltd to AE 1000
T2701AA/BA	7.0/7.5x	Upgrade AE 250 to AE 1000
T2705AA/BA	7.0/7.5x	Upgrade AE 1000 to AE 5000
T2709AA/BA	7.0/7.5x	Upgrade AE 1000 to Unlimited
T2713AA/BA	7.0/7.5x	Upgrade AE 5000 to Unlimited
T2638AA/BA	7.0/7.5x	Upgrade 6.x 250 to 7.0/5 SE 250
T2641AA/BA	7.0/7.5x	Upgrade 6.x 250 to 7.0/5 AE 250
T2644AA/BA	7.0/7.5x	Upgrd 6.x Enpr to 7.0/5AE 1000
T2652BA	7.5/7.5x	Upgrd 6.x Enpr to 7.0/5SE Unltd
T2496AA/BA	7.0/7.5x	Advanced Edition 250 Nodes
T2501AA/BA	7.0/7.5x	Advanced Edition 1000 Nodes
T2506AA/BA	7.0/7.5x	Advanced Edition 5000 Nodes
T2512AA/BA	7.0/7.5x	Advanced Edition Unlimited
T2580AA/BA	7.0/7.5x	Developers Toolkit

Windows:

J5321BA	6.4	NNM 250 Edition
J5321BA	6.4	Enterprise Edition (Unlimited)
J5314BA	6.4	Upgrade NNM 250 to 6.4 250
J5398BA	6.4	Upgrade NNM 250 to 6.4 Entp
J5326BA	6.4	Upgrade NNM Entp to 6.4 Entp
J1242AB	6.4	NNM 250 Node Increment
J1242UB	6.4	NNM 250 Node Incr. Upgrade
J5312BA	6.4	Developer's Toolkit
T2486AA/BA	7.0/7.5x	Starter Edition 250 Nodes (SE)
T2648BA	7.5x	Starter Edition Unlimited
T2690BA	7.5x	Upgrade SE 250 to SE Unlimited
T2493AA/BA	7.0/7.5x	Upgrade SE 250 to AE 250
T2694BA	7.5x	Upgrade SE Unltd to AE 1000
T2702AA/BA	7.0/7.5x	Upgrade AE 250 to AE 1000
T2706AA/BA	7.0/7.5x	Upgrade AE 1000 to AE 5000
T2710AA/BA	7.0/7.5x	Upgrade AE 1000 to Unlimited
T2714AA/BA	7.0/7.5x	Upgrade AE 5000 to Unlimited
T2639AA/BA	7.0/7.5x	Upgrade 6.x 250 to 7.0/5 SE 250
T2642AA/BA	7.0/7.5x	Upgrade 6.x 250 to 7.0/5 AE 250
T2645AA/BA	7.0/7.5x	Upgrd 6.x Enpr to 7.0/5AE 1000
T2653BA	7.5x	Upgrd 6.x Enpr to 7.0/5SE Unltd
T2497AA/BA	7.0/7.5x	Advanced Edition 250 Nodes
T2502AA/BA	7.0/7.5x	Advanced Edition 1000 Nodes
T2507AA/BA	7.0/7.5x	Advanced Edition 5000 Nodes
T2513AA/BA	7.0/7.5x	Advanced Edition Unlimited
T2581AA/BA	7.0/7.5x	Developers Toolkit

Linux:

T2487AA/BA	7.5x	Starter Edition 250 Nodes
T2649AA/BA	7.5x	Starter Edition Unlimited
T2691AA/BA	7.5x	Upgrade SE 250 to SE Unlimited
T2582AA/BA	7.5x	Developers Toolkit

Notes: Product numbers ending in AA refer to 7.0/7.01 versions and those ending in BA refer to version 7.51 and 7.53. Product numbers for

NNM 6.4 and 6.41 are the same and product numbers for NNM 7.0 and NNM 7.01 are the same.

Support package numbers (North America only)

A new support structure was introduced at the end of 2003. Several companies deliver SPI-support on behalf of HP, and have add-ons to the support packages from HP. Those are not listed here.

Old Support Options	New HP Care Pack #s	Description
OS2, OS3	HA106A1	Software Sppt – Business hrs, updates, 1 yr
3Y2, 3Y3	HA106A3	Software Sppt - Business hrs, updates, 3 yrs
OS6	HA107A1	Software Sppt – 24x7, updates, 1 yr
3Y6	HA107A3	Software Sppt – 24x7, updates, 3 yrs
OS3	HA109A1	SW & HW sppt - Business hrs, updates, 1 yr
3Y3	HA109A3	SW & HW sppt - Business hrs, updates, 3yrs
OS6	HA110A1	SW & HW sppt – 24x7, updates, 1 yr
3Y6	HA110A3	SW & HW sppt - 24x7, updates, 3yrs
n/a	HA111A1	Old PSS (Personalized system sppt) – 1 yr
n/a	HA111A3	Old PSS (Personalized system sppt) – 3 yrs
OTx	HA112A1	Old CSS (Critical Systems sppt) – 1 yr
n/a	HA112A3	Old CSS (Critical Systems sppt) – 3 yrs
U5008AA	HA287A1	OpenView Premier Services
005	n/a	U2461AA Developer Support 5-pack
012	n/a	U2461AA Developer Support 12-pack
025	n/a	U2461AA Developer Support 25-pack

Glossary

A	DNS A Record or Address Record per RFC 1035
ACL	Access Control List, sets access rights (MS, Cisco, etc)
AE	Acronym for HP OpenView NNM Advanced Edition
AIX	IBM's proprietary UNIX system V variant
Alarm	An NNM depiction of an event conveying relations, etc.
Alpha	A 64-bit chip architecture introduced by DEC in 1992
AMI	Alternate Mark Inversion, an older DDS T1 encoding
ANSI	American National Standards Institute, www.ansi.org
APA	Active Problem Analyzer, NNM's ET-based Poller
ARF	NNM Application Registration Files, page 6
ARP	Address Resolution Protocol per RFCs 826, 1293
ASN.1	Abstract Syntax Notation One, an OSI-defined syntax
ATM	Asynchronous Transfer Mode per RFC 1932
B8ZS	Binary 8 Zero Substitution, Clear Channel T1 coding
BECN	A FR Backward Explicit Congestion Notification
BER	Basic Encoding Rules are ASN.1 encoding rules
BES	Binary Event Store, NNM's raw event store
BGP	Border Gateway Protocol, an EGP per RFC 1771
BIND	Berkeley Internet Name Domain, DNS, www.isc.org
BRI	Basic Rate Interface, a type of ISDN interface
BSD	Berkeley Software Distribution, www.bsd.org
CA	Computer Associates, Inc. www.ca.com
CERT	Computer Emergency Response Team, www.cert.org
CCO	Cisco Connection Online – Cisco registered support site
CDC	Cisco Discovery Configuration, controls ET discovery params
CDP	Cisco Discovery Protocol, advertises Cisco device data
CFA	NNM's Connectivity Fault Analyzer, an APA subsystem
CGI	Common Gateway Interface for Web, RFC 3875
CISC	Complex Instruction Set Computing CPU architecture
CIDR	Classless Inter-Domain Routing, RFC 1518, 1519, 1817
CIM	Compaq Insight Manager, now called SIM
CIR	Committed Information Rate, see Frame Relay
CLI	Command Line Interface, accesses OS commands

CNAME	DNS Canonical Name Record (Alias), RFC 1035
CS	NNM Collection Station: a DIM term
CSOV	Chip Sutton's OV Perl API Module, www.cs-net.com
CSV	Comma Separated Variable text file for DB imports
CW2K	CiscoWorks 2000, Cisco's router management tool
CWSI	CiscoWorks for Switched Internetworks; part of CW2K
DB	Generic term for Data Base
DBM	UCB's flat file database libraries; embedded in UNIX
DBMS	Database Management System, e.g. Oracle, SQL Server
DDS	Dataphone Digital Service, AT&T's pre-T1 link service
DE	Discard Eligible Frame Relay packet
DEC	Digital Equipment Corp. A defunct computer company
DFM	CiscoWork's Device Fault Manger, subset of SMARTS
DIM	NNM Distributed Internet Discovery
DOD	United States Department of Defense
DOS	Denial of Service attack or MS Disk Operating System
DMI	Desktop Management Interface, a DMTF standard
DMTF	Desktop Management Task Force, a standards body
DMZ	Demilitarized Zone between internet and intranet
DNS	Domain Naming Service; Many RFCs, primarily 1035
DP	HP OpenView Data Protector; enterprise backup tool
DS1, DS3	1.544Mbit(t1), 43Mbit(t3) serial lines, RFC 1232, 2495
Duplex	Synonymous with Full Duplex; bi-directional traffic
DW	OpenView NNM data warehouse, a relational DB
E1/E3	See DS1/DS3
ECS	OpenView Event Correlation Services product
EGP	Exterior Routing Protocol, generic for internet routing
Envvars	Contraction of environment variables
Event	NNM-encapsulated trap conveying status, source, etc
ET	Extended Topology, NNM's Level 2 topology tool
Ethernet	A LAN architecture defined by IEEE 802.3 standard
FDB	Acronym for Bridge Fowarding Database,
FECN	A FR Forward Explicit Congestion Notification
FQDN	Acronym for Fully Qualified Domain Name
Frame	The OSI Layer 2 (data link) encapsulation
FR	Frame Relay, WAN packet switching, RFC 1315, 2115
grep	UNIX command to search for a pattern
GNU	Short for GNU's Not UNIX, a free OS, www.fsf.org
GPL	Short for GNU Public License, www.gnu.org
GUI	also UI, an acronym for Graphical User Interface
HC	High Capacity MIB variables support 64-bits counters
HP	Hewlett-Packard Corp., a large computer company

HP-UX	HP's proprietary UNIX Sytem V variant
HPOV	Hewlett-Packard OpenView, synonymous with OV
HSRP	Hot-Swappable Routing Protocol, A Cisco protocol
IANA	Internet Assigned Numbers Authority, www.iana.org
IBM	Int'l Business Machines, a large computer company
ICMP	Internet Control Message Protocol, Packet IP, RFC 792
IGP	Interior Gateway Protocol, generic for intranet routing
IEEE	Int'l Institute of Electronic Engineers, www.ieee.org
IE	Microsoft's Internet Explorer web browser
If	Contraction for Interface, see NIC
IfMIB	Interface Mib, RFC 1573, 2233
IIS	Microsoft Internet Information Server, a web server
IOS	Internal Operating System; Cisco et al.
IETF	Internet Engineering Task Force, www.ietf.org, see RFC
IP	Internet Protocol, See RFCs 791, 793, 1180, etc
IPV4	Internet Protocol Version 4, 32-bit IP addr, RFC 791
IPV6	Internet Protocol Version 6, 128-bit IP addr, RFC 2460
ISO	International Org. for Standardization, www.iso.org
ISDN	Integrated Services Disgital Netwrok; a telephony network
IT	Acronym for Information Technology
IT	Short for Itanium in OS software support matrix (page 304)
ITRC	HP's IT Resource Center; online db at www.itrc.hp.com
J2EE	Java 2 Platform Enterprise Edition, dev platform from Sun
Java	Sun's high-level object-oriented programming language
JPI	Java Plug-In, equivalent to JRE
JRE	Java Runtime Environment, http://java.sun.com/j2se/
JVM	Java Virtual Machine, a virtualized JAVA processor
Kermit	Serial communications from www.columbia.edu/kermit
LAN	Acronym for Local Area Network
LRF	NNM Local Registration File
MAC	Media Access Control Address, ANSI/IEEE Std 802
Man	UNIX Man pages provide online help facilities
MAU	Media Access Unit, e.g an Ethernet transceiver
MD5	Message Digest Encryption algorithm, RFC 1321
MIB	SNMP Management Information Base, per RFC 1212
mib2	MIB holding the most common agent data, RFC 1213
MibExpr	NNM Mib Expression, combines variables using RPN
MLT	Multi-Link trunking, an aggregated port protocol for Nortel
Motif	OSF GUI guidelines for look and feel, opengroup.org
MS	NNM Management Station (DIM); also: Microsoft
MTU	Maximum Transmission Unit. A packet size limitation
NAT	Network Address Translation, RFC 1631 et al.

NDBM	A flat file DB library set used by NNM based on DBM
NDE	Cisco's Netflow Data Export, a switch traffic monitor
Netbios	Network Basic Input/Output System, A Microsoft API
NetBT	Netbios over TCP/IP, an older Windows service
Netmask	Contraction of IP Subnet network mask, RFC 950
netmon	NNM's discovery and polling daemon
NetView	An IBM NMS based in part on OpenView code
NIAP	A US Govt IT securityt initiative, see niap-ccevs.org
NIC	Network Interface Card, a media access device
NIS	Network Information Service (Yellow pages) (Sun)
Node	A system or device connected to a network
NMS	A generic term for Network Management System
NNM	Hewlett-Packard's OpenView Network Node Manager
Nortel	A large provider of network equipment
OAD	Overlapping Address Domain (TCP/IP)
Object	In NNM, a uniquely identified object database entity
Octet	A single byte of data, or 8 bits
ODBC	Open Data Base Connectivity; SQL Access Group Std
OEM	Original Equipment Manufacturer's embedded product
OID	Object ID, dotted number for SNMP MIB variable
OOID	OpenView Object ID, unique no. assigned in object db
OpenSSH	Secure open source logon tool from www.openssh.com
OpenView	HP's suite of enterprise management software products
OQL	A subset of SQL with HP extensions for NNM/ET
OUSPG	Oulu Univ. Secure Programming Group, ee.oulu.fi/?en
OV	A contraction of OpenView, a suite of HP software
OVO	OpenView Operations for UNIX (A systems manager)
OVOW	OpenView Operations for Windows
OVPI	OpenView Performance Insight (formerly Trend Micro)
OVR	OpenView Reporter Product
ovw	OV Windows, the NNM static Map foreground process
OS	Operating System, e.g. Solaris, Windows 2000, HP-UX
OSF	Open Software Foundation, now www.opengroup.org
OSF/1	Proprietary 64-bit UNIX variant from DEC; now Tru64
OSI	Open System Interconnect, set of ISO-defined protocols
OSI	Ontario Swine Improvement, Inc – www.osi.org
OSPF	Open Shortest Path First IGP routing, RFC 1583,2328
Packet	See PDU
PA	Short for PA-RISC, HP's CPU chip architecture
PAgP	Cisco's Port Aggregation Protocol
Perl	Practical Extraction and Reporting (scripting) Language
PID	Process ID. A unique number assigned by the OS

ping	A program that issues ICMP Echo requests and replies
PD	HP OpenView Problem Diagnosis, an NNM built-in
PDU	Package Data Unit, the OSI Layer 3 data encapsulation
PPP	Point-to-Point Protocol, RFC 1661, 1990 (Multilink) etc.
PPTP	Point-to-Point Tunneling Protocol, RFC 2637
PRI	Primary Rate Interface, a type of ISDN interface
PTP	Acronym for Point To Point
PTR	DNS Pointer Record for reverse lookup, RFC 1035
RARP	Reverse Address Resolution Protocol, RFC 903, 1931
RAMS	OpenView Route Analytics Management System
RANCID	Really Awesome New Cisco conflg Differ
rc	UNIX Remote Control files, auto daemon start and stop
Ref	Reference pages. Accessible from NNM Help menu
RDMI	HP's Remote DMI access protocol
RFC	IETF Request for Comment. Search web for RFC 3160
RISC	Reduced Instruction Set Computing CPU architecture
RIP	Routing Information Protocol, an IGP per RFC 1058
RME	Cisco Resource Manager Essentials, part of CW2K
RMON	Remote Monitoring SNMP extensions, RFC 1757
RMONII	Extends RMON from layer 2 to 3 and more, RFC 2021
RPN	Reverse Polish Notation, math via Postfix Notation
SAA	Cisco Service Assurance Agent; monitors performance
SAM	HP-UX's System Adminstration Manager GUI
SANS	SysAdm, Audit, Network, Security Inst. www.sans.org
SE	Refers to HP OpenView NNM Starter Edition
SEA	Solstice Enterprise Agent, an SNMP agent, sun.com
sed	Unix stream editor command
SID	Oracle System Identifier, used to uniquely ID a DB
SIM	Acroynym for HP Systems Insight Manager
Simplex	synonymous with Half Duplex; one-way transmission
SMI	Structure of Management Information, see RFC 1155
SMLT	Split Multi-Link Trunking, an aggregate protocol for Nortel
Solid	Embedded DBMS (with NNM). www.solidtech.com
SOX	Boston Red Sox, 2004 World Series Champions, Yeeha!
SPAN	Cisco's term for port spanning or port mirroring
SPI	Smart Plug-In: add-on functionality for NNM, OVO
SQL	Structured Query Language, a DBMS access method
SMTP	Simple Mail Transport Protocol, RFC 821, 2821, et al
SNMP	Simple Network Mgmt Protocol, RFC 1157, 1905
SNNP	Simple Network Paging Protocol, RFC 1568, 1645
SSH	Secure Shell, generic for SSH1, SSH2, OpenSSH, etc
SSH1,2	Secure UNIX logon tool from SCS, www.ssh.com

SSL	Secure Sockets Layer, an encryption protocol, RFC 2246, et al
syslog	BSD-based error logging facility, RFC 3164
T1/T3	See DS1/DS3
TAC	Cisco Technical Assistance Center (Support center)
TAP	IXO/Telocator Alphanumeric Protocol, see SNNP
TCP	Transmission Control Protocol, connection-oriented IP
tail	A UNIX command that delivers the last part of a file
telnet	A terminal emulation program/protocol, RFC 854 et.al.
Tivoli	IBM's enterprise management product suite
Tomcat	Apache's Jakarta JAVA servlet
Trap	An SNMP unsolicited notification, per RFC 1215
UDP	User Datagram Protocol, connectionless IP, RFC 768
UCB	University of California, Berkeley
UNIX	A trademark of the Open Group, see www.unix.org
VAX	A proprietary CISC-based OS produced by DEC
Varbind	Contraction of Variable Binding: SNMP trap attributes
VLAN	Virtual LAN, logical groups of devices, RFC 3069
VLSM	Variable Length Subnet Mask, Internal CIDR,RFC1817
VNC	Virtual Network Computing, www.vnc.com
VOIP	Voice Over IP, Many RFC's, e.g. 1889, 2543, 2885, 3261
VPDN	Virtual Private Dialup Network, Cisco, RFC 2764, et al
VRRP	Virtual Router Redundancy Protocol, RFC 2338, 3867, 2787
WMI	Intel's Wired for Management Initiative

Index

www.ingramcontent.com/pod-product-compliance
Lightning Source LLC
Chambersburg PA
CBHW071403050326

40689CB00010B/1736